Thinking Poetics

MODERN AND CONTEMPORARY POETICS

Series Editors
Charles Bernstein
Hank Lazer

Series Advisory Board
Maria Damon
Rachel Blau DuPlessis
Alan Golding
Susan Howe
Nathaniel Mackey
Jerome McGann
Harryette Mullen
Aldon Nielsen
Marjorie Perloff
Joan Retallack
Ron Silliman
Jerry Ward

Thinking Poetics

Essays on George Oppen

Edited by Steve Shoemaker

THE UNIVERSITY OF ALABAMA PRESS

Tuscaloosa

Copyright © 2009
The University of Alabama Press
Tuscaloosa, Alabama 35487-0380
All rights reserved
Manufactured in the United States of America

Typeface: Caslon

∞
The paper on which this book is printed meets the minimum requirements of
American National Standard for Information Sciences-Permanence of Paper for
Printed Library Materials, ANSI Z39.48-1984.

Library of Congress Cataloging-in-Publication Data

Thinking poetics : essays on George Oppen / edited by Steve Shoemaker.
     p.   cm. — (Modern and contemporary poetics)
   Includes bibliographical references and index.
   ISBN 978-0-8173-1662-4 (cloth : alk. paper) — ISBN 978-0-8173-5546-3 (pbk. : alk.
paper) 1. Oppen, George—Criticism and interpretation. I. Shoemaker, Steve.
   PS3529.P54Z89 2009
   811'.54—dc22

                                   2009012616

Contents

Preface
Meaning a Life

> I went to the woods because I wished to live deliberately, to front only
> the essential facts of life, and see if I could not learn what it had to
> teach, and not, when I came to die, discover that I had not lived.
> —Henry David Thoreau, *Walden*

If one were to seek a central, defining theme in George Oppen's life, one could certainly do worse than to begin with the title of Mary Oppen's autobiography *Meaning a Life.* The title seems to apply equally well to both Mary and George; or better, it evokes the shared life they lived together. The dedication page to George's *Collected Poems,* which reads "For Mary, whose words in this book are entangled inextricably among my own," makes clear the depth of their mutual commitment, as well as the importance that that commitment had for George's poetry. To "mean a life" suggests living intentionally, "deliberately" as Thoreau put it, seeking an honest engagement with what George Oppen's poetic mentor Louis Zukofsky called "historic and contemporary particulars."[1] When Zukofsky used that phrase he was inaugurating the "Objectivist" movement in American poetry. And after George had become, eventually, one of the more well known Objectivists, he adopted a definition of "Objectivist" poetry that emphasized deliberateness, vision, and conviction: "The point for me, and I think for Louis too, was the attempt to construct meaning, to construct a method of thought from the imagist technique of poetry— from the imagist intensity of vision. If no one were going to challenge me, I would say, 'a test of truth.' If I had to go back and back it up I'd say anyway, 'a test of sincerity'—that there is a moment, an actual time, when you believe something to be true, and you construct a meaning from these moments of conviction" (Dembo interview 174). Oppen's goal was to use poetry to think, to "construct a meaning," and to arrive at points of "conviction." The kind of thinking Oppen had in mind did not take place in a vacuum; instead, he was trying to think through the lived particulars of what turned out to be a fascinating life.

With a few exceptions (Rimbaud running guns in Africa and Byron rallying the Greek troops come to mind), poets are not generally known for leading especially dramatic lives; Oppen is one of those exceptions. His life is eventful, adventurous, and notably marked by violence. When he was a young child his mother committed suicide; when he was an adolescent he was the driver in a car crash that killed his companion; he was expelled from high school and nearly expelled from college. As a young man in his, and the century's, twenties he hitchhiked across the country with Mary, and upon reaching New York City he encountered the poets Louis Zukofsky and Charles Reznikoff and soon launched his own small press, To Publishers (from France, he and Mary having continued on from New York to Europe).[2] In 1934 he published his first book of poetry, *Discrete Series,* as part of another publishing venture, the Objectivist Press, but not long afterward he stopped writing poetry and joined the Communist Party to work on behalf of the homeless and unemployed. In the forties, he joined the antifascist cause as a U.S. soldier, seeing heavy action, and receiving serious wounds, as an infantryman in France. In the fifties, he fled McCarthy-era persecution, taking up residence in Mexico, with Mary and their daughter Linda, as part of the same community of exiles sheltering members of the notorious Hollywood Ten. Only in the late 1950s, after twenty-five years of silence, did he return to the United States and to the writing of poetry. Even then, however, his life was far from a settled one. He lived variously on the West and East coasts, and he and Mary would remain restless travelers for the rest of their lives. Mary describes that peripatetic life, which began with their cross-country hitchhiking adventure, as follows:

> We were constantly searching—searching in our travels, in our pursuit of friends and in our conversation concerning all that we saw and felt about the world. We were searching for a way to avoid the trap that our class backgrounds held for us if we relented in our escape from them. We understood from our experiences while hitchhiking that in the United States we were not required to remain in the class into which we were born. We wanted to see a great deal of the world, and the education of which we talked for ourselves was

to leave our class and learn our life by throwing ourselves into it.
(*Meaning a Life [ML]* 76)

To "learn our life by throwing ourselves into it." The emphasis is double,
encompassing headlong commitment and a drive toward action, on the
one hand, and the imperative to stop and reflect, to try to understand what
it all means, on the other.

But before that lifelong education could properly begin there had to
be, as Mary tells us, an "escape," an extrication from the "trap" of class.
The need for such an escape was fundamental for both George and Mary,
rendered urgent by the fact of the Oppen family's wealth. Eluding the
subtle and not-so-subtle nets that this wealth threatened to throw over
the young couple is one of the more important subjects of Mary's narrative in *Meaning a Life,* and we find this personal escape coded into the un-
characteristically "literary" first poem of George's first book, *Discrete Series.* In that poem, keyed to a Henry James short story, the protagonist
Maude Blessingbourne, the restless inhabitant of a claustrophobic, bric-
a-brac-filled interior, "'approached the window as if to see what was really
going on'" (the line is quoted directly from James). What Maude sees is
"the world, weather-swept, with which one shares the century," and this
approach to the window, an act of vision, could be said to be central to all
of Oppen's subsequent work. It speaks as well to the twenty-five years of
poetic silence, which began, after all, with Oppen's turn to political action, his desire to engage the heavy weather of the twentieth century's unfolding history. The escape from class brings exposure to a wider range of
people and "life experience," and so begins the sentimental education of
Oppen as person and poet.[3]

It might seem odd, and indeed it *is* a bit odd, for this "call to action" to
come in such oblique, subtle, and *textual* form as a poem paying homage to
Henry James, but such angular, arduous "approaches" are not unusual for
Oppen, and the presence of James here is illuminating. Decades after the
poem's original publication, Oppen wrote to L. S. Dembo, who had identified the quotation from James, as follows:

of course you are right about the Henry James: I wanted the phrase
BUT I wanted James in the book—secretly, superstitiously, I carved
his initials on that sapling book.

I argued, shortly after Discrete was printed, that James and not

Hemingway was the useful model for "proletarian" writers —— and realized, in the ensuing discussion, if one could call it a discussion, that I must stay away from left-wing "cultural workers." (*Selected Letters [SL]* 241)

That Oppen would argue in the thirties for Henry James as "the useful model for 'proletarian' writers" tells us something about his obstinacy, and also about his definition of clarity of vision, which must allow not just for "direct treatment of the thing" (as the Imagist motto had it) but for subtlety and even obliquity. And his reference to the ensuing "discussion" with those "left-wing 'cultural workers'" helps illuminate at least one of the reasons for his ensuing poetic silence. Though he would join the Communist Party, Oppen didn't want his writing to be reduced to propaganda, and he didn't want to adopt a set of literary values that would threaten to lead him to such a result. We don't know how exactly Oppen made the case for James as a "proletarian writer," but we might guess that he appreciated James's insight into social forces, the vagaries of class, and the pervasive operation of "cultural contradictions." Further, the contrast with Hemingway shows us that Oppen didn't adopt the view, common in the period, that plain prose style was the necessary vehicle of authentic political insight. It seems likely, in fact, that it is above all James's style itself—difficult and elaborate, yet a vehicle of fine perception—that Oppen admired. But to reconcile a "modernist" devotion to formal complexity and aesthetic sophistication with a political commitment to concrete action would prove no easy matter. As I've already said, Oppen stopped writing poetry in the thirties, and much later, in his long poem *Of Being Numerous* (1969), he would pose the question "'Whether, as the intensity of seeing increases, one's distance from Them, the people, does not also increase'" (*New Collected Poems [NCP]* 167).[4] That question would haunt him continually, for even as he valued "intensity," and the difficulty it often brings with it, he also admired what he called a "Populist" strain in literature, and more specifically, in American poetry.

In his essay "The Mind's Own Place," Oppen took stock of the field of American poetry and situated himself within that field upon his return to writing. In so doing, he described the Populist legacy as he saw it, articulating its values and making clear that he wished to see his own poetic project in similar terms. In this account, James is not mentioned, but William Carlos Williams is. Williams, Vachel Lindsay, Carl Sandburg, and Alfred Kreymbourg, identified as "the poets of the little magazine *Others* which came off a hand press in a garage somewhere in New Jersey about 1918," are classified by Oppen as "almost a populist movement" (*Selected Poems [SP]* 175). And even Ezra Pound and T. S. Eliot find a place in this quasi-movement, by virtue of their devotion to "clarity," their "freedom from the art subject," and their dedication to recording "the data of experience" (*SP* 175). Oppen argues that for these first-generation modernists the exercise of vision required a rejection of "the accepted poetry of their day," and he suggests that devotion to registering the world of actual experience "was and is the core of what 'modernism' restored to poetry, the sense of the poet's self among things" (*SP* 175). This emphasis on the "data of experience," on lived reality, is central to what Oppen means by the term "populist," and his search for that data would characterize his own poetry for the rest of his life.

For despite his wealthy and protected childhood, his lifelong habit of world travel, the period of exile in Mexico, and a serious engagement with European philosophy, George Oppen did think of himself as definitively a product of the American scene. Or to put it more precisely, Oppen saw himself as part of a generation of writers who found themselves *becoming* American:

> I belong to a generation that grew more American—literarily at least—as it approached adult estate: we grew up on English Writing— and German fairy tales—as I think no American any longer does. Starting with Mother Goose . . . and proceeding to Kipling and Robert Louis Stevenson and the Rover Boys, perhaps the only American writing we saw was in the Oz books and in Mark Twain. I have not discussed this with other writers and risk the statement, but I believe that many a young American writer-to-be was astonished on reaching adolescence to discover that he was not easily going to take his place as the young master, or even as a Thackereyan young man who manages, with whatever difficulty, to equip himself with fresh linen and varnished boots for his crucial morning call on the Duchess. We found ourselves below stairs, possibly: certainly among the minor characters. Which was a factor I believe in our need to make our own literature. Huck Finn, if this were a scholarly work, might be contrasted to Tom Brown, or even to Christopher Robin of Pooh Corner. Alice wandered from her governess; Dorothy of Oz ran too late for the storm cellar and was caught in a Kansas cyclone. Together and contrastingly they dawned on our infant minds, and

may have contributed to the aesthetic, if not social sentiment which went in search of the common, the common experience, the life of the common man. ("Mind's Own Place" [MOP] 135)

The violence of a Kansas cyclone was part of life in the new world and called for new forms of expression, a new literature. And that new literature, in Oppen's view, could only arise from a full engagement with "common experience." If from a literary standpoint Oppen imagined himself, despite his family's wealth, to be "below stairs," then that was no handicap, and maybe even an advantage, given his convictions. For Oppen there is something inevitably "populist" about the best and most important American literature and art (MOP 135–136), and he thought of his own work as possessing this "American grain," to use Williams's phrase. As I've already suggested, the trajectory outward, the arc of a search for the "ground under [his] feet" (MOP 136), was the dominant movement in the narrative of his life.

From Sherwood Anderson, the Oppens derived a sort of populist motto, "we wanted to see if we were any good out there," which describes their feeling that there were important things to be done and a kind of test to be undergone. Even if one leaves school, as the Oppens did, there is apparently no education without tests.[5] Just as Oppen described poetry as a "test of truth" and "a test of whether one's thought is valid" (Dembo interview 175), the years of political action were to be judged by accomplishment. Decades later Oppen described the effort as follows:

> It was a matter of going from house to house, apartment to apartment; I think we knew every house in Bedford-Stuyvesant and North Brooklyn and all the people in them. We wanted to gather crowds of people on the simple principle that the law would have to be changed where it interfered with relief and that settlement laws would have to be unenforceable when they involved someone's starvation. And we were interested in rioting, as a matter of fact— rioting under political discipline. Disorder, disorder—to make it impossible to allow people to starve. It also involved the hunger march on Washington as well as local undertakings. (Dembo interview 188)

The emphasis was pragmatic, geared toward concrete action rather than toward party factionalism and ideological hair-splitting: "we made sure what we were doing was not politicalizing but what we really intended to do" (Dembo interview 188). The Oppens were also carrying out their imperative to expand their horizons, to increase their range of experience. It was important that they came to know the people in the houses, and that the action they took arose from "grass roots" needs rather than ideological dictates.

Indeed, the major thrust of their organizing activity was designed to meet the most basic of needs—food and shelter. Here is Oppen's description of the urgency of the situation:

> I think it was fifteen million families that were faced with the threat of immediate starvation. It wasn't a business one simply read about in the newspaper. You stepped out your door and found men who had nothing to eat. . . . [F]or some people it was simply impossible not to do something. . . . And if you decide to write poetry, then you write poetry, not something that you hope or deceive yourself into believing, can save people who are suffering. That was the dilemma of the thirties. In a way I gave up poetry because of the pressures of what I'll call conscience. But there were some things I had to live through, some things I had to think my way through, and some things I had to try out—and it was more than politics, really; it was the whole experience of working in factories, of having a child, and so on. Absurd to ask myself whether what I undertook was right or wrong for the artist and the rest of that. Hugh Kenner interrupted my explanation to him of these years by saying, "In brief, it took twenty-five years to write the next poem." Which is the way to say it. (Dembo interview 187)

It was the sense that "we didn't know enough," and that "there were some things I had to live through, some things I had to think my way through," that led Oppen to turn, as a response to "the dilemma of the thirties," from writing to political action and lived experience. As it happens, there was a lot to live through, more than Oppen could have known at the time, and so the poetic silence ended up lasting twenty-five years.

But this is to get a bit ahead of the story. Before there was silence there was the first book, *Discrete Series,* and the confluence of poets who would come to be known as the "Objectivists"—the core of the group consisting of Oppen himself, Louis Zukofsky, Charles Reznikoff, and Carl Rakosi. When George and Mary completed their cross-country trip, sailing the last leg of the journey and arriving in New York City in 1928, they soon met both Louis Zukofsky and Charles Reznikoff. Zukofsky was only a few years older than Oppen, but much more savvy about the current state of American poetry, and more broadly, literary modernism. Indeed, he had been corresponding steadily with Ezra Pound and was also in close contact with William Carlos Williams.[6] As a result of Pound's sponsorship, Zukofsky secured a guest editorship for the February 1931 issue of *Poetry* magazine, the most influential poetry journal of the time. With the encouragement of Harriet Monroe, the magazine's regular editor, Zukofsky rather reluctantly fashioned a manifesto of sorts, consisting of two prose pieces, "Program: 'Objectivists' 1931" and "Sincerity and Objectification, with Special Reference to the Work of Charles Reznikoff." Zukofsky determinedly, and rather slyly, resisted defining an "ism," preferring to talk of "Objectivists" rather than "Objectivism," and it is in reference to the individual yet related practices of a small group of poets that the descriptor "Objectivist" makes the most sense. The "Objectivist" issue of *Poetry* featured two of George's poems, and though the initial response to the number was less than overwhelming, the eventual influence of the Objectivist poets would be large.[7] By the early 1930s, the circle of Oppen's poetic colleagues and mentors included Zukofsky, Charles Reznikoff, Ezra Pound, and William Carlos Williams, and the work of all these men would remain important to him for the rest of his life, even though his relations with Zukofsky and Pound in particular would suffer considerable strain over the years. Oppen would go on to supply the money for the short-lived small press To Publishers, which would publish *An "Objectivists" Anthology* (1932), a book-length, Zukofsky-edited follow-up to the *Poetry* number.

From there, Oppen, Zukofsky, Williams, and Reznikoff went on to form the Objectivist Press, a publishing endeavor devoted to a series of books by the Objectivists, with each volume paid for by the author. As Oppen describes the operation of the press,

It was a matter of a group of writers who in varying degrees—in sharply varying degrees—approved each others' work. My own interest in the group was probably greatest. I was interested in getting my own work out, I was eager to contribute to Williams' influence on poetry, I considered and consider Reznikoff the most important of living poets, and I considered it important to get Zukofsky out. It's unfortunate that we failed to accomplish that.[8] Like the others I attached no particular importance to the idea of a group, much less of a school. (*SL* 46–47)

As with Oppen's political endeavors, the goals here are limited and pragmatic and the approach is cooperative, without anything like the cult-like emphasis on group identity that characterized, say, the Surrealist movement under the forceful hand of André Breton, with his famous insistence on doctrine and his elaborate rituals of either inclusion or "excommunication." In later years, Oppen was fond of quoting the description of the Objectivist Press that Charles Reznikoff had written for the dust jackets of the books: "an organization of writers who are publishing their own work and that of others whose work they think ought to be read" (*SL* 46). If the rhetoric here is modest, Oppen nevertheless felt the commitment to be a deeply serious one: "I don't know if any group of people in the next few years seriously committed their lives, their fortunes, and their honor—sacred honor, was it?—to an organization based on an agreement concerning the use of words. But we had certainly published good work, and in fact only good work" (*SL* 46).[9]

When Oppen's own Objectivist Press book, *Discrete Series,* appeared in 1934, it bore a preface from Ezra Pound hailing Oppen as a "serious craftsman," thus firmly positioning him as part of the next wave of modernist activity. But Oppen's situation as a modernist inheritor was an uneasy one. As we have already seen, he had begun to find his poetic work inadequate to the times, and Pound's growing fascism, anti-Semitism, and as the Oppens saw it, general wrongheadedness, was also a cause for serious concern. Indeed, George and Mary had found themselves unable to print Pound's *ABC of Economics,* which had been slated to appear from To Publishers. Here is Mary's account of the difficulty:

We had read Pound's *ABC of Economics* and discussed it between ourselves; we thought it absurd. Pound wrote, "When I gather chestnuts on the hills of Rapallo I step outside the Capitalist system"—Pound trying to circumvent Marx, Pound who could not have read Marx and hold the views he aired. Pound, we knew, lived on income derived through capitalism, and without confronting capitalism he was trying to change the system, proposing as an example his grandfather's scrip issued to workers for trade at his grandfather's store. To us this seemed to be the company store of the fur-traders or the tenant-farm system of our southern states, in which workers are compelled to trade at the company store at the trader's or the owner's prices. Perhaps Pound could not think clearly about economics; at any rate, we could not agree to publish the book. (*ML* 135–136)

Like Pound, the Oppens were driven toward politics by the crises of the thirties, but they reached very different conclusions about the form political action should take, and these conclusions grew directly out of their experiences during that decade.

When the Oppens moved to Europe, where publishing costs were cheaper, to establish To Publishers in 1929, they were continuing their education, especially their political education. Once they based their publishing operation in France, they encountered both alarming poverty and a politically aware and activist French working class. Their conversations with the members of that working class, especially the butcher and the hotel keeper in the small town where they lived, helped to shape their emerging politics, as did their reading of Trotsky's *History of the Russian Revolution*. Further, by 1932 they began to see Jewish refugees from Hitler's Germany arriving in France. So when they went to Italy to meet Pound in Rapallo, they were deeply alarmed by his fondness for Mussolini (whom he liked to call "The Boss") and by his new economic theories. During the visit with Pound, Mary was often excluded from the conversation between the men, but she and George continued to sift and evaluate their experiences: "It must be remembered that we were always *two;* we learned from reading and from what we saw, but conversation never ceases between us, and our critical views of our elders kept us from depending on them for intellectual sustenance. We made our visits brief, but our discussion of these visits was long, sometimes life-long" (*ML* 135). So when they came to read Pound's *ABC of Economics,* the meaning of their experience, the result of the bottom-up political education they were in the act of pursuing, was that they could not in good conscience publish the book. In a pattern Oppen would come to emphasize, experience comes to a head in a moment of choice, when one must decide, sometimes painfully, to do either one thing or another.

As with Heidegger, the philosopher most important to Oppen, Oppen's thinking is grounded in the twists and turns of "existential" life, and such thinking is sometimes pushed to resolution by moments of choice. The existential emphasis on the moment of decision has been well characterized by Rudiger Safranski, and the description seems quite relevant to Oppen: "Amid the complexities of life, we find ourselves time and again in situations in which we must decide who we wish to be. We leave the sphere of the merely thinkable; we must take a stand, assume responsibility; we cannot avoid turning from a possibility person, who can consider everything, into a reality person, who from the thinkable selects that which binds him in internal and external action" (83). Oppen brought deliberative care to those moments when the whole realm of "the thinkable" narrows to a single choice, a single course of action; his thinking was attuned to those crucial and often difficult moments when we most powerfully shape who we become.

We've already seen how a series of decisive moments shaped Oppen's life: when he abandoned the scene of his family's wealth and social position; when he left college and embarked on his travels with Mary; when he stopped writing and became a political activist. Each of these is both a renunciation and an embrace; in each case, Oppen turns aside from one path and launches down another with dedication and enthusiasm. But if commitment is the result, it is also the case that many if not all of Oppen's key decisions are marked by difficulty, doubt, and ongoing struggles of conscience. This struggle is nowhere more evident than in the next major crisis facing Oppen, when the full efflorescence of fascism resulted in his decision—despite his reservations, and his age (he was thirty-four)—to fight in World War II. In the poem "Route," written many years after the fact, he recorded the dilemma as follows:

Wars that are just? A simpler question: In the event,
will you or will you not want to kill a German. Because, in the
event, if
you do not want to, you won't.
(*NCP* 196)

Here he recasts an unworkably abstract, and therefore unanswerable, question into a more limited and pragmatic—though still intensely difficult—one. By March 1933, the Oppens had returned to the United States, but by then they had already seen firsthand the building threat to the world's Jews, and this threat seemed to demand a response. As Mary puts it: "George wanted to go to the war. The enemy was fascism, and we agreed that the war must be fought. It seemed to us that the lives of all Jews were endangered by fascism; our lives were in danger, and not to fight in the war was to ask of others what we would not do for ourselves" (173). In

"The Mind's Own Place" Oppen wrote, commenting on his decision to stop writing poetry in the thirties, that one needn't fiddle precisely at the moment the house next door is burning. The overwhelming poverty and homelessness of the thirties had called for immediate political action. In the forties, the house next door seemed once again to be burning, so Oppen went to war.

But the question "will you or will you not want to kill a German" remains a difficult one, and one that probably has to be answered anew day by day rather than decided once and for all. In the poem, the question is immediately followed by a tortured commentary on Oppen's war years, and on the cost, or one cost, of his decision to fight:

> ... and my wife reading letters she knew were two weeks
> late and did not prove I was not dead while she read. Why
> did I play all that, what was I doing there?
> (*NCP* 197)

For the rest of his life, he continued to wrestle with that decision, but Oppen was well aware that he wasn't the only one for whom the war had meant confrontation with excruciating choices. The remarkable narrative of "Route" grapples with the things Oppen saw and heard during the war and frames a whole series of such choices. In a bare factual presentation we learn, as Oppen himself learned from an encounter with a Frenchman named Pierre, of the Alsatian practice of digging a hole in the woods (*faire un trou*) and going into hiding to avoid conscription into the German army, even though such an action might put one's family at risk ("He knew, of course, what he was telling me. You must try to put yourself in those times. If one thought he knew anything, it was that a man should not join the Nazi army."). Then, too, there, is the conversation, between a man and wife who are afraid they will be separated from their children, over whether they should tattoo the children's names and addresses on their chests so they can be found later—a conversation that must take into account the fear that the tattoos might be cut out of the children. And finally, we learn of a Frenchman facing conscription who throws a party at the conclusion of which he drives his bicycle down a hill and into a tree with enough force to end his life. Oppen comments:

> It must be hard to do. Probably easier in an automobile. There is, in an automobile, a considerable time during which you cannot change your mind. Riding a bicycle, since in those woods it is im-

possible that the tree should be a redwood, it must be necessary to continue aiming at the tree right up to the moment of impact. Undoubtedly difficult to do. And of course, the children had no father hereafter.

Tellingly, Oppen points to the literally unswerving nature of the decision, and to the consequence, specifically its impact on the children, the next generation. Oppen was also thinking, no doubt, of his own "abandonment" of his family in order to go to war. And more broadly, he is wondering about how our decisions affect the fate of future generations. In a key passage in the same poem, Oppen writes, "Tell the beads of the chromosome like a rosary, / Love in the genes, if it fails / We will produce no sane man again." What is at stake in our collective decision making is nothing less than the ultimate fate of man, hinging on the success or failure of "love in the genes."

How, then, are we to understand one of Oppen's most important decisions, the decision to stay away from writing poetry for so long? The decision to fall silent, which has become almost legendary among those who know his work, may have been precipitated by his turn toward communism and the political activism of the thirties, but to understand its twenty-five-year stretch we have to consider much more than this initial moment. As we can see in retrospect, his decision to fight in World War II deepened and extended this poetic silence, and the problem of war in general bears a close relation to the larger problem of silence for Oppen. Indeed, he hadn't been writing again for very long (he started again in 1958) before he once again had to wrestle with the decision of whether to stop. The occasion was the advent of the Vietnam War, which brought his thinking about both war and poetry to a new level of intensity and soul searching. In "Of Being Numerous," one of his most important poems and the centerpiece of a book that won the Pulitzer Prize in 1969, Oppen wrote of war as follows:

—They await

War, and the news
Is war

As always

That the juices may flow in them
Tho the juices lie.
(*NCP* 174)

World War I was the war of Oppen's childhood; World War II was the war in which he fought and was seriously wounded; and Vietnam the war of his disillusioned old age. The pervasiveness, the constancy, of war sparked horror for Oppen, threatening his very ability to write poetry, just as the Depression had earlier deflected his energy from writing. As he observed at the time of Vietnam: "I perhaps cannot write poetry in war time. I couldn't before, and perhaps cannot now. I become ashamed, I become sick with shame" (quoted in Lowney, this volume). There may be many reasons for the sense of shame and guilt that Oppen expresses here and elsewhere. But his difficulty in writing during wartime is surely related to the "lies" alluded to in the lines of poetry I have quoted ("That the juices may flow in them / Tho the juices lie"). Oppen is haunted by the sense that lies, like atrocities, are "in the air"; in fact, *are* the air ("the air of atrocity"), the medium through which we live and breathe. In this stultifying atmosphere, language itself seems to fail us.

War is a crucial impetus toward silence in Oppen's work, but the entangling of language and silence in that work runs deeper still. In one of the palimpsestic "overwritings" Oppen habitually engaged in, he riffed on Ezra Pound's assertion that "Poetry must be at least as well written as prose," transforming it into a quite different yet intriguingly parallel claim: "Poetry must be at least as good as dead silence."[10] Pound was arguing against sloppiness in poetry, and taking well-written prose as a provocation, a challenge that poetry should try to meet. Just so, silence seems to have been for Oppen an ever-present provocation and challenge and even a palpable presence hovering over the poetry. For Oppen, to write bad poems, or dishonest ones, or perhaps just unnecessary ones, was a worse thing than to write no poems at all.

In a letter to Harvey Shapiro, Oppen describes how he stopped writing in mid-poem: "When I quit writing I was attempting a poem that began: 'twenty-first birthday / stitch taken without thread'" (*SL* 247). As is clear from Oppen's comments elsewhere, we can gloss the missing "thread" here as the thread of Experience, literally the material out of which the poems would, or would *not*, be made. In another gloss on Kenner's observation that it took him "25 years to write the next poem" Oppen explained as follows: "When the [political] crisis occurred we knew we didn't know what the world was and we knew we had to find out so it was a poetic exploration at the same time that it was an act of conscience." Here the turn toward silence is seen not only as "an act of conscience" but also as a "poetic exploration." If there was a turn away from art (and of course there was, since poetry was not, in fact, being written), there was also, apparently, a "turn back" already in mind, already in preparation—as well as a sense that poetic "activity" was being carried on even if actual writing was not. When Oppen returned to writing, he looked back and took stock of the earlier work in *Discrete Series*, while also casting an eye toward the future: "The early poems just have to stand as is—Some of them come up against the limit of my understanding at the time, and sort of break to pieces. Those that stay solidly within what I had grasped seem to me good. But I am starting now as if from scratch to write of things I knew nothing about when I was twenty. I just have to say it as best I can" (*SL* 26). Here Oppen is ready to write again, ready to begin turning the "poetic exploration" that had consumed nearly twenty-five years into actual poetry.

But here again we see his sense of a lack in the early poems, of having "come up against the limit of [his] understanding," and to his corresponding feeling that some of the poems consequently "break into pieces." Though this account favors the poems that "stay solidly within what [he] had grasped," I would suggest instead that this "breaking into pieces" remains a pervasive element of Oppen's poetics. It takes different forms as his investigation pushes from one book to the next, but this breaking up, this shattering encounter with limits, is always part of the challenge of reading Oppen. And indeed it becomes a more and more explicit *theme* of the poetry, as in these lines coming at the very end of his 1975 *Collected Poems*:

> Say as much as I dare, as much as I can
> Sustain I don't know how to say it
>
> I say all that I can
> ("Two Romance Poems," *NCP* 261)

But it is the most literal sense of breaking up, of shattering, that carries us to Oppen's experience during World War II, which brought, in a moment of extremity, a kind of return to poetry, to words and lines of poetry, before Oppen's actual re/turn to writing after the war.[11] In war, as everyone "knows," but only some *know*, bodies and lives are broken apart, shattered, blown to bits. Oppen was one of those who came to know. While he was driving a truck for the 103rd Antitank division, which had landed in Marseilles and then moved north to participate in the Battle of the Bulge, Oppen came under fire and was badly wounded. He lay trapped in a foxhole

amid heavy shelling, alongside two other men who were killed in the attack. As he would later describe (*much* later), the foxhole became for him a
kind of terrible listening chamber:

> lost to be lost   Wyatt's
> lyric and Rezi's running thru my mind
> in the destroyed (and guilty) Theatre
> of the War

Oppen's word "Theatre," which is capitalized, is interesting here. The
"Theatre of the War" is, of course, the military "scene of operations," but
it seems also in this poem to be a site for the staging of a kind of psychic
drama, a *psychomachia* we might say. In the medieval senses, a *psychomachia*
can be described as a battle for the soul, or of soul against body (often pit-
ting the seven virtues against the seven vices). And a meaning not too different from this seems appropriate to Oppen's experience in the foxhole,
which transforms the war into a shattered ("destroyed") theater of guilt
and fragments in which Oppen fights for his life, fights for his soul, grappling with guilt and terror while lines of poetry by Sir Thomas Wyatt and
Oppen's old friend Charles Reznikoff offer some solace, some means to
keep going.

Oppen turned aside from the writing of poetry to search for experience,
and then, in the foxhole, at the very extremity of Experience, found poetry. Or poetry found him, the lines running through his head. As he described in a letter, the stay in the foxhole lasted something like ten hours
and the poems "ran thru my mind over and over, these poems seemed to
fill all the space around me and I wept and wept" (*SL* 338). Given the importance of this moment, and the central role poetry plays, it is surprising to realize how long it took Oppen to render this experience in poetry
of his own. Tracing the thread of "war" through his work, one encounters
important "war poems," or substantial sections of poems, in each of the
books he produced after his return to writing: *The Materials* (1962), *This
in Which* (1965), and *Of Being Numerous* (1968). But it isn't until 1972, with
Seascape: Needle's Eye—in other words, twenty-eight years after the fact—
that Oppen's experience in the foxhole is directly described. And not until
still later, with *Myth of the Blaze* (and the title poem I have cited), does Oppen grapple with the full emotional intensity and complexity of the incident. Oppen seems, like many veterans, to have been reluctant to relive the
trauma by speaking or writing about it, even as the experience continued

to haunt him. He stopped writing because of the problem of too little experience, and he seems to have taken so long to write about the war—and more particularly his experience in the foxhole—because of the problem of too *much* experience. Like many survivors, Oppen was haunted, filled with guilt at the thought of his lucky break. "Why had they not killed me?" he asks.

> why did they fire that warning
> wounding cannon only the one round I hold a
>   superstition
> (*NCP* 247)

The winds of chance, of history, blow through this battlefield, this poem, through Oppen's life, and through the deaths of his two companions in the foxhole. The scene of the foxhole is a primal one for the development of what might be called the poetics of exposure in Oppen's later poetry, a development growing out of Oppen's dedication to an aesthetic of Heideggerian disclosure, of making what is hidden visible. But with the poetics of exposure this stripping or laying bare is taken to an extreme, as when flesh is flayed from the bone.

Again, the war is an important impetus toward silence for Oppen, but silence serves, in fact, as a kind of larger context, a larger fact, for language, for poetry, and for living. In another of Oppen's remarkable meditations on his poetry, from about the time of *Seascape: Needle's Eye*, he returns again to the tentative beginning to a lifelong project achieved in *Discrete Series*. The poems provided, he says:

> —a place a place at least to begin. But place in another sense: place
> without the words, the wordless sphere in the mind—Or rather the
> wordless sphere with things including a word or so in it. . . . That
> I still believe to be, as they say, Poem: the thing in the mind before
> the words to be able to hold it even against the language—
> (*SL* 236)

Here we have an attitude that is both fundamental and mysterious in Oppen's work, the sense that the poem must somehow hold allegiance to "the thing in the mind before the words," that it must somehow "be able to hold it even against language—." One of the most striking things about Oppen is that he so strongly feels *both* the tug of silence and the necessity of speaking. In another letter, where he is wrestling yet again with his doubts about poetry, he writes, poetically, gropingly: "What one wants, to know what one wants, to move toward it — What is it? Fear of loss of oneself as one knows himself?? . . . I don't know I suppose fear's a great part of our lives I don't know" (*SL* 231). And there the letter ends, with Oppen pushing once more against the limit of his understanding: "To know what one wants, to move toward it." This is a continuation, the ultimate continuation, of the theme of education and the deliberate effort to "mean" a life. Oppen is writing of a schooling of desire, but not in a selfish sense. Desire as Oppen treats it here is both individual and social, and we see in this formulation his abiding concern with how we define "the good life." The struggle to keep moving is in the most brute sense the struggle of life itself, and the need for us to keep moving *in the right direction,* to live ethical and sustainable lives, was for Oppen one of the great problems. If Oppen's poetry displays a poetics of thinking, then the condition "of being numerous," of the individual amid the collective, seems to be the problem he thought about most assiduously. Writing with and through the surrounding silence, Oppen tries to help us decide what we want and what we need.

Notes

1. Zukofsky's phrase comes from his "Program 'Objectivists' 1931" in the "Objectivist" number of *Poetry* magazine.

2. They actually hitchhiked from the West Coast to Detroit, and then, in a feat that would be impossible today, sailed from Detroit to New York City, by way of Lake Erie, the Erie Canal, and the Hudson River.

3. For the biographical facts of Oppen's life, I'm indebted both to Mary Oppen's *Autobiography* and Rachel Blau DuPlessis's introduction to Oppen's *Selected Letters,* and also to the chronology of Oppen's life DuPlessis provided for his *Selected Poems,* edited by Robert Creeley. As for the Oppen family wealth, Oppen's father was a successful businessman in San Francisco. Though Oppen sought to escape his class background, he was also well aware throughout his life that the family money, from which he drew an inheritance when he reached twenty-one, remained a significant source of his freedom. See, for example, this statement from the working papers: "I have been in the habit of doing things my own way. And I have been able to pay for it. I realize, tho, that it has been my pure good fortune that I have been able to afford it." Oppen worked to make money during much of his life, and he held many kinds of employment, including carpenter, builder, and machinist. He observed that he had been freed not from the necessity of working but from the necessity of "success."

4. Oppen is quoting a letter from Rachel Blau DuPlessis, then a young poet in regular correspondence with Oppen, now a mature poet and important critic of Oppen's work. See her essay, "Uncannily in the Open," in this collection.

5. Mary and George met in 1926 at the Agricultural College at Corvalis. Mary was expelled after she and George didn't come back to the dorms the night of their first date, and George left the college soon afterward. See *Meaning a Life,* 61ff.

6. See my essay, "Between Contact and Exile," for an account of Zukofsky's relations with Pound and Williams during this period.

7. The whole present collection testifies to the wide range of Oppen's influence, and the other Objectivist writers have all had a significant impact on American poetry, though in every case it has taken many decades for that impact to be really felt.

8. Oppen is referring to the fact that the press was unable to publish a book by Zukofsky, who could not afford the cost.

9. In addition to Oppen's *Discrete Series,* the Objectivist Press published William Carlos Williams's *Collected Poems 1921–1931,* and four books by Reznikoff: *Jerusalem the Golden, Testimony, In Memoriam: 1933,* and *Separate Way.*

10. I take the term "overwritings" from DuPlessis.

11. I am indebted to Kristin Prevallet's essay in the present volume for the suggestion that Oppen's foxhole experience brought a kind of return to poetry and writing.

Works Cited

Oppen, George. *Collected Poems.* New York: New Directions, 1975.

——. *Discrete Series.* New York: Objectivist Press, 1934.

——. Interview with L. S. Dembo. *The Contemporary Writer.* Ed. L. S. Dembo. Madison: University of Wisconsin Press, 1972.

——. "The Mind's Own Place." Reprinted in *Selected Poems.*

——. *New Collected Poems.* Ed. Michael Davidson. New York: New Directions, 2002.

——. *The Selected Letters of George Oppen.* Ed. Rachel Blau DuPlessis. Durham, NC: Duke University Press, 1990.

——. *Selected Poems.* Ed. Robert Creeley. New York: New Directions, 2003.

——. *Selected Prose, Daybooks, and Papers.* Ed. Stephen Cope. Berkeley and Los Angeles: University of California Press, 2007.

Oppen, Mary. *Meaning a Life.* Santa Barbara, CA: Black Sparrow Press, 1978.

Reznikoff, Charles. *In Memoriam: 1933.* New York: Objectivist Press, 1934.

——. *Jerusalem the Golden.* New York: Objectivist Press, 1934.

——. *Separate Way.* New York: Objectivist Press, 1936.

——. *Testimony.* New York: Objectivist Press, 1934.

Safranski, Rudiger. *Martin Heidegger: Between Good and Evil.* Cambridge, MA: Harvard University Press, 1998.

Shoemaker, Steve. "Between Contact and Exile: Louis Zukofsky's Poetry of Survival." In *Upper Limit Music: The Writing of Louis Zukofsky,* ed. Mark Scroggins, 23–43. Tuscaloosa: The University of Alabama Press, 1997.

Thoreau, Henry David. *Walden.* Princeton, NJ: Princeton University Press, 1989.

Williams, William Carlos. *Collected Poems 1921–1931.* New York: Objectivist Press, 1934.

———. *A Novelette and Other Prose (1921–1931).* Toulon, France: To Publishers, 1932.

Zukofsky, Louis. "Program 'Objectivists' 1931." *Poetry* 37 (February 1932): 268–272.

Thinking Poetics

Introduction
Thinking Poetics

Steve Shoemaker

George Oppen was a founding member of the Objectivist movement, his book *Of Being Numerous* won the Pulitzer Prize in 1969, he is considered by many to be one of the major American poets of the twentieth century, and his work has had a powerful influence on subsequent generations of poets. Yet his poetry is still curiously neglected in academic circles. Thus far, only two book-length collections of essays devoted to his work have appeared; the most recent of these volumes was published over twenty years ago, in 1985, and the more substantial of the two collections appeared even earlier, in 1981.[1] In recent years, however, there have been encouraging signs that the appreciation of Oppen's poetry is on the rise. Certainly, Michael Davidson's crucial edition of the *New Collected Poems* (New Directions, 2002) has given us an important opportunity to reconsider the entirety of Oppen's challenging body of poetic work. And we may add to this Robert Creeley's new presentation of Oppen's *Selected Poems* (New Directions, 2003), which convincingly makes the case for Oppen as "one of America's most important poets." Further, the latest edition of the *Norton Anthology of Modern Poetry*—an influential and widely distributed teaching anthology—includes a substantial selection of Oppen's poetry. Indeed, this last development seems particularly telling, since it represents a striking reversal of earlier editorial decisions, which had given little weight to the Objectivist tradition of American poetry in general and *no* weight to Oppen's poetry in particular. But if Oppen's inclusion in the *Norton* anthology represents an important inroad into notably conservative poetic territory, his work has already proven indispensable to anthologies more aggressively devoted to innovative twentieth-century poetry. These would include the following: Jerome Rothenberg and Pierre Joris's *Poems for the Millennium, Volume One* (University of California Press, 1995); Douglas Messerli's *From the Other Side of the Century: A New American Poetry 1960–1990* (Sun & Moon, 1994); Eliot Weinberger's *American Poetry since 1950: Innovators and Outsiders* (Marsilio, 1993); and the remarkably adventurous Library of America collection, *American Poetry: The Twentieth Century, Volume Two* (2000). Further, a collection of Oppen's prose writings, edited by Stephen Cope, has recently appeared from the University of California Press, providing a welcome and illuminating complement to the poetry; and Susan Thackrey's perceptive critical essay *George Oppen: A Radical Practice* has been published in book form by O Books (2001).[2]

All of these developments signal the presence of a strong current of interest in Oppen's poetry; in addition to the anthologies and other publications I've already mentioned, one might point as well to the frequent references to Oppen's work on internet listservs devoted to poetry (like the one administered by the University of Buffalo), and in the fugitive but myriad publications of the thriving "little mag" scene (in both print and electronic incarnations); or one might take note of the annual George Oppen Memorial Lecture in Twentieth-Century Poetics, sponsored by the San Francisco State University Poetry Center. And indeed, the gathering of contributors for this collection can itself provide an impressive index of the continuing importance of Oppen's work for readers and writers of poetry. I have been pleased to be able to bring together a formidable assemblage of poets, poet-critics, and scholars who write about this work with energy and intelligence, and the readiness with which this gathering has coalesced says much about the powerful attraction Oppen's poetry holds in the context of the contemporary poetry scene. In a sense, this collection seems to have a quality of immanence, to have been already "in the air" (to cite Louis Zukofsky's way of speaking about poetic "influence"). Before previewing the contributions in more detail, however, I'd like to suggest a few of the reasons for the value of Oppen's work: his poetry offers us a subtle and original weave of sociopolitical engagement and formal innovation; it relentlessly returns us to fundamental, metaphysical questions, reminding us of the need for such investigations, *especially* in an age of epistemological skepticism; it displays a sophisticated historical awareness, which informs a sustained ethical confrontation with the great events of twentieth-century history, including its prominent "disasters" (the Great

Depression, the rise of fascism, World War II, the Holocaust, the Vietnam War, and so on); it mounts a sharp-eyed critique of the workings of "power"; and it presents us with a "lyric reaction to the world" of great intensity and beauty.

In this collection, these qualities of Oppen's work—along with many others—are explored by a diverse range of writers, adopting a variety of critical stances. Theodore Enslin, John Taggart, Michael Heller, Rachel Blau DuPlessis, and Henry Weinfield all write as fellow poets who knew Oppen well during his lifetime and who have been deeply influenced by his example in their own work. Their critical insights are enriched by their personal knowledge of the man and are in many cases interlaced with moving testimonies to the integrity of Oppen's thinking, living, and writing (such an approach seems especially apt given how intertwined these activities are in Oppen's practice). Charles Bernstein, Ron Silliman, Lyn Hejinian, and Michael Davidson all write as poet-critics affiliated with the Language Poetry movement, and as such, they bring to Oppen's work a keen appreciation for its relevance to contemporary avant-garde poetics. Forrest Gander approaches Oppen as a poet-critic of roughly the same generation as the Language group, but with distinct, and in some ways complementary, poetic concerns. John Lowney and Peter Nicholls offer trenchant scholarly accounts of two crucial sociocultural contexts for Oppen's work (considering, respectively, its engagement with the Vietnam War and its intertextual relation to the philosophy of Martin Heidegger). And finally, Kristin Prevallet and I come to Oppen as members of a younger generation of readers and writers working to articulate a new stage in Oppen's reception. The result of this mix is a rich and productive critical dialogue, touching on many of the most significant facets of Oppen's life and work. The multiplicity of interpretations, the variety of possible lineages, even the dilemmas and contradictions that emerge—these all open up a compelling horizon of reading, so that we may begin to arrive at a truer understanding of Oppen's place in twentieth- and twenty-first-century poetic culture.

Thinking Poetics

I put down my cup and examine my own mind. It is for it to discover the truth. But how? What an abyss of uncertainty whenever the mind feels that some part of it has strayed beyond its own borders; when it, the seeker, is at once the dark region through which it must go seeking, where all its equipment will avail it nothing. Seek? More than that:

create. It is face to face with something which does not so far exist, to which it alone can give reality and substance, which it alone can bring into the light of day.

—Marcel Proust, *Swann's Way*

Like Proust, George Oppen is a writer who participates in the modernist revolution of Mind; that is, he writes in an age when the mind itself has become the preeminent object of contemplation, even as he also maintains, as we shall see, an unwavering commitment to the existence of the world outside the mind. The title of the only essay he ever published, "The Mind's Own Place," signals his concerns. As is so often the case, Oppen's phrase is a subtle rewriting and recasting of earlier lines, in this case the famous declaration of Milton's Satan: "The mind is its own place, and in itself / Can make a Heaven of Hell, a Hell of Heaven." Oppen's reworking emphasizes both the "placeness" of the mind and the possessive relation, the relation of the mind to itself. For Oppen, the seeking, questioning, investigative mind is central to the project of poetry, but as for Proust, the mind is also a "dark region," an elusive and shifting ground that can only be explored fully by means of the sliding and shifting prosodies of the poem. To remind ourselves that the mind "must confront an abyss of uncertainty" whenever it "feels that some part of it has strayed beyond its own borders" is to begin to prepare to read Oppen.

My own title for the present volume, *Thinking Poetics,* is intended to suggest both that these essays enact a process of "thinking poetics" in their engagement with Oppen's work and that Oppen himself was committed to a poetry of thinking, a poetics of thought. This sense of Oppen's work runs, in one form or another, through all of the essays included here, but receives particularly detailed attention in two contributions: Peter Nicholls's "Oppen's Heidegger" and Rachel Blau DuPlessis's "'Uncannily in the Open': In Light of Oppen." Nicholls undertakes a thorough, rigorous exploration of the influence that Oppen's extensive reading of Heidegger had on his poetry, attending both to the evidence of the poetry itself and to the record provided by the ample collection of "working papers" housed in the New Poetry Archive at the University of California, San Diego. Building on Heidegger's distinction between "calculative" and "meditative" thinking, Nicholls shows how Oppen is committed to a kind of "poetic thinking" conceived as "not a matter of articulating a thought already had, but rather of deploying the resources of writing to disclose the texture of thinking as it takes shape." Whereas calculative thinking "is rooted in the will and sees the world as nothing more than a resource to be exploited," meditative thinking involves a kind of "letting go" that preserves the integrity of being itself. As Oppen himself puts it, the poem seeks a "cadence of disclosure," so that the poem's "prosody" becomes "the pulse of thought, of consciousness," and therefore also the pulse of "human *Dasein*, human 'being there.'" For DuPlessis, who was urged by Oppen, as she struggled to launch her own vocation as a poet, to make "poems of thinking," poems that demonstrate "a commitment to thought," Oppen's poetry evokes "a kind of ontological arousal to thought itself—not to knowledge as such, but to the way thought feels emotionally and morally in time."

But if the experience of thinking, of "consciousness" itself, is crucial to Oppen's work, consciousness is always consciousness of *something*. As Oppen put it in the epigraph to his book *The Materials:* "We awake in the same moment to ourselves and to things" (*New Collected Poems* 38). That line is taken from Jacques Maritain's *Creative Intuition in Art and Poetry*, where Maritain defines "poetry" in its broadest sense not as "the particular art which consists in writing verses, but [as] a process both more general and more primary: that intercommunication between the inner being of things and the inner being of the human Self which is a kind of divination" (3). Or, as he elaborates:

> The poet does not know himself in the light of his own essence. Since man perceives himself only through a repercussion of his knowledge of the world of things, and remains empty to himself if he does not fill himself with the universe, the poet knows himself only on the condition that things resound in him, and that in him, at a single wakening, they and he come forth together out of sleep. In other words, the primary requirement of poetry, which is the obscure knowing, by the poet, of his own subjectivity, is inseparable from, is one with another requirement—the grasping, by the poet, of the objective reality of the outer and inner world. (83)

To know oneself is the same as to know the world, and vice versa. One might even say that the two, self and world, give birth to each other. If Proust insists that the act of thinking is an act of creation, one that calls into being "something which does not so far exist, to which [the mind] alone can give reality and substance," Oppen balances this insistence with the claim that the poem must be concerned with "a fact which it did not create, the world."[3] Though he was adamant about the importance of "the life of the mind," Oppen unequivocally rejected solipsism.

But what exactly does one mean by the "things" which must "resound" in the poet? Maritain called "things" the "poorest and tritest word of the human language," explaining that he wished "to invest this empty word with the feelings of primitive man looking at the all-pervading force of Nature, or of the old Ionian philosophers saying that 'all things are full of gods'" (9). In "The Mind's Own Place," Oppen describes a similar problem with the word "reality":

> There comes a time in any such discussion as this when the effort to avoid the word *reality* becomes too great a tax on the writer's agility. The word of course has long since ceased to mean anything recognizably "real" at all, but English does seem to be stuck with it. We cannot assert the poet's relation to reality, nor exhort him to face reality, nor do any of these desirable things, nor be sure that we are not insisting merely that he discuss only those things we are accustomed to talk about, unless we somehow manage to restore a meaning to the word. (132)

Here Oppen is talking about a specific word, "reality," but more generally, the project of "restoring meanings to words" is central to the task of poetry and to what Oppen means by poetic thinking. Genuine thinking can only arise from a clear, considered use of language, but language itself has too often been corrupted by habit and by deception. For Heidegger, as Peter Nicholls reminds us, poetry is "the inaugural naming of being and of the essence of all things—not just any speech, but that particular kind which for the first time brings into the open all that which we then discuss and deal with in everyday language." But in carrying out this "naming of being" poetry must address a kind of "rift" between language and reality. If language is often inadequate or corrupt, the world, for its part, is often intransigent, or as Oppen put it, "impenetrable." Poetry, and poetic thinking, can work to heal the rift, but the healing is always temporary; the wound is continually reopened. And so new poems, poems *in* and *of* the world, must be continually brought into being.

I. Working Papers / The Mind Thinking

It may not be true for all poets, but for Oppen making poems demands what we might call the larger activity of *writing*. And it is from Oppen's working papers themselves that we can get a full appreciation of his meditative habit, or practice, of mind, and for what he means by poetry as an act of thinking and a test of truth. As a former curator of the Oppen archive at the University of California, San Diego, Michael Davidson explores Oppen's writing and thinking by bringing to bear his extensive firsthand familiarity with Oppen's "working papers" or "daybooks."[4] Consisting of thousands of sheets of both typed and handwritten manuscripts, these papers are unusual and compelling both at the level of the individual page and in aggregate. Accordingly, Davidson coins the term "palimtext" in order to emphasize both the "intertextual" quality of the writing and its dense materiality. A given page of Oppen's working papers might include lines of Oppen's own poetry, quotations drawn from a variety of sources, meditations building on, or rewriting, or otherwise engaging in dialogue with those quotations, and so on. Further, the pages themselves are shaped and grouped in distinctly thingy, materialist fashion. New lines or even stanzas of poetry are glued on top of old lines "so that the revised draft seems to rise vertically off the page in a kind of thick, textual impasto." Papers are joined by a quirky array of fasteners including "safety pins, pieces of wire, pipestem cleaners . . . [and] ring binders" (86). One sheaf of papers is even joined by a nail driven into a piece of wood. As Oppen himself puts it, he is engaged in a process of "piling up pieces of paper to find the words." The archive helps us to see that "for Oppen, the poem does not represent the mind thinking; it *is* the thinking itself, including its marginal references, afterthoughts and postscripts" (80). As the literal enactment and physical record of that thinking, the archive shows us the full extent of Oppen's dialogic, processual, materialist method of writing.

And that thinking, it should be noted, engages with what Davidson calls an "extraordinary range of subjects." Here is his brief but suggestive survey: "the youth culture of the 1960's, the Civil Rights movement, rock and roll, the poetics of Imagism, the work of John Berryman ('shameless but seductive'), Jung, the Vietnam War, the Altamont concert, Elizabeth Bishop's 'The Fish' ('I had always thought "o to be like the Chinook" was the silliest line ever written, but I see that it is not'), Charles Olson on PBS ('giving birth to the continent out of his head like Jove'), Plato, Hegel and Marx" (87).

Such a survey, which could be easily matched by any number of alternate listings substituting other poets and other social concerns, demonstrates the full breadth and depth of Oppen's investigation of the meaning "of being numerous." His approach to any given subject may be playful, thorny, cantankerous, or "controversial" (that is, if these writings had been originally intended for public consumption), but Oppen is engaged in a rich dialogue with other writers and thinkers and the process is always a deeply thoughtful one. Like one of his heroes, William Blake, Oppen believes in the necessity of ongoing "mental fight," a continual struggle that questions both his own assumptions and those of others.[5]

II. On *Discrete Series* / Of the World, Weather-Swept

Oppen's first book, *Discrete Series,* established many of the central concerns Oppen pursued for the rest of his life, and we can see each book as a continuation of the thinking begun here. At the same time, the twenty-eight-year gap between the publication of *Discrete Series* and the publication of Oppen's next book, *The Materials* (1962), is far from negligible. Oppen's thinking changes and develops between each of his books, but there is a particularly large jump between these two; a great deal of personal life and a crisis-ridden slice of twentieth-century history occupy the interval. In order to make sense of *Discrete Series* both within its own historical moment and within the shape of Oppen's poetic career, we need reading strategies that can encompass the book's thorny particularity while also staying attuned to Oppen's continuity of concerns. All of Oppen's books have their difficulties, their "arduous" approaches to the materials at hand, requiring and rewarding effort on the part of the reader. But in this early, strikingly "postmodern" book, Oppen was at his most avant-garde.[6]

Lyn Hejinian's essay is concerned with laying the groundwork for a close reading of Oppen's first book, the "preliminary" quality of the effort acknowledging the difficulty, even intransigence, of the work. Hejinian's richly suggestive contribution offers a number of approaches or strategies for reading one's way into this poetry. Perhaps most strikingly, Hejinian is interested in the way Oppen's deployment of "seriality" engages with a thoughtful, complicated, historically attuned sense of temporality running through the book. If Pound's Imagism is famously grounded in the idea of the "image" as "that which presents an intellectual and emotional complex in an instant of time," then Oppen's use of the poetic series is keyed to "image/instants" that become "events," which are "suffused with contingency and transience." In its serial arrangement, and in its response to the crisis in the perception of time instigated by the advent of capitalist modernity, the book investigates truth as "a temporal matter." Anyone encountering Oppen's serial work has to confront the problem of how to leap the gaps between one poem/unit and the next, and Hejinian addresses this difficulty by proposing the useful notion of the "blank connector," a kind of "flickering" that "occurs between the frames or image/instants of the series." In that "between" space there is a kind of co/incidence of continuity and discontinuity, and this paradox is something we have to engage in order to understand the jagged "flow" of time in Oppen's work.

My own essay shares Hejinian's interest in Oppen's engagement with capitalist modernity, but focuses more particularly on the way Oppen's serial poetry records and responds to the pressures of the urban scene. In this reading, Oppen anticipates the concerns of postmodern theorists like Donna Haraway and Katherine Hayles. In a "posthuman" order emphasizing "informational pattern over material instantiation" (Hayles) there is a kind of crisis of dis/embodiment. We can read the confusions and interpenetrations of subject and object in *Discrete Series* as reflecting this problem; moreover, his use of what I call "serial topography" works to map the crisis, registering the abstraction and immateriality of a universe of Heideggerian "mathematical projection," while also remaining stubbornly grounded and persistently "empirical." Reading Oppen's series is like negotiating a fragmented, disorienting landscape where frames of reference and even the ground under one's feet are constantly shifting. Even so, he resists treating the poem as a disconnected language machine generating its own realities; instead, he insists that the poem must be concerned with "a fact which it did not create, the world." In light of this insistence, I argue for a reading strategy that is attuned to an aesthetic of *translucence*, one that seeks clarity but acknowledges the obstacles to clear vision. Like Walter Benjamin, Oppen registers the densities and obscurities of our age, writing with an acute awareness of how technological transformation restructures thought, emotion, and the daily patterns of living.

III. Among the Philosophers

Oppen's "thinking poetics" is a kind of philosophical practice, or at least a *writing* practice that benefits from engagement with the kinds of questions that have occupied philosophers. Questions of epistemology, metaphysics, and ethics are all crucial for Oppen's poetic endeavor. His work demonstrates a lifelong concern with the problem of how we know what we know, addressing itself particularly to the problem of how we manage doubt and belief; he investigates the nature of the world, and of being, bearing in mind at all times what Heidegger also emphasized: that any inquiry into metaphysics begins with acknowledgment of the awe-ful fact that there is *something* where there might, after all, have been nothing; and he persistently addresses the problem of how we can lead ethical lives, and of what the "good life" consists. But for Oppen, a poet first and foremost, this engagement with philosophical concerns is a matter not of establishing a body of propositional truths, but of the *activity* of writing, of writing one's way toward conviction. In this sort of practice, the questions are never settled, and so there are always new poems demanding to be written.

As I have already suggested, Peter Nicholls's essay is crucial to this collection's emphasis on poetic thinking. As Nicholls writes: "Poetic thinking [in Oppen's work] is not a matter of articulating a thought already had, but rather of deploying the resources of writing to disclose the texture of thinking" (Nicholls 17). Poetry, in Oppen's view, is an enactment of thought, not a receptacle, and Nicholls's word "texture" attunes us to the palpable, physical nature of poetic thinking. Beyond this, Nicholls reminds us in other ways that poetic thinking goes beyond merely rational or calculative thought. Tracing Oppen's extensive, enduring engagement with Heidegger's writings in painstaking detail, Nicholls shows how Oppen takes from Heidegger not a body of thought, a set of conclusions to be applied to, or illustrated by, poetry. To be sure, Oppen did take certain key terms from Heidegger. As Nicholls writes, "Words like 'encounter,' 'disclosure,' 'world,' and 'occurrence' retain their specific Heideggerian inflection in Oppen's usage" (8), and the insistence on the role of poetry as "disclosure" or "unconcealment" or "revelation" is certainly one of the most profound connections between Heidegger's work and Oppen's. But Heidegger's affinity with Oppen is not a matter of settled philosophical "conclusions," but rather of a kind of approach or stance to the world, a stance that can be taken up in the service of further work, further thinking. As Nicholls shows, *thinking with Heidegger* is for Oppen a kind of poetic activity in itself—not straightforwardly logical, but angular, oblique, even mysterious.

If Heidegger is clearly the most important philosopher for Oppen, Forrest Gander nevertheless makes a compelling case for the affinity between Oppen's writing and the work of the philosopher Maurice Merleau-Ponty. We know from a letter Oppen wrote to Michael Heller that Oppen did read "quite a bit" of the philosopher's work, and Gander argues that Oppen's poetics aligns with the philosopher's emphasis on "a stance that acknowledges perception as the product of a participatory relationship with the world" (4). Merleau-Ponty's insistence on the bodily grounding of the act of perception, and on the "participatory" or "collaborative" relation between subject and object (and indeed, subject and subject) finds an analogue in Oppen's own experientially grounded, embodied, and socially embedded approach to poetry. Gander echoes the views of a number of other contributors to this collection when he argues that Oppen's version of poetic thinking cuts against the categories and preconceptions of conventional rationalism, registering instead "the very act of perception and thought coming into being, of language and feeling arising as experience" (11). Further, that act of thinking is fundamentally *inter-subjective* in nature, a matter of "subjectivity opening out onto otherness" (8).

IV. Two Wars

Though Oppen's work is deeply philosophical, it is also true that Oppen's thinking arises from the events of lived experience and that it is attuned to larger political and historical realities. Both the essays in this section deal with the relation of writing and politics, writing and history, as played out in Oppen's response to war, or rather his two sets of responses to two different wars: World War II and the Vietnam War. The biggest difference between the two wars in biographical terms is just that Oppen fought in the first but not the second. Both wars, however, demanded that Oppen make agonizing decisions, and both brought the vexed relation of politics and writing to a kind of crisis. During Vietnam, Oppen sometimes doubted whether he could continue writing, but ultimately he did keep going. Nonetheless, the question of whether to write or not seems to have remained painfully open, even as Oppen was writing one of his most important books of poetry, *Of Being Numerous*.

Kristin Prevallet's attentive tracking of Oppen's actual war experience—particularly her emphasis on the way Oppen experienced a kind of return to poetry in the midst of this battlefield trauma—gives us powerful new insight into the experiential grounding of the poetry. Her essay deepens our understanding of the crucial series of "war poems" Oppen wrote over the course of his career, as well as of his body of work as a whole, marked (scarred) as it is by some of the more dramatic, and horrific, events of twentieth-century history. Oppen's project is both historical and personal; he seeks a larger understanding of the events, and patterns, of twentieth-century history even as he also maintains a rigorous commitment to writing directly from what he knows. This attempt to bridge the personal and historical is remarkable, and the particulars of his experience put Oppen in a unique position. There is no other American poet of Oppen's stature who saw such heavy combat or experienced such serious wounds during World War II (or any other war for that matter). Oppen's testimony about the war is vivid, pained, and profound, even as he avoids, as Prevallet argues, the kinds of images and approaches that typify conventional war poetry. Prevallet gives us a new way to understand the fragmentation that sometimes characterizes Oppen's language, as in his remarkable late poem "Myth of the Blaze" where "the very form of the poem is a body encountering shrapnel." Her essay shows just how powerfully the experience of rending violence runs through Oppen's sense of the world, of being, and of art—an awareness lying in wait behind even images that are also touched by beauty and joy.

Just as Prevallet's essay demonstrates how Oppen's critique of U.S. imperialism grew out of his experience in World War II, John Lowney's essay shows us just how far that critique was extended as Oppen observed, and wrote about, the American experience in Vietnam. As Lowney shows, Oppen's long poem "Of Being Numerous" is both a "Vietnam poem" and a continuation of Oppen's career-long investigation of "the concept of humanity." As a Vietnam poem, the work stands alongside the massive literature of social protest generated during the period; as a philosophical investigation, and an elaboration of Oppen's larger social vision, the poem illuminates social, political, and cultural concerns of relevance to the twentieth century as a whole.

In Lowney's reading, Oppen's language in this poem records not the outpouring of a single poetic voice, but rather an embodied, enmeshed "network of voices," including poetic precursors, friends, family members, and poetic contemporaries, especially members of the younger generation. Two key intertexts are part of this network: Thomas Hardy's "poem of Christmas," which also happens to be a poem of World War I; and a letter from Walt Whitman to his mother written during his harrowing experience as a nurse at the time of the Civil War. Both intertexts are marked by the war, but both are also surprisingly domestic, and Lowney shows the extent to which Oppen's questioning of the rigid separation of masculine and feminine spheres is a theme of this "war poem." In order to keep writing during the Vietnam War, Oppen engaged with the social movements of the day, with the growth of a national counterculture, with the writings of his contemporaries, and with the dialogues of domestic life.

The language of the poem, as Lowney shows, is marked by a continual personal and cultural act of questioning, yet Oppen also demonstrates a determination to keep going, even amid the choking "air of atrocity." During the thirties he had decided that one needn't fiddle precisely while the house next door was burning, and during the sixties he continued to struggle deeply with his concerns about the inadequacy of language, including poetic language, in the face of social and political disaster. But this time around, the struggle led to a resolution opposite to that of the thirties, when he had turned aside from writing in favor of political action. At the time of the Vietnam War, Oppen addressed himself more and more to the fear that if we stop talking, and *writing,* we in fact "abandon one another." So despite his nearly overwhelming doubts, he continued to write.

Obviously, if he hadn't made that decision to keep writing, if we had been left with only *Discrete Series,* we wouldn't have the profound contribution to American poetry that makes up his later body of poetry. The intertexual, dialogic, interrogative nature of this later work testifies to the wide range of his concerns, and to the strength of his desire for larger social vision. He writes through, and with, the larger cultural moment, even as he also draws deeply on his experience of having lived through the Great Depression and World War II. The result is a remarkable act of bearing witness, both deeply personal and penetratingly historical in its sweep.

V. Receptions

The contributions in this section chart the thorny, varied reception history of Oppen's work. These essays give us a sense of some of the obstacles to reading Oppen, but also an understanding of the importance of his work for a whole range of poets and critics. Although Oppen was uncomfortable with cutting any sort of "figure" as a poet, his nearly legendary twenty-five years of "committed" silence, coupled with the integrity of his poetic vision, has made him a kind of model of poetic seriousness and honesty. And as the contributors to this collection show, his work demonstrates the power of a lifelong project of poetic thinking. Oppen's poetry makes clear that such a project must engage recalcitrant political and historical "facts," pursue linguistic investigation and innovation, and acknowledge those places and moments where poetry abuts silence.

One could trace many paths through these essays, but I would like to concentrate on one particular concern: the problem of the role of poetic "statement." This problem opens a debate that is taken up in one form or another by many of the contributors here. Briefly, the question is whether poetry can properly be said to make "statements" at all, or whether its role is to engage in a process of formal investigation that scrupulously avoids "closure" or "resolution." Ron Silliman's approach to this question is bound up with his early and influential account of the reception history of Objectivist poetry, an account situating Oppen's post–*Discrete Se-*

ries work as the most significant contribution to what Silliman calls "third-phase Objectivism." In Silliman's reading, the first phase of Objectivism is the period of the thirties, which produced both Zukofsky's *An "Objectivists" Anthology* and Oppen's *Discrete Series*; the second phase is the long interval of silence and/or neglect that ran from the midthirties to the sixties; and the third phase marks the group's resurgence, beginning, roughly, in the sixties. Silliman describes this third phase as "the most problematic of that literary tendency's phases, simultaneously its most influential and least cohesive time, mixing a resurgence of interest in existing texts with the production of new writings." As others have noted, the Objectivists can be seen as a kind of "missing link" between Pound/Williams modernism and the explosive appearance of the New American Poetry in the fifties and sixties; that is, when the New Americans discovered the Objectivists they found a poetry that made sense to them where there had seemed before to be only a kind of gap.[7] Such a reading situates the Objectivists in an interesting and peculiar niche in the history of twentieth-century poetry, but must be further complicated, as Silliman suggests, by the fact that Objectivist poets also ended up, during "third-phase Objectivism," writing alongside the younger generation—in fact younger *generations*—of American poets. For Oppen in particular, this meant occupying a status rather awkwardly situated somewhere between "elder" and "contemporary."

To understand how this reception history intersects with the problem of poetic statement we have to consider more closely the nature of the poetry Oppen was actually writing during third-phase Objectivism. Silliman's story of Oppen's place in the Objectivist lineage is also a detailed account of an important shift in Oppen's prosody as he moved from *Discrete Series* to the work he produced after his return to writing in the late fifties. Here Silliman makes his most controversial claim: that Oppen's post-return work "transforms [Objectivism] from the aesthetically radical and oppositional poetry of the early thirties to a more conservative (aesthetically, if not politically) phenomenon that then served as the foundation" for what he (Silliman) calls a poetic "middle road." The claim is provocative, and it will ultimately be up to readers of the collection, and of Oppen's poetry, to make their own assessment of its validity. For my purposes here, though, one of the most interesting elements of Silliman's critique is that the question of whether one sees Oppen's later poetry as "oppositional" or "conservative" seems to come down largely to how one views the role of poetic statement.

Silliman's essay, and the polemical stance it adopts, is itself conditioned by Silliman's own leading role in the Language Poetry movement, which achieved its first mature stage as Silliman was writing the book, *The New Sentence*, containing his reception history of the Objectivists. Further, Silliman's preference for the "aesthetically radical" early work of *Discrete Series* seems to be one held by a number of Language poets, and can be understood in light of Language Poetry's preference for syntactical and semantic disjunction and the refusal of poetic "closure."[8] To make his case regarding Oppen's later work, Silliman draws on William Carlos Williams's contemporaneous review of *Discrete Series*, in which Williams argues—in support of Oppen's early aesthetic—that a poem's "importance cannot be in what the poem says, since in that case the fact that it is a poem would be redundancy." Rather, Williams asserts, "the importance lies in what the poem *is*" (emphasis added), and "its existence as a poem" is fundamentally a question of its "mechanical structure." Here Williams is writing in the same mode, and from the same set of assumptions, that gave us his now famous definition, "the poem is a small (or large) machine made of words." Silliman's point here, his reason for drawing on Williams, is to show that Oppen's later poetry is inconsistent with this early "Objectivist" dictum, that "beginning with *The Materials*, Oppen . . . demonstrated himself to be a master in calling attention to what the poem *says*" (emphasis added). The implication seems to be that the earlier, radical mode of first-phase "Objectivism" has been tamed and vitiated, the concern with "what the poem *says*" coming at the expense of what the poem *is*.

As becomes clear when Silliman's reading of Oppen is itself read in light of the larger polemical context of *The New Sentence*, what is at stake is the question of whether a poetics allowing for "statement" can adequately "challenge the perceptual limits of the reader." But as Susan Thackrey's contribution to this collection argues, a poetics of statement need not be a poetics of the status quo. Indeed, Thackrey sees in Oppen's later poetry a continuing struggle with the problem of how to achieve fresh perception in the face of stale and restrictive cultural norms. To understand Oppen's complicated attitude toward statement we have to pay close attention both to poetry and poetics, taking into account, for example, Oppen's observation from a letter of 1959 that revisits the experience of the thirties: "Maybe I admire myself . . . for simply not attempting to write communist verse. That is, to [write] any statement already determined before the verse. Poetry has to be protean; the meaning must begin there. With the perception" (*Selected Letters [SL]* 22). So if this is Oppen's position, where does the disagreement with Silliman/Williams lie? In Thackrey's acute gloss, the real problem may be that in the later poetry Oppen's definition of "perception" comes more and more to include thoughts themselves. As Thackrey puts it, this "shift in perceptual focus" operates according to the realization that "Thoughts, in the sense of whatever might arise in one—sensations, cognitions, feelings, percepts, memories, and not least words—are part of what is perceivable, part of world, in which mind is." The disruptions of the conventional perceptual order can be harder to detect because the poetry now allows for the more "fully formed" expression of entire thoughts, of poetic *statements,* even as these thoughts/statements arise fluidly and mutably from the dynamic, "protean" nature of the poem, and even as they are subject to Oppen's poetic process of testing (poetry as a test of truth). The key point, for Oppen, is that the "statement" cannot be "already determined before the verse"; instead it must arise from the act of writing itself and from the process of weighing and testing that is a crucial element of this act.

And as it happens, Oppen was never very happy with Williams's definition of the poem as a "small (or large) machine made of words." This may be a little surprising, given Oppen's keen, if often critical, interest in technology, but Oppen had serious objections to the attempt to formulate a "mechanical" conception of the poem. In his notebook writings and letters, one finds instead the insistence that the "the poem is not built out of words, one cannot make a poem by sticking words into it, *it is the poem which makes the words* and contains their meaning" (emphasis added, *SL* 123). This approach to composition suggests that even though "statement" cannot *precede* the poem there is nevertheless a level of conceptualization, or perhaps a kind of "global" intuition, that interacts with, and indeed checks, the bottom-up impetus of the individual words jostling to become part of the poem. And Oppen's critique of Williams's dictum gets further clarification in the following observation: "In despair, so many turn to 'the machine of words' and arrive, if anywhere, at the Hermetic . . . 'the machine of words' which resolves everything — until one steps out the door" (*SL* 144–145). Here we see again Oppen's insistence on his own version of "realism," with its orientation to the brute fact of the physical world, the inescapable historical "weather," and the shaping, defining role of individual action (one steps out the door, presumably, to *do* something). Oppen's own touchstone definitions of poetry are consistent; rather than taking a mechanistic view they build on Heideggerian notions of "disclosure" to emphasize the "revelatory" nature of poetry.

Placed in juxtaposition, Michael Heller's and Charles Bernstein's essays stage a mini-debate on "clarity" that is close kin to the debate over "statement" we have just been considering. Bernstein praises the sophistication of Oppen's prosody and the integrity of his poetry of "witness," but comes close to Silliman's critique when he suggests that Oppen sometimes uses "clarity as a tactic," meaning that Oppen sometimes "fall[s] back onto clarity as a self-justifying means of achieving resolution through scenic motifs, *statement* [my emphasis] or parable in poems that might, given his compositional techniques, outstrip such controlling impulses."[9] In addition to "clarity," the keywords "statement" and "resolution" are both obviously important here. Like Silliman and other Language poets, Bernstein places a high value on "openness" and holds a suspicion of "resolution," which is taken to be an attempt to close down possibilities prematurely. But for Heller, Oppen's use of statement, clarity, and resolution are all crucial to his (Oppen's) poetics. As Heller puts it, Oppen practices a kind of "*supra*literalism consisting of statements that 'cannot not be understood.'" Further, the poet's concern with "clarity" is a form of love and "finally a way into praise of the world." Here Heller's argument resembles John Taggart's, with both writers pointing to something primal in Oppen's work. Heller calls the work "a kind of first poetry"; Taggart labels it "essential song," and identifies a quality of "stripping down that at the same time opens out and takes on depth." In similar fashion, Henry Weinfield writes that "Oppen's great gift is to allow . . . the simplest utterances . . . to be heard, as if for the first time," even as those utterances are also part of a rich intertextual weave condensing an astonishingly wide-ranging dialogue with other thinkers and writers.

Ultimately, the debate over poetic statement impinges on the question of what we can mean in speaking of a "poetics of thinking." Is it possible to have "conviction," to reach "truth" in Oppen's sense, without having some sort of "resolution," however tentative? One might argue that "conviction" is posited on resolution; one needs "resolve" in order to act, in order to know how to act—and even just to know what one thinks. But one of the most striking things about Oppen's work is that it is, as Rachel Blau DuPlessis argues, a poetry of both "negativity" and "commitment." If it is true that "every word of Oppen questions what art is possible," it is also true that the poetry is written toward belief. DuPlessis writes about what she calls Oppen's "black verse" as follows: "Black verse is Oppen's metaphor for his poetry of negativity: an unconsoled poetry of turning and searching, an unconsoling poetry of hope." DuPlessis finds that in

Oppen's work "commitment has migrated into form," and thus we are returned once again to the crucial importance of Oppen's innovative and investigative prosody. And perhaps close attention to Oppen's prosody offers a way out of the dilemma of "statement." One cannot really talk about statement in poetry without talking about form, but neither can one talk about form in Oppen's later work without also discussing "what the poem *says*." Oppen's poetic line holds its fruitful tension, seeking truth yet worried by doubt.

~

Whatever their perspectives, the essays in this collection have in common the fact that they pay detailed, thoughtful attention to Oppen's poetry and poetics. In combination, they offer a rich array of valuable approaches to the work. As becomes clear in these pages, Oppen is a historical thinker, not passively reflecting the trends of his day but actively addressing them by means of a restless, innovative poetics. Without slighting the power of historical currents or ignoring the fact that Poetry, and Language, and Thinking, are collective enterprises, we can find in Oppen's poetry a vision of great individuality and originality—one that tends to slip the nets of our conventional categories and modes of reading. To read Oppen well, we need to be ready to forget some of what we think we know and to remember the pleasures of seeing afresh. And if Oppen is not yet as thoroughly ensconced in the "the anthologies of influence" as one would wish, he has nevertheless left us with a body of work that gives sustenance.[10] As Theodore Enslin writes, in a brief essay that is both illuminating memoir and instructive criticism, Oppen's poetry is spare yet rich, providing us "only those things which a man might take if he were going on a long and dangerous journey and must travel light." Having witnessed the various disasters of twentieth-century history, Oppen did indeed come to believe that the journey ahead was both long and dangerous, that our whole civilization was—in a favorite Oppen word—"precarious." Yet he wrote toward that journey with a difficult hope.

Notes

1. The two collections are Burton Hatlen's *George Oppen: Man and Poet* and Jonathan Griffin's *Not Comforts, but Vision*. As critic, editor, and publisher, Hatlen, who passed away just recently, has been of tremendous importance for readers of modern American poetry; his volume on Oppen remains a crucial resource. Michael Cuddihy also published important material on and by Oppen in the jour-

nal *Ironwood,* particularly the George Oppen special issues, *Ironwood* 5 (1975) and *Ironwood* 26 (1985).

2. This long essay is excerpted in the present collection.

3. Oppen's phrase appears in "Three Oppen Letters with a Note."

4. Michael Davidson and Rachel Blau DuPlessis have both edited and presented selections from Oppen's archive. DuPlessis prefers the term "working papers"; Davidson prefers "daybooks."

5. Rachel Blau DuPlessis points to this quality of Oppen's thinking in her contribution to this collection.

6. We should note Oppen's insistence, however, that avant-gardism for its own sake was never his aim.

7. Silliman is no doubt thinking especially of Charles Olson, Robert Duncan, Robert Creeley, Allen Ginsberg, and Denise Levertov, all of whom appeared in Donald Allen's groundbreaking anthology *The New American Poetry,* and all of whom express a strong debt to the poetry of the Objectivists, Oppen included.

8. See, for example, Lyn Hejinian's essay "The Rejection of Closure."

9. The phrase "clarity as a tactic" takes up an old quarrel, reversing Oppen's critique of Zukofsy. Oppen accused Zukofsky of using "obscurity as a tactic" in his work.

10. The term "anthologies of influence" comes from John Taggart's contribution to the present volume.

Works Cited

Allen, Donald, ed. *The New American Poetry.* New York: Grove Press, 1960.

Griffin, Jonathan. *Not Comforts, but Vision.* Budley Salterton, Devon: Interim Press, 1985.

Hatlen, Burton. *George Oppen: Man and Poet.* Orono, ME: National Poetry Foundation, 1981.

Hejinian, Lyn. "The Rejection of Closure." In *Writing/Talks,* ed. Bob Perelman. Carbondale and Edwardsville: Southern Illinois University Press, 1985.

Library of America. *American Poetry: The Twentieth Century, Volume 2.* New York: Library of America, 2000.

Maritain, Jacques. *Creative Intuition in Art and Poetry.* New York: New American Library, 1974.

Messerli, Douglas, ed. *From the Other Side of the Century: A New American Poetry 1960–1990.* Los Angeles: Sun & Moon, 1994.

Oppen, George. *Discrete Series.* New York: Objectivist Press, 1934.

———. *The Materials.* New York: New Directions, 1962.

———. *New Collected Poems.* Ed. Michael Davidson. New York: New Directions, 2002.

———. *Of Being Numerous.* New York: New Directions, 1968.

———. *The Selected Letters of George Oppen.* Ed. Rachel Blau DuPlessis. Durham, NC: Duke University Press, 1990.

———. *Selected Poems.* Ed. Robert Creeley. New York: New Directions, 2003.

———. "Three Oppen Letters and a Note." *Ironwood* 5 (1975): 78–85.

Proust, Marcel. *Swann's Way.* Excerpted in *The Modern Tradition,* ed. Richard Ellman and Charles Feidelson Jr. and trans. C. K. Scott Moncrieff, 730–737. New York: Oxford University Press, 1965.

Ramazani, Jahan, ed. *Norton Anthology of Modern and Contemporary Poetry.* New York: W. W. Norton, 2003.

Rothenberg, Jerome, and Pierre Joris. *Poems for the Millennium, Volume I.* Berkeley and Los Angeles: University of California Press, 1995.

Silliman, Ron. *The New Sentence.* New York: Roof Books, 1987.

Thackrey, Susan. *George Oppen: A Radical Practice.* Oakland, CA: O Books, 2001.

Weinberger, Eliot. *American Poetry Since 1950: Innovators and Outsiders.* New York: Marsilio Publishers, 1993.

Zukofsky, Louis, ed. *An "Objectivists" Anthology.* Var, France: To Publishers, 1932.

I
Working Papers / The Mind Thinking

1
Palimtexts

Postmodern Poetry and the Material Text

Michael Davidson

```
Rembrandts's Old Woman Utting Her Nails


An old woman
As if I saw her now
For the first time, cutting her nails
In the slant light



WE HAVE A LONG TRADITION OF CONTEMPT FOR MATTER, AND HAVE
CEASED TO NOTICE THAT ITS EXISTENCE __ AND ONLY ITS EXISTENCE __
REMAINS ABSOLUTELY UNEXPLAINED


   No raod now ends   : a network of roads.
        _____


   Wespeak of people's death, except the deaths of the extremely
old, as if they might have lived forever   Of course tney could
not have, and therefore the difference bewteen thirty years of
life and seventy years does not in itself define thexdifference
tragedy

       But the wives or husbands and parents and children!!
That is, when the young die, there are the bereaved  By the time
the old man or woman dies, no on e is bereaved?  Dare we say that?

By the time a man or woman is very old, the tragedy has already
happened
        _____


   'Mankind' is a conversation
             _____



It would be hard for human nature to find a better ally in this
enterprise than love'   Symposium

One knows what he thinks   but not what he will find

   the classic love of the finite has no relevance to our knowledge
```

1. George Oppen, "Rembrandt's Old Woman Cutting Her Nails." The Estate of George Oppen. © Linda Oppen. Used with permission. From the George Oppen Papers at the Mandeville Special Collections, University of California at San Diego. The sheet is located at UCSD collection 16, box 16, file 5.

Piling up pieces of paper to find the words.

—George Oppen

The page (figure 1) is relatively free of penciled marks or emendations. Brief prose remarks are spaced at intervals, sometimes separated by typed underlining. At the top of the page is a short lyric entitled "Rembrandt's Old Woman Cutting Her Nails":

An old woman
As if I saw her now
For the first time, cutting her nails
In the slant light

It is a poem whose brevity, economy of imagery and lack of editorializing embody many of the values one associates with Imagism and Objectivism. The only concession to a larger theme is the phrase beginning "As if," which introduces the absent poet, a third participant in the conversation between painter (Rembrandt) and old woman. This "As if" finds its visual correlative in the "slant light" of the last line which hints at the indirect source of sight, mediated through a painter, a period of time, an aesthetic frame, a rhetorical displacement: "As if I saw her now."

Below the poem, perhaps serving as a commentary to it, is a prose remark, typed in caps:

WE HAVE A LONG TRADITION OF CONTEMPT FOR MATTER, AND HAVE CEASED TO NOTICE THAT ITS EXISTENCE—AND ONLY *ITS* EXISTENCE—REMAINS ABSOLUTELY UNEXPLAINED

To some extent this prose extends the poet's meditation on Rembrandt's design but shifts the emphasis from the painting's subject—the old woman—to its materiality, a shift that, as subsequent lines make clear, has distinctly existential implications:

We speak of people's death, except the deaths of the extremely old, as if they might have lived forever. Of course they could not have, and therefore the difference between thirty years of life and seventy years does not in itself define tragedy.

But the wives or husbands and children!! That is, when the young
die, there are the bereaved. By the time the old man or woman dies,
no one is bereaved? Dare we say that?

What began as a depiction of an old woman has now become an interrogation of the life beyond her. The author seems anxious to interrogate the
painting by understanding the world he shares with it, a world in which
matter "matters." And to the degree that both painter and poet engage
the problem of mortality, they share the same world. What links poet and
painter, youth and age, painting and subject is care: "It would be hard for
human nature to find a better ally in this enterprise than love," the poet
quotes from *The Symposium.* But human care alone is not enough; the material expression of that care, as presented in painting, poem, and prose is
the form that care takes. "Mankind is a conversation," and one might add
that the page itself, in its wandering and questioning, is the material analogue of that conversation.

This page by George Oppen, one of thousands like it among his papers
housed at the Archive for New Poetry at the University of California, San
Diego, represents a crucial problem for any consideration of postmodern
genres: that of the poem's materiality, its existence as writing.[1] Once we
have seen the "poem" in this context it becomes difficult to isolate it from
its written environment. Indeed, can we speak of "poetry" at all when so
much of it is embedded in other quotations, prose remarks, and observations? Does Oppen's oeuvre end in the work we know as *The Collected
Poems* or does it end on the page on which it began? I would like to answer
some of these questions by thinking about the status of the manuscript
page, not out of some antiquarian interest in early drafts but out of a concern for epistemological questions that lie at the heart of genre theory. For
if genre implies a way of organizing knowledge, then to "think genericity"
is to think thinking.

The question of genre in postmodernism has most often taken the form
of a debate over "new" genres (various forms of nonnarrative prose, sound
poetry, procedurally derived forms) or the rediscovery of previously mar-
ginalized genres (the manifesto, the fragment, the epistle). And while this
discussion has had a useful taxonomic function, it has not addressed the
issue of genericity itself, the degree to which postmodernism challenges
notions of categorization altogether. It could be said that the current debate extends a more pervasive romantic skepticism over formal categories,
manifesting itself on the one hand by a pursuit of some idealized, Mallar-

méan livre, or on the other by a ruthless exhaustion of types through forms of appropriation, quotation, and parody. It could equally be said that both positions rest on an opposition between literary and ordinary language (or in the case of Mallarmé, between poetry and journalism), which can be transcended only by exploiting the possibilities of the former.[2]

The most significant critique of genericity has occurred within the context of post-Structuralism with its emphasis on *écriture* as the recognition of difference (differance) within the linguistic sign. The writer is no longer "one who writes something, but the one who writes" (Barthes 18), leaving in place of novels, poems, and plays, the process of writing itself. Literature ceased to be defined by its "signs of literariness" but rather by its intransitivity, its refusal of all rhetorical and generic markers. I would like to retain post-Structuralism's emphasis on writing as trace, as inscription of an absence, but emphasize the material fact of that trace, an inscribing and reinscribing that, for lack of a better term, I have called a "palimtext." By this word I mean to emphasize the intertextual—and inter-discursive—quality of postmodern writing as well as its materiality. The palimtext is neither a genre nor an object, but a writing-in-process that may make use of any number of textual sources. As its name implies the palimtext retains vestiges of prior writings out of which it emerges. Or more accurately, it is the still-visible record of its responses to those earlier writings.

We can easily see evidence of such palimtextual writing in recent writers like Susan Howe, Bob Perelman, Kathy Acker, Bruce Andrews, Michael Palmer, Ken Irby, Paul Metcalf, and Clark Coolidge, who make extensive use of documentary or "found language." In these poets, the material nature of the sign and its specifically social and discursive context become major features of composition. Susan Howe's *Defenestration of Prague*, for example, makes use of documentary histories of the Thirty Years War (from which her title is derived) but also of etymological glosses, philological research, and word lists embodying qualities of linguistic fragmentation and materialization that inaugurate the modern era. But we can see many of these same features in a modernist lyric poet like George Oppen, especially if we treat his manuscript page as a text in its own right. It is precisely because Oppen's work so little challenges generic boundaries that his material text becomes so important for reconsidering the authority of those boundaries.

Poetry, according to Louis Zukofsky, "is precise information on existence out of which it grows" (28). It is seldom observed, however, that this growth begins and ends on a page. Traditional textual research has provided us with a methodology for investigating such materiality, but always with an eye toward some definitive version out of which to establish a copy text. As Jerome McGann points out, textual criticism has had one end in sight recently: "to establish a text which . . . most nearly represents the author's original (or final) intentions" (15). That desire to recover the author in the work is part of a "paradigm which sees all human products in processive and diachronic terms" (119). These intentions can be discovered by locating the last text upon which the author had a primary hand before it came under the influence of copy editors, compositors, and house style. The textual editor must master the corrupt text, deleting any superfluous or extraneous material not directly related to the work in question. Genre becomes an ally in such mastery insofar as it provides a codified set of rhetorical and textual expectations to which the text must ultimately conform. The editor's service to the author therefore is mediated by his generic expectations.

Postmodern poets, in this context, are no different from previous generations in the way that they keep notebooks, use paper, and revise their work. But recent poets have incorporated the material fact of their writing into the poem in ways that challenge the intentionalist criteria of traditional textual criticism. At the same time that poets have foregrounded the page as a compositional field, they have tended to "think genericity" to an unprecedented degree, making the issue of formal boundaries a central fact of their poetics. Indeed, for many poets today, it has become meaningless to speak of "the poem" but rather of "the work," both in the sense of oeuvre and of praxis. We can see the evolution of such a poetics not just in the writing of poets but in their papers and manuscripts, which, in increasing numbers, have been deposited in academic libraries. What we see in such collections is the degree to which writing is archeological, the gradual accretion and sedimentation of textual materials, no layer of which can ever be isolated from any other. George Oppen's page, to return to my initial example, is only one slice through a vast, sedimented mass that quite literally rises off the page, carrying with it the traces of prior writings. That page is part of a much larger "conversation" for which the published poem is a scant record.

One of the most important implications to be derived from studying the material text is the way that the page reinforces certain epistemological concerns of contemporary writers, notably the idea that writing is a form of knowing. Robert Creeley's remark, "One knows in writing," Charles Olson's equation of Logos and Muthos (thought and saying), and Allen Ginsberg's poetics of spontaneity are but three examples of a pervasive postmodern attempt to ground thought not in reflection but in action (Creeley 279; Olson 20). George Oppen is no exception. In a letter to Rachel Blau DuPlessis he speaks of the poem as a "process of thought" and then goes on to qualify this remark: "but it is what I think. A poem which begins with an idea—a 'conceit' in the old use of the term—doesn't learn from its own vividness and go on from there unless both terms of the conceit or one at least is actually *there*. I mean, had it begun from the parade, the experience of the parade and stuck to it long enough for the thing to happen it could have got one into the experience of being among humans—and aircraft and delivery trucks—?" (Oppen, "Letters to Rachel Blau DuPlessis" 121). For Oppen the poem does not represent the mind thinking; it *is* the thinking itself, including its marginal references, afterthoughts, and postscripts. One may begin with a "conceit," but, if one attends to the "parade" of passing things, one will find oneself "among humans—and aircraft and delivery trucks." Like one of his favorite philosophers, Heidegger, Oppen understands that knowledge is gained not by bracketing experience but by finding oneself already in the world, engaged in human intercourse. The poet strives to reduce the words to their barest signification, prior to their subordination to various cognitive or intellectual schemes.

The ideal of a poetry that no longer represents but participates in the process of thought is hardly new. It is part of the romantic movement's desire to escape forms of associationism and empiricism by a belief in the poem's creative nature. George Oppen is seldom mentioned in such contexts, but this is because we have tended to read his poetry through modernist spectacles. Critics have tended to see his work as the logical extension of certain Imagist principles involving "direct treatment of the thing" and economy of language. It is as though we have focused only on the first word in the title to his first book, *Discrete Series*, to the exclusion of the second. And by doing so we have reified the processual—and I would argue dialogical—nature of his thought in an ethos of the hard, objective artifact. Such a reading is not surprising; many of Oppen's own comments speak of the poem as "discrete" object among others, a "girder among the rubble," as he liked to quote from Reznikoff. This emphasis on the single poem is supported by his oft-stated desire to find the final real and indestructible things of the world, "That particle of matter, (which) when you get to it, is absolutely impenetrable, absolutely inexplicable" (Dembo interview 163).

My contention is that rather than being regarded as a series of single lyric moments, George Oppen's poetry should be seen as "a lyric reaction to the world" (Dembo interview 164), a fact that becomes dramatically evident once one looks at a page like the one described earlier. His poems represent the outer surfaces of a larger "conversation" that appears partially in broken phrases, ellipses, quotations, and italics throughout his work. We know, for example, that *Of Being Numerous* is constructed largely around quotations from Meister Eckhart, Kierkegaard, Whitehead, Plato, Whitman as well as friends like Rachel Blau DuPlessis, Armand Schwerner, and John Crawford, all of whom enter the poem silently in the form of inverted commas. And even where such obvious quotation does not occur, as in the poems from *Discrete Series,* Oppen's paratactic logic, truncated syntax, and ambiguous use of antecedents embody the shifting attentions of a mind dissatisfied with all claims to closure. Like the "Party on Shipboard," in that volume, Oppen's narrative movement is "freely tumultuous" (*New Collected Poems [NCP]* 15).

This idea of poetry as a "lyric reaction" can be understood best by comparing a poem from *Of Being Numerous* with a page from which it emerged. In the fourth section of "Route" we encounter the image of a sea anemone, which serves to focus a series of observations on language:

Words cannot be wholly transparent. And that is the "heartlessness" of words.

Neither friends nor lovers are coeval . . .

As for a long time we have abandoned those in extremity and we find it unbearable that we should do so . . .

The sea anemone dreamed of something, filtering the sea water thru its body,

Nothing more real than boredom—dreamlessness, the experience of time, never felt by the new arrival, never at the doors, the thresholds, it is the native

Native in native time . . .

The purity of the materials, not theology, but to present the circumstances
(*NCP* 194)

As a poem, "Route" deals with the difficulties of achieving clarity, the lure of the finite and indestructible. The section quoted here appears to be a qualification of that clarity, an attempt to express the "heartlessness" of words that refuse to become transparent to the world.[3] This qualification takes the form of a meditation on boredom, a state in which the world is reduced, as Oppen says, to "dreamlessness." The reality of boredom is, as he says elsewhere, "the knowledge of what *is*" (Dembo interview 169), a state in which things have been divested of significance and are encountered spontaneously and without reflection. It is a state in which one is naturalized in one's environment, "Native in Native time." Things have lost their novelty and may now be encountered in their instrumentality, ready-to-hand. In this condition, rather than in dreams or in conscious reflection, the "purity of the materials" may be experienced.[4]

The most confusing lines of this passage are those concerning the sea anemone. It is the only concrete image of the section and so becomes all the more important in focusing exactly how Oppen understands boredom. On the one hand, the sea anemone could represent a kind of ultimate boredom in which the organism's whole existence is conceived around "filtering the sea / water thru its body." This interpretation would seem to be borne out by a brief prose remark included among Oppen's papers: "Boredom, the sense of lack of meaning—In the cities from the sense of being submerged in the flood of people, of not being able to see out, of being a passenger—In the small cities from the sense of shallowness, the shallowness of affairs. Actually, of nothing happening." Here boredom is compared to "being submerged in the flood of people," a sort of urban analogue to the anemone's condition. On the other hand, because it is capable of dreaming, the sea anemone might represent the endurance of concern and novelty against the deadening effects of routine. However the "conceit" is being used, Oppen is clearly trying to find an image of reduced nature, a biological reality that challenges the theological and metaphysical. In its published version, the image of the sea anemone cannot be interpreted allegorically; it is one of those "heartless" words that must be interrogated and as such becomes "real."

This refusal of the anemone to become symbol is all the more evident when we look at a page upon which it makes an earlier appearance. Unlike the final published version in which all lines are relatively long, the typescript page (figure 2) contains a variety of prose and lined verse forms. The image of the sea anemone is contained in considerably shorter lines than in the later version and seems to respond to a previous prose remark: "Impossible to use a word without finally wondering what one meant by it. I would find that I mean nothing, that everything remained precisely as it was without the word, or else that I am naming absolute implausibilities, which are moreover the worst of all nightmares." The attempt to name, to "use a word without wondering what one means by it," leads to a cycle of repetition in which the only thing to say is that "we die":

We die we die we die

All there is to say
The sea-anemone dreamed of somethong
No reason he shoul d not

Or each one does
Filtering the sea water thru his body

I have retained Oppen's typos and misspellings to indicate how, at least in his early writing of it, the sea anemone was closely identified with the individual. The pronoun "one" is hidden in the word "anemone" and the misspelled "somethong" and is explicitly developed in the penultimate two lines (deleted from the published version). These two lines also provide an alternate antecedent for "his" in the final line, uniting anemone and human subject. Oppen wants to link human mortality with that of other creatures—as if to say "each one of us is like the sea anemone, living in a perpetual state of boredom, filtering the world rather than reflecting upon it. In this state all we can say of existence is that 'we die.'"

This existential fact is not alleviated by theological alternatives. In the published version, Oppen stresses "The purity of the materials, *not theology*, but to present the circumstances" (emphasis added), but in the typescript version the attack on theology is much more forceful, directly linked to Oppen's concern with language: "Because some people wrote a book a long time ago, they think they know what god is." This remark on the limitations of an authorizing Logos is extended later in a definition of the trinity as "the man, the spirit, and the mystery. / Which is man. And says nothing about god." In pencil, Oppen has added "Job's God," a remark which may very well have inspired the final remark: "an inconceivably brutal universe; it is possible that sea anemones dream continually." Clearly, a logocentric worldview is inadequate to the brutality of the universe, a view given secular force by the image of the anemone and salvific force by the story of Job.

What we see in the page that we do not see in the published poem is the dialogue between individual sections, each responding to and qualifying the previous. I see the sections as linked, one to the next, in a debate or ar-

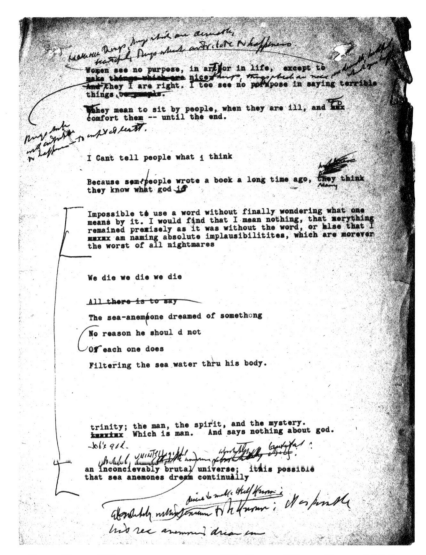

2. George Oppen, "Women see no purpose . . ." The Estate of George Oppen. © Linda Oppen. Used with permission. From the George Oppen Papers at the Mandeville Special Collections, University of California at San Diego. The sheet is located at UCSD collection 16, box 19, file 2.

gument over the efficacy of language in a "brutal universe." Language is both the vehicle and the object of Oppen's speculations as he oscillates between competing propositions. Such dialectical progress can be seen in the published version to be sure, but the page—with its spelling mistakes, its holograph emendations and variable lineation—provides a "graphic" indication of how immediate and personal that progress is. That is, the published page provides us with a series of more or less balanced (if truncated) prose statements on the theme of language; the typescript page provides us with the "graphic voice" out of which that theme emerges. The page shows Oppen grousing about difficulties of self-expression, the image of the sea anemone serving as a satiric version of the poet himself dreaming in his watery environment. The sea anemone, rather than serving as an icon of either boredom or conscious reflection, is a term around which all other sections constellate. It does not "serve" the poet's purpose but gets in his way, forces him to ask each question anew.

The varieties of intentions that I have described on one page are synecdochic for Oppen's archive in general. Like the individual page, the archive returns a quality of voice and physicality to work, which may seem, in its published version, hermetic and isolated. In terms that I have already employed, the archive revises generic expectations, turning lines of poetry into quotations, queries, and questions. As my epigraph suggests, Oppen was engaged in "Piling up pieces of paper to find the words" that would ultimately become poems. The archive is the physical remains of that "piling up" and deserves to be described as a text in its own right.

As the then curator of the Archive for New Poetry, I had a unique chance to view Oppen's papers in their pristine state, prior to being divided up into separate categories according to genre (manuscripts, notes, correspondence, daybooks, etc.). When we first opened the boxes in which the papers were sent, we were not prepared for the chaos that appeared. Where some archives come in folders or envelopes with dates or other identifying marks on them, Oppen's papers appeared as a great midden with shards of writing in every conceivable form, no one page related to the next, no recognizable order to the whole. A page containing a verse from the early 1960s would be followed by a page with scribbles from his last days. Prose and poetry were interspersed with grocery lists, phone numbers, quotations from philosophers, observations on films, tables of contents from books (his own and others). Every conceivable type of paper had been used, from cheap, high-acid newsprint (seriously decaying and flaking) to letterhead bond. Writing had been performed equally by typewriter and pen, the former often heavily annotated by the latter. Occasionally, passages of particular importance had been circled by crayons or felt-tipped pencil. Each manuscript page was like a collection as a whole: a marvelously scribbled, jumbled, and chaotic written field.

Although the bulk of the collection consists of individual pages like those already discussed, there are numerous larger manuscripts made up of anything from two to several hundred pages. In some cases, these manuscripts consist of a final typed draft of poems for a book, but in most cases, the gathering is simply a heterogeneous scatter of poems, jottings, and typings. The methods by which these groupings are held together deserve some comment. Oppen used a variety of fasteners—from safety pins, pieces of wire, pipestem cleaners to ring binders. The manuscript for the poem "The Little Pin" is held together, appropriately enough, by a little pin. Another batch of pages is held together by a nail driven though the upper-left-hand corner into a piece of plywood. A better definition of Objectivism cannot be imagined.

Oppen's method of composition can be best glimpsed by considering what I will call his "palimpsestic" manuscripts: pages of individual poems onto which new lines or stanzas have been glued so that the revised draft seems to rise vertically off the page in a kind of thick, textual impasto. Rather than add new lines on fresh sheets of paper, he would build his poem on top of itself, adding new lines in many cases ten or twelve pages thick. One such palimpsest, containing work from *The Materials,* appropriately enough, is "built" out of a ring binder. On the front and back inside covers, Oppen has glued the entire script for a reading given at the Guggenheim Museum, including his own interlinear commentary. The binder's metal clasps hold part of a manila folder (addressed to the Oppens in Brooklyn) to which other drafts and fragments are glued. The whole pile of pages is held together by pipestem cleaners which are wrapped, at the top, around a number 2 pencil and a one-inch roundhead screw.[5]

My purpose in describing the material component of Oppen's work is to suggest the degree to which writing was first and foremost a matter of something ready-to-hand, something as immediate as a coat hanger or piece of wire. The pipestem cleaners, metal clasps, and glue are visible representations of those "little words" that Oppen liked so well, the basic materials of a daily intercourse. "Gone for Breakfast in Z coffee shop across the street," reads the back of one heavily scribbled folder, indicating that the recto of poetry easily became the verso of daily living. And just as he used whatever writing surface was nearby, so he drew upon the "signage" that surrounded him: newspapers, books, magazines, and of course, conversations, parts of which can be found recorded through the collection. Oppen did not keep a separate notebook for poems and another for quotations and another for prose, but, rather, joined all of them together in a continuing daybook.[6] One finds drafts of letters to friends on pages that contain the beginnings of poems. In many cases, a quotation from a newspaper would become the genesis of a poem, a poem the genesis for a prose commentary on an article in the newspaper.

This daily, unbound diary covers an extraordinary range of subjects: the youth culture of the 1960s, the civil rights movement, rock and roll, the poetics of Imagism, the work of John Berryman ("shameless but seductive"), Jung, the Vietnam War, the Altamont concert, Elizabeth Bishop's "the Fish" ("I had always thought 'o to be like the Chinook' was the silliest line ever written, but I see that it is not"), Charles Olson on PBS ("giving birth to the continent out of his head like Jove"), Plato, Hegel, and Marx. His comments on Robert Lowell's "Skunk Hour" are worth quoting in full: "perhaps I simply do not understand the Christian sense of 'sin.' I do not understand a sin by which no one was injured. If the people in the love cars were embarrassed by his peeking, then it was a sin. If not, it was merely undignified"; or his remarks on Pound "and if Pound had walked into a factory a few times the absurdity of Douglas' theory of value, which Pound truculently repeats in the *Cantos,* would have dawned on him—it sometimes pays to have a look. And to keep still till one has seen."

Treated palimtextually, such remarks elucidate that trinity of concerns that informs Oppen's entire life: politics, epistemology, and poetics. The archive suggests that all three are inextricably united like those jerry-rigged manuscripts held together with pipestem cleaners. As he meditated on contradictions in American politics, so he drafted poems; as he drafted poems, so he thought about the relationship of old age to love. The manuscripts do not suggest a man working toward the perfect lyric but of a man struggling for a vision of society in which the poem plays an instrumental role. To adapt a remark on the page mentioned earlier, Oppen "knows what he thinks but not what he will find."

John Taggart records a conversation in which Oppen claimed that "he did not think of his books as collections of individual poems but as developments of a thought" (259). The study of Oppen's manuscript certainly verifies this developmental aspect of his writing and suggests the need for an alternative mode of analysis that takes the entire archive—including its material form—into account.[7] Unfortunately, much modernist criticism has defined "materiality" in strictly rhetorical terms—the foregrounding of poetic devices and the defamiliarizing of language—thus validating artisanal aspects of the poem to the exclusion of the world in which it is produced. For Oppen, materiality implies "objects" and the realms of value that objects constellate:

> There are things
> We live among 'and to see them
> Is to know ourselves'
> (147)

Oppen's processual mode of writing, his incorporation of nonliterary genres, his use of the page as speculative field or "conversation" are all dimensions of his Objectivism and cannot be separated from the final published poem.

What we have seen in Oppen as an explicit materialization of writing is reflected implicitly in numerous contemporary poets for whom the page has become a "field" or "score." Charles Olson's oralist poetics, for example, emphasizes the typewriter as score for the voice and the physical page as a map or graph. And Robert Creeley, speaking with Allen Ginsberg at the Vancouver Poetry Conference, comments on the importance of typewriters, pens, and paper in creating the measure of his verse: "Habits of this kind are almost always considered immaterial or secondary. And yet, for my own reality, there is obviously a great connection between what I physically do as a writer . . . and what comes then out of it" (30). Creeley goes on to qualify this remark by speaking of his dependence on the typewriter: "I wanted to be able to [write] with a typewriter. Now equally I never learned to type. So I mean my typing is a habit that's developed, with two fingers . . . Think again—that begins to be a qualification of how *fast* I can write. In other words, I find that the pace of my writing is concerned with the speed with which I can type" (30).[8] Such remarks could be seen as the poet's version of an action aesthetic, shared by painters and musicians of Creeley's generation, in which the physical medium becomes as much the subject as the means of production. The typographic and concrete experiments of Pound, Williams, Apollinaire, cummings, Mallarmé, the Dadaists and Futurists provided a variety of important new models for what the graphic poem might be, and the poets of "field verse" extended those modernist experiments into distinctly physiological dimensions.

The most characteristic form that field composition takes is the long, open-ended notebook poem.[9] Works like Olson's *Maximus Poems* or Robert Duncan's *Passages* are based on historical and literary researches that incorporate documentary evidence as well as the methodologies of that research into the poem.[10] History, for both poets, is a matter of the record—a written record—and their poems incorporate not only references to American history or Renaissance theology but to specific editions, translations, and volumes in which that evidence was first encountered. More important, Olson and Duncan make their inaugural entries into these other sources part of the poem. Olson, for example, corrects details about Gloucester's history in "Maximus to Gloucester, Letter 15" that he had made in a previous "Maximus" poem (71). Similarly, Robert Duncan in "Poem Beginning with a Line by Pindar" provides a parenthetical comment about his edition of the Greek poet: "(An ode? Pindar's art, the editors tell us, was not a statue but a mosaic, an accumulation of metaphor. But if he was archaic, not classic, a survival of obsolete mode, there may have been old voices in the survival that directed the heart" (69). The fact that this remark concerns genre nicely illustrates my point: that reference to a canonical genre—the ode—occurs in a passage that denies the genre's authority. Duncan's "ode," at least in his editor's definition, will be like Pindar's, a "mosaic, an accumulation of metaphor." The open parenthesis suggests that what had begun as an afterthought continues into the poem as a generative element in its composition. Olson's and Duncan's self-reflection marks a desire to make the means and materials of research part of the poem—a dance, as Olson says, "sitting down" (39).

The idea of the poem-as-notebook coincides with the poets' increasing desire to have greater control over the means of reproduction. Robert Duncan has insisted that his recent work be reproduced directly from his own typescript and has produced several facsimile volumes of his holograph copy. Olson's *Maximus Poems* involves typographic and notational formats that provide an idiosyncratic "map" of the poet's vocal and visual intentions. George Butterick chronicles the difficulties of transferring those intentions to the printed page, and in at least one case simply reproduces the author's holograph version of "*Migration in Fact . . .*" with its spiraling, interlocked notation (Butterick v–xvi). Several of Philip Whalen's actual notebooks have been reproduced in order to show his extraordinary calligraphic hand in concert with his designs and drawings. Pages of Robert Creeley's notebook have been reproduced in facsimile by Bouwerie Editions. And in a more general sense, works like A. R. Ammons's "Tape for the Turn of the Year," John Ashbery's "Vermont Notebook," Paul Blackburn's *Journals,* Robert Creeley's *A Day Book,* Ed Dorn's *Yellow Lola,* Ted Enslin's *Synthesis,* Allen Ginsberg's *Planet News,* Joanne Kyger's *Desecheo Notebook,* Denise Levertov's "Entr'acte," Bernadette Mayer's *Midwinter Day,* Ron Silliman's *Tjanting,* Gary Snyder's *Mountains and Rivers without End,* and Philip Whalen's *Scenes of Life at the Capital,* to name only a few, in some way or another incorporate the idea or format of the notebook into their form.[11]

At one level the poem-as-notebook seeks to establish some kind of authenticity and immediacy.[12] The poem becomes the record of its own growth, form replicating the sudden shifts of attention in a desultory speculation. But at a more complex level such emphasis on the process rather than the product of writing dissolves boundaries between literature as artifact and literature as daily record. This could be said for a work like Bernadette Mayer's *Midwinter Day,* a poem that incorporates observations, readings, and routines of a twelve-hour period of time in December 1978. Although on the surface it appears to be a rather typical personalist lyric, balancing local details with reflective comments, it is animated by the urgency of staying within certain imposed temporal boundaries. The notebook, rather than being the course for materials used retrospectively, is the activity *of* and *for* that day. Writing and living are so closely united that incidents like shopping or doing the wash merge imperceptibly with the act of writing about them.

> You go out for cigarettes,
> As if love is not the food
> Of those of us satisfied enough to write
> To write to lend urgency pleasure, to sing
> To celebrate, to inspire, to reveal
> You put on
> Your gotten shoes and coat in an image
> And say you will be right back
> While you're out love is stored
> In intensest house, this cave of it, . . .
> (116)

More traditional "domestic lyrics" would find the poet looking back upon an incident, using details to inspire reflections "on" or "about" those actions. In Mayer's work, there is no separation between incident and reflection. Time is happening "right now"; the writer is "this person";

>   Today I'm the present writer
>   At the present time the snow has come
>   At this moment we won't starve
>   At once the ferries terrify us and
>   We knead red and green peppers with
>   Our contrasting hands
>   At a time
>   Very close to the present I want to get
>   A tight pair of pants and dance
>   With you with things as they are
>   (16–17)

The last lines play a nice variation on Stevens's "Man With a Blue Guitar," in which "things as they are / Are changed upon the blue guitar" (165). By making her poem coincide with the day it records (and the notebook in which it is written) Mayer claims a kind of presence unmediated by any appeal to the transforming imagination. At the same time, because the time of writing is the present, she must suspend until the future a time when she can "dance / With you" and truly participate with "things as they are."

Although one feature of the notebook-as-poem is an antiformalist gesture in the direction of more authentic experience it also imposes its own formal limitations upon writing. Mayer's decision to record *everything* on one day determines a strict limit on materials that will be permitted. The same could be said for the overtly procedural poetics of Ron Silliman, who uses notebooks as a way of generating long, rule-determined books like *Ketjak* or *Tjanting*. In composing such works, Silliman draws from a vast body of materials, some derived from the newspaper and much derived from observation. Unlike the personalism of Mayer, however, Silliman subjects this material to formal operations that remove the incident from its experiential context. In *Tjanting*, for example, the account of a muscle pull, spilled grease, and a blistered lip are subjected to radical transformation. Individual sentences are removed from their normal narrative progression and organized according to the Fibonacci number series. Each paragraph of the book expands incrementally as numbers of sentences are added according to the formulation 1,2,3,5,8,13 . . . and so forth. The opening paragraphs give some indication of how this occurs:

> Not this.
> What then?
> I started over & over. Not this.
>
> Last week I wrote "the muscles in my palm so sore from halving the rump roast I cld barely grip the pen." What then? This morning my lip is blistered.
>
> Of about to within which. Again & again I began. The gray light of day fills the yellow room in a way wch is somber. Not this. Hot grease had spilld on the stove top.
>
> Last week I wrote "the muscle at thumb's root so taut from carving that beef I thought it wld cramp." Not so. What then? Wld I begin? This morning my lip is tender, disfigurd. I sat in an old chair out behind the anise. I cld have gone about this some other way. (Silliman 11)

Not only does each paragraph increase according to the Fibonacci series, each sentence counteracts or contrasts the previous, thus extending the dialectic of the opening lines: "Not this. / What then?" My point in using this example is to show how the use of materiality (the notebook-as-source for poetry), when subjected to procedures, points to a second-order materiality, that of language itself. And since language is the barrier as well as the object of the poem, its radical defamiliarization points to the conventional, rather than the natural, qualities of communication. Silliman's larger point is not how poetry can accommodate the quotidian by ever-more effective representations but how the quotidian is already materialized *as* representation. And to return to my point about Oppen, it is only when the language of passive observation ("This morning my lip is tender") is fractured that the mood of boredom is erased and a critical perspective becomes possible.

Genre theory has no name for this kind of writing and so falls back on hybrid terms like "greater romantic lyric" or "prose poem." Such terms are useful in mapping a general area of shared features, but they ignore the specific discursive properties of each work. A palimtextual study of poetry would look not only at the poem in relation to similar poems (the traditional task of genre study) but to the writing each poem displaces, a displacement that is "represented" in the manuscript as a kind of over-writing. Far from rejecting theories of genre I see this study of poetry as emphasizing the presentational aspect of genre, the degree to which literary works are addressed to an audience. Northrop Frye sees this aspect as central to generic distinctions, whether a work is intended to be played on a stage or recited to a community or sung to the Muse. "The basis of generic criticism in any case is rhetorical, in the sense that the genre is determined by the conditions established between the poet and his public" (247). Precisely, but I would go a step further and see this relationship as being embodied in the way the poem engages the materiality of both written and speech genres.

We can see this presentational relationship to an audience best in those areas where an audience is least invited: in the poet's papers and manuscripts. What we learn from the material fact of archive and page is the degree to which poems are a temporal process of marking and remarking, of response and contention. George Oppen's poems exist in relation to other texts and are part of his larger interrogation of the world. As Jack Spicer says, "Poems should echo and reecho against each other. They should create resonances. They cannot live alone any more than we can" (61). And it is this temporal process that is foregrounded in more recent postmodern works. These more self-consciously anti-generic texts—far from distinguishing themselves from the past—force us to look at traditional forms from new perspectives. Shakespeare's heavily annotated acting texts, Blake's illustrated books, Emily Dickinson's fascicles and Pound's ideograph-encrusted late Cantos are but four examples of a materializing tendency in every writer, a tendency that tends to get lost in the attempt to interpret and unify the text. So long as we search for "new" genres in the interstices of the old, we will be searching within the terms of normative criticism that seeks consensus among dissimilar elements. We will fail to see processes that occur at (or *in*) the margins of the material artifact, an object that can never be recovered strictly within textual terms. If that object fails to stay in one place, perhaps it is because it is the trajectory rather than the fulfillment of writing.

Notes

1. All references to George Oppen's papers are to the George Oppen Manuscript Collection at the Mandeville Department of Special Collections, University of California, San Diego, La Jolla, California.

2. On Mallarmé and genre, see Marjorie Perloff, "Postmodernism and the Impasse of Lyric," 172–181. On Romanticism and the attack on genre, see Philippe Lacoue-Labarthe and Jean-Luc Nancy, "Genre," *Glyph* 7 (1980): 1–14; and Michel Beaujour, "Genius Universum," *Glyph* 7 (1980): 15–31.

3. In earlier drafts of the poem, section 4 directly follows those which, in the published version, now conclude section 2: "I have not and never did have any motive of poetry / But to achieve clarity."

4. Eric Mottram glosses these lines as stating, "Knowledge of boredom becomes a philosophic Tool to ascertain what the facts are" ("The Political Responsibilities of the Poet" 151).

5. Many of the palimsestic manuscripts had originally been pasted to the wall of Oppen's study, suggesting that he not only wrote *on* paper but lived quite literally *within* it.

6. I have edited a selection from Oppen's "daybooks" in *Ironwood* 26 (1985): 5–31. Excerpts appear, as well, in *Conjunctions* 10 (1987).

7. Susan Howe has begun such a project in her recent work on American women writers. See *My Emily Dickinson* (Berkeley, CA: North Atlantic Books, 1985); "The Captivity and Restoration of Mrs. Mary Rowlandson," *Temblor* 2 (1985): 113–121.

8. Creeley's remarks on the relationship between his characteristically short lines and his typing become even more interesting when set beside the fact that Robert Duncan, who writes in extremely long lines and open forms, earned his living as a typist when younger.

9. Of course by referring to "field" verse and "notebook poem" I am participating directly in the genre-naming tendency I wish to call into question. The difficulty of discussing poetics without depending on classifications shows how completely genre structures our thought. I can only look forward to a time in which a "notebook poem" also refers to a notebook and not just a series of stylistic features.

10. I have discussed the fuller implications of this methodology in "From the Latin *speculum:* the Modern Poet as Philologist," *Contemporary Literature* 28, 2 (Summer 1987): 187–205.

11. Works referred to in this section: Philip Whalen, *The Invention of the Letter: A Beastly Morality* (New York: Carp and Whitefish, n.d.); Philip Whalen, *Highgrade* (San Francisco: Coyote's Journal, 1966); Robert Creeley, *Notebook* (New York: Bouwerie Eds., 1972); A. R. Ammons, *Tape for the Turn of the Year* (Ithaca, NY: Cornell University Press, 1965); John Ashbery, *The Vermont Notebook* (Los Angeles: Black Sparrow Press, 1975); Paul Blackburn, *The Journals* (Santa Barbara, CA: Black Sparrow Press, 1975); Robert Creeley, *A Day Book* (New York: Charles Scribner's, 1972); Ed Dorn, *Yellow Lola* (Santa Barbara, CA: Cadmus Eds., 1981); Ted Enslin, *Synthesis 1–24* (Plainfield, VT: North Atlantic Books, 1975); Allen Ginsberg, *Planet News: 1961–1967* (San Francisco: City Lights, 1968); Joanne Ky-

ger, *Desecheo Notebook* (Berkeley, CA: Arif Press, 1971); Denise Levertov, "Staying Alive," in *To Stay Alive* (New York: New Directions, 1971), 21–84; Robert Lowell, *Notebook* (New York: Farrar, Strauss and Giroux, 1970); Bernadette Mayer, *Midwinter Day* (Berkeley, CA: Turtle Island Press, 1982); Ron Silliman, *Tjanting* (Berkeley, CA: The Figures, 1981); Gary Snyder, *Six Sections from Mountains and Rivers without End* (San Francisco: Four Seasons Foundation, 1965); Philip Whalen, "Scenes of Life at the Capital," in *Heavy Breathing: Poems 1967–1980* (San Francisco: Four Seasons Foundation, 1983). Many of these poems or books have been subsumed into larger collections, but I have cited the original publication data in order to emphasize the form of the "book" as it first appeared.

12. Obviously the very fact of such immediacy rules out a work like Robert Lowell's *Notebook* for inclusion in the preceding list, even though it would seem an obvious variation. The sonnets of *Notebook* with their ornate rhetoric, complex rhymes, and reflective mood stand at quite the opposite end of the continuum from what I have been developing here.

Works Cited

Barthes, Roland. "To Write: An Intransitive Verb?" *The Rustle of Language.* Trans. Richard Howard. New York: Hill and Wang, 1986. 11–21.

Beaujour, Michel. "Genius Universum." *Glyph* 7 (1980): 15–31.

Butterick, George. *Editing the Maximus Poems.* Storrs: University of Connecticut Library, 1983.

Creeley, Robert. "An Interview with Robert Creeley." *The Poetics of the New American Poetry.* Ed. Donald Allen and Warren Tallman. New York: Grove Press, 1973. 273–292.

———. "Contexts of Poetry: With Allen Ginsberg in Vancouver." *Contexts of Poetry; Interviews 1961–1971.* Ed. Donald Allen. Bolinas, CA: Four Seasons Foundation, 1973. 29–43.

Duncan, Robert. *The Opening of the Field.* New York: Grove Press, 1960.

Frye, Northrop. *Anatomy of Criticism: Four Essays.* Princeton, NJ: Princeton University Press, 1973.

Howe, Susan. *Defenestration of Prague.* New York: Kulcher Foundation, 1983.

Lacoue-Labarthe, Philippe, and Jean-Luc Nancy. "Genre." *Glyph* 7 (1980): 1–14.

Mayer, Bernadette. *Midwinter Day.* Berkeley, CA: Turtle Island Press, 1982.

McGann, Jerome. *A Critique of Modern Textual Criticism.* Chicago: University of Chicago Press, 1983.

Mottram, Eric. "The Political Responsibilities of the Poet: George Oppen." *George Oppen Man and Poet.* Ed. Burton Hatlen. Orono, ME: National Poetry Foundation, 1981. 149–167.

Olson, Charles. *The Maximus Poems.* Ed. George F. Butterick. Berkeley and Los Angeles: University of California Press, 1983.

———. *The Special View of History.* Ed. Ann Charters. Berkeley, CA: Oyez, 1970.

Oppen, George. *Collected Poems.* New York: New Directions, 1975.

———. Interview with L. S. Dembo. *Contemporary Literature* 10, 2 (Spring 1969): 159–177.

———. "Letters to Rachel Blau-DuPlessis." *Ironwood* 24 (Fall 1984): 119–138.

Perloff, Marjorie. "Postmodernism and the Impasse of Lyric." *The Dance of the Intellect: Studies in Poetry of the Pound Tradition.* Cambridge: Cambridge University Press, 1985. 172–200.

Silliman, Ron. *Tjanting.* Berkeley, CA: The Figures, 1981.

Spicer, Jack. *The Collected Books of Jack Spicer.* Ed. Robin Blaser. Los Angeles: Black Sparrow Press, 1975.

Stevens, Wallace. *The Collected Poems of Wallace Stevens.* New York: Knopf, 1968.

Taggart, John. "Deep Jewels: Oppen's *Seascape: Needle's Eye.*" *Ironwood* 26 (Fall 1985): 252–262.

Zukofsky, Louis. "A Statement for Poetry." *Prepositions.* New York: Horizon Press, 1968. 27–31.

II

On *Discrete Series* / Of the World, Weather-Swept

2
Preliminary to a Close Reading of George Oppen's *Discrete Series*

Lyn Hejinian

With the publication of *George Oppen: New Collected Poems* (New Directions, 2002) under the careful editorship of Michael Davidson, we have *Discrete Series* once again almost exactly as George Oppen intended it and as it originally appeared in 1934 when published under the imprint of his own Objectivist Press. The salient feature left out during interim publication (in New Directions' 1975 *Collected Poems of George Oppen*) is the placement of the poems one to a page. In the original Objectivist Press edition of the poem, after the initial prefatory poem, which appears on the right opposite a blank page, the thirty short poems that constitute the rest of the series are printed in pairs on facing pages. New Directions' space-saving decision in 1975 to run the poems continuously, with only a small amount of space between them (an amount of space so small as to make it at times difficult to know where one poem ends and another begins), all but suppressed the dialogical character and dialectical theme of the work; it became almost impossible to track the contrapuntal development that is one of the poem's most important features. Happily, the *New Collected* remedies the mistake of the cold war–era volume; the only feature of the Objectivist Press edition that the *New Collected* version doesn't replicate is the blank page separating Ezra Pound's "Preface" from the opening poem.

Discrete Series has, in fact, two prefaces. The first is Pound's—brief but not much to the point. The tone is predictably authoritative and paternalistic, and his principal concern is to admit the book's obscurity (he seems to have found it obscure himself) while testifying to the originality of Oppen's sensibility. Neither of these points is illuminating, but one assumes Pound's gesture in writing the preface was well meant.

The real "Preface" to *Discrete Series* is its opening poem, written of course by Oppen but partially in the words and very much in the mood and mode not of Ezra Pound but of Henry James. Though James is not named directly, his presence is invoked allusively, through the name of Maud (or Maude—Oppen, probably inadvertently, adds an e to the name) Blessingbourne, one of the two principal characters in James's short 1902 work, "The Story in It."

The pertinent passage, containing the phrase that Oppen quotes directly, reads as follows:

> Nothing had passed for half an hour—nothing, at least, to be exact, but that each of the companions occasionally and covertly intermitted her pursuit in such a manner as to ascertain the degree of absorption of the other without turning round. What their silence was charged with, therefore, was not only a sense of the weather, but a sense, so to speak, of its own nature. Maud Blessingbourne, when she lowered her book into her lap, closed her eyes with a conscious patience that seemed to say she waited; but it was nevertheless she who at last made the movement representing a snap of their tension. She got up and stood by the fire, into which she looked a minute; then came round and approached the window as if to see what was really going on. (James 403–404)

The quotation was apparently identified by L. S. Dembo. Writing to him in 1972, Oppen acknowledges the debt:

> of course you are right about the Henry James: I wanted the phrase BUT I wanted James in the book—secretly, superstitiously, I carved his initials on that sapling book . . .
> I argued, shortly after Discrete was printed, that James and not Hemingway was the useful model for 'proletarian' writers —— and realized, in the ensuing discussion, if one could call it a discussion, that I must stay away from left-wing 'cultural workers'
>
> 'to know what, really, was going on'
>   and the story in it (*Selected Letters [SL]* 241)

A return not just to the literary and philosophical significances suggested in the opening of the *Discrete Series* but to the actual poem itself—
to the materialization of those significances—occurs in "Of Being Numerous," in which Oppen again quotes James and again evokes boredom:

> . . . approached the window as if to see . . .
>
> The boredom which disclosed
> Everything——
> ("Of Being Numerous," #37, *New Collected Poems [NCP]* 186–187)

As Oppen himself admitted, "The word 'boredom' is a little surprising there" (i.e., in *Discrete Series;* Dembo 169). But the boredom Oppen
has in mind (and indeed aspires to sustain) is neither the alienated ano-
mie of the disaffected nor the boorish boredom of the disdainful; what he
proffers is a precognitive, pretemporalizing threshold of wonder not yet
attached to anything but across which everything can travel. In James's
story, the mood of boredom is what *animates,* and ultimately what breaks,
the static silence in the room where Maud Blessingbourne and her hostess,
Mrs. Dyott, are passing a rainy afternoon. It is in boredom and as an act of
boredom that Maud goes to the window. The poem "means, in effect, that
the knowledge of the mood of boredom is the knowledge of what is, 'of
the world, weather-swept'" (Dembo 169).

Though he came to his understanding of boredom on his own, Oppen
was delighted (again "superstitiously") to discover that at the very time he
was acknowledging the fundamental role that boredom has to play in the
imperative drama of apperception, Martin Heidegger was doing the same.
Writing to Frederic Will in 1967, Oppen explains:

> The poem which happens to be printed as the first poem in Discrete
> Series—my first book—was written in 1929. That, I've learned, was
> the year in which H. was giving his Inauguration Speech, in which
> he spoke of the mood of boredom (in the translation I have) which
> leads, again in the translation I have, to 'the knowledge of what-is.'
> The poem—I don't know if you have the book—begins with 'the
> knowledge of boredom' and ends with 'the world, weather-swept,
> with which one shares the century.' [. . .] I am touched by super-
> stition remembering my hesitation over that word and the sense of
> having been given it. (*SL* 156)

The "Inauguration Speech" to which Oppen refers was given on the occasion of Heidegger's acceptance of the chair of Philosophy at Freiburg in 1929 and subsequently published in English as "What is Metaphysics." In this essay, as in the series of lectures he gave in 1929–30 on "The Fundamental Concepts of Metaphysics: World—Finitude—Solitude," Heidegger presents boredom as a condition of incipience, a condition, in other words, that is also a precondition; it offers itself as a conceivable goal that consists of preparedness—nothing. In the context of this idea—that we begin with nothing—Heidegger enters into the astonishing and fundamental bewilderment in which all thought about the material universe begins: "Why are there beings at all, and why not rather nothing?" (Heidegger 110).

Oppen (or his "Maude") transits boredom into a slightly different experience, though with equally paradoxical results. The mood, whether we have driven ourselves into it or simply find that it has come upon us, hovers like natural light or the weather (which are often much the same thing), permeating both the world as a whole and our interior individual response to it, our sense of the state of ourselves within it. Boredom, in other words, is both self-limiting (cosmic) and self-determining (experienced). It resembles the window (and one cannot help but notice the recurrence of windows in the *Discrete Series*): it offers aperture and barrier, a view into the limitless distance but one that is closely framed. Even as it isolates one and overcasts things in an alienating fog (or blurs things through a drizzling rain), it also both casts one loose, leaving one free to wander (either literally or in one's thoughts—and in *Discrete Series*, Oppen does both), and casts things loose, leaving them free to shift position and to flicker in and out of view. Boredom induces something of a Keatsian negative capability, then, but the capability belongs as much to objective conditions as to the subjective state of mind.

From the initial vantage (or vantaging) point of a depersonalizing mood, in the lull of dulled interest and lackluster sensation typical of boredom, Oppen gains access to "'the world, weather-swept' as the great thing to see, the thing that must be seen, the universe" (DuPlessis 154). Out of the flow of unfocused thought, with vision vaguely obscured, Oppen becomes precise. "I fight automatically and fiercely against derangement of the senses, and have been consciously doing so since I was nineteen. As witnessed by the first poem in Discrete Series" (*SL* 105).

Boredom, then, serves as even more than the hospitable condition for the exercise of a complex form of "negative capability." It is as a temporal condition, and therefore as a linking condition, albeit and paradoxically in the form of an extended discontinuity, that boredom is of particular and detailed interest to Oppen (and to us) at the opening stage of his series.

Discontinuity is inconceivable apart from continuity, of course, and indeed what we see as discontinuity in *Discrete Series* is the prolonged flickering of the blank (and cinematic) connector, a "sudden vacuum / Of time," as Oppen puts it in "Of Being Numerous" (*NCP* 181), that occurs between the frames or image/instants of the series. Coexisting but contradictory, discontinuity and continuity coincide in the space of this blank connector; like boredom it is interstitial and yet also pervasive, serving as the screen onto which the *Discrete Series* are projected.[1]

Oppen's dialectical approach in this respect as in others contributes both to the logic (the thought that is brought to bear on the images presented by the poems) and to the dynamics propelling the logical processes that discover and/or generate the images in the first place.

To discover what is in the poem is implicitly to speak of why the poem is as it is. Flowing like light through the series of events—the image/ instants of the poem—are empiricist and political currents on whose character the series is predicated. Or, to put it another way, these currents provide the (not so) missing predicates of the poem. Being fundamentally ethical in character, the work emerges out of troubled encounters with capitalist modernity. In response, and from the very start, Oppen developed a phenomenological (and, as I've already suggested, inherently cinematic) methodology, heuristic in intent, empiricist in approach, and grounded in particulars (or as he put it, "the commonplace"), with strong political overtones. Despite the seemingly measured calm and apparent minimalism of the short poems that comprise it, the work opens up a rigorously nuanced (and undoubtedly sometimes anguished) social as well as perceptual analysis. As it proceeds, Oppen's testing of the character and "truth" of reality is a conceptually materialist, and thus at least implicitly Marxist, undertaking. Though not yet members of the Communist Party (they joined the party in 1935), George and Mary were reading Marx as well as Trotsky's *History of the Russian Revolution*; as George noted to John Crawford, "FROM DISCRETE SERIES TO THE MARXISM WAS NOT A 'BREAK'————BY ANY MEANS" (*SL* 255).

The question of "truth," for Oppen, was multifaceted, but it was not, strictly speaking, a question of being right. At a fundamental level, his concern was with ascertaining, literally as well as figuratively, what matters. The result is primarily a record of things; "even my vocabulary is affected by that conviction, that 'the Truth' is not a pronouncement but a thing" (*SL* 89). Such a record, however, must also inevitably be an account of our affective relationship with things, an account that recognizes the contemporary bond we share with them. As he says in a letter to Rachel Blau DuPlessis, "There are certain things, appearances, around which the understanding gathers. They hold the meanings which make it possible to live, they are one's sense of reality and the possibility of meaning" (*SL* 123).

Oppen's notion of *things* takes reality as a given, at least at a pragmatic, if not at a supernal, level. "I speak of a Realist poetry: Realist in that it is concerned with a fact which it did not create" (*SL* 140). His writing, as a result, has an indexical character; "the nouns do refer to something; that it's there, that it's true, the whole implication of these nouns; that appearances represent reality, whether or not they misrepresent it: that this in which the thing takes place, this thing is here, and that these things do take place" (Dembo 163).

Oppen's object was "to produce the realization of reality" and "the sense of the poet's self among things" (Oppen, "Mind's Own Place" 4) and he took care to do so without imposing on them an overlay of interpretation. "I'm really concerned with the substantive, with the subject of the sentence, with what we are talking about, and not rushing over the subject-matter in order to make a comment about it. It is still a principle with me, of more than poetry, to notice, to state, to lay down the substantive for its own sake" (Dembo 161). As he put it in a letter to Jerome Rothenberg: "Discrete Series is not concerned with predicates" (*SL* 179), though as I've suggested above, predication saturates the series—that a substantive has "its own sake," for example.

Oppen's avoidance of explicit commentary is not solely the result of his sympathies, genuine though they were, for the basic tenets of Ezra Pound's Imagist program ("Direct treatment of the 'thing' whether subjective or objective," "To use absolutely no word that does not contribute to the presentation," etc. [Pound, 31]). In the wake of his rupture with his family and class, Oppen at the beginning of his career was shaping a methodology whose perpetually paradox-ridden and mobile but always sound principles he never abandoned. "The important thing is that if we are talking about the nature of reality, then we are not really talking about our comment about it; we are talking about the apprehension of some *thing*, whether it is or not, whether one can make a thing of it or not. [. . .]

I'm trying to describe how that test of images can be a test of whether one's thought is valid" (Dembo 162).

The materialist philosophy underlying this comment seems to have taken into account Marx's correctives to Feuerbach, particularly with respect to Marx's emphasis on the dynamic, ongoing, and "self-changing" character of a properly materialist relation to things: "The chief defect of all hitherto existing materialism (that of Feuerbach included) is that the thing, reality, sensuousness, is conceived only in the form of the object or of contemplation, but not as sensuous human activity, practice, not subjectively. . . . The question whether objective truth can be attributed to human thinking is not a question of theory but is a practical question. Man must prove the truth, i.e. the reality and power, the this-sidedness of his thinking in practice" (Marx 156).

Earnest, self-critical, rigorous, and alert to antinomies, Oppen proceeded not in a spirit of detachment (because he was not in quest of authority) but, on the contrary, in order to forge attachments, that being what the affirmation that things simply matter achieves. "O what O what will / Bring us back to Shore," he asks, and he answers, "the shore" (*NCP* 32).

The images and moments that comprise the *Discrete Series* are neither special nor precious. Oppen's imagism is almost militantly resistant to the sentimentality that followed "in the wake of the Amy Lowells" (*SL* 82), for reasons that are political as much as aesthetic. "The 'Marxism' of Discrete Series is, was felt as, the struggle against the loss of the commonplace" (*SL* 254), that is, the loss of the materialist attention to the practice of everyday life, "the real individuals," as Marx says, "their activity, and the material conditions under which they live, both those which they find already existing and those produced by their activity" (Marx 160).

The "objective" that Louis Zukofsky announced in both the 1931 essay that launched "Objectivism" (including two poems from what would become the *Discrete Series*) in the pages of *Poetry* magazine and in the Sixth "Movement" of his poem *"A"* has strong affinities with Marx's historical materialism: "experience perfecting activity of existence, making it," "everything aptly, perfectly, belonging within, one with, a context," "desire for what is objectively perfect, inextricably the direction of historic and contemporary particulars" (Zukofsky 20, 23).

The poems that were assembled into the *Discrete Series* (published in 1934) were written between 1928 and 1933,[2] a period in which the shock effects so characteristic of capitalist modernity were particularly acute, occurring, as they were, against a backdrop of widespread historical trauma, marked by the Depression and the politically conservative decade that led up to it. Prohibition was in effect, the execution of Sacco and Vanzetti had taken place (in 1927), the Nazis were rising to power in Germany and Austria, and in the United States the Ku Klux Klan was extending both its power (its membership is estimated to have grown to around 4 million by the mid-1920s, with branches flourishing in the Midwest as well as the South) and its range of hostility (adding anti-Semitism, xenophobia, and anti-Catholic statements to its rhetoric), while also gaining a degree of legitimacy (the Klan openly campaigned on behalf of Herbert Hoover during his [successful] campaign for the presidency in 1928).

This was a period for Oppen of considerable personal disillusionment as well, but, despite the negativity that no doubt informed his critical disavowal of his class background and brought about a break with his family, the disillusionment was intentional—a conscious process of dis-illusioning. In George Oppen's occasional comments on the period as well as in Mary Oppen's account of it in her autobiographical *Meaning a Life,* one can sense Oppen's underlying vitality and sense of purpose as he set about putting geographical and ideological distance between himself and the relatively privileged class background his family represented.

By early 1928, George and Mary Oppen had left the West Coast and were living in New York City. They were just twenty years old. Beginning their adventures "on the road" as hitchhikers, they had traveled as far as Detroit, but once there, according to Mary's later account, they had realized that "wind was free and George could sail, and when we examined our road map we saw that we could sail to New York," and this they did (*Meaning a Life [ML]* 17).

Living in New York, Mary notes that she was discovering "Virginia Woolf's novels, just appearing in 1928" (*ML* 84) and was also, at the time, reading Proust and Henry James. Given the allusion to James at the beginning of *Discrete Series,* we can speculate that George too was reading James. They had also discovered Louis Zukofsky, first in the pages of *Exiles* 3, where his "Poem beginning 'The'" had just appeared, and then in person shortly thereafter.

Throughout the spring and summer, they continued to do a lot of sailing. "We sailed every weekend past the estates, villages, harbors and beaches along the Long Island shore. . . . We also sailed with big sailing ships, lumber-schooners bringing lumber from Maine. We sailed faster than they, but while we were alongside we talked to the crew, then came about and sailed with them again" (*ML* 95).

The following year, as soon as George turned twenty-one (and had access to a significant sum of money), they moved to France. The journey, from San Francisco to Le Havre, took a month, during which, Mary says, "We spent hours each day in our cabin; George worked at poetry" (*ML* 119).

Many of the nautical poems in the *Discrete Series* depict image/instants from George and Mary's experiences, both in the sailboat and on shipboard, and it is important to note in them a critical, rather than pleasure-seeking, purpose. Despite the leisure-class connotations that sailboating inevitably suggests to the reader (unless, presumably, he or she is in the navy or works as a merchant mariner), the images comprising the boating series of Oppen's *Discrete Series* in fact often allude to elements of class conflict. Of particular interest in this regard is the following poem (*NCP* 10):

> The three wide
> Funnels raked aft, and the masts slanted
>
>   the
> Deck-hand slung in a bosun's chair
> Works on this 20th century chic and
>   efficiency
> Not evident at "The Sailor's Rest."

With the funnels raked aft as if oppressed by the very conditions of the work, and with the deckhand in a pose the very opposite of leisurely, this could almost be a description of a montage from Eisenstein's *Battleship Potemkin*.[3] Though, ironically, some interpreters of this poem have assumed that the "bosun's chair" is for lounging, in fact the deckhand "slung in a bosun's chair" is no resting sailor. On shipboard, the bosun, or boatswain, is an officer who has "direct charge of all work on deck . . . and details the crew to carry out the day-to-day work of the ship"; his eponymous chair consists of a short board suspended between two ropes on which a sailor can be pulled aloft to attend to the masts, rigging, and so on.[4] The deckhand, in other words, is hard at work in a precarious and uncomfortable position, as exposed as the funnels. The contrast between the passengers (who may or may not be lounging) and the deckhand underscores the character "Of the world, weather-swept, with which one shares the century" with its "20th century chic and efficiency."

Eisenstein's film came out in 1925, and though it seems unlikely that Oppen would have seen it, it is not impossible. Certainly Oppen was familiar with films generally (Oppen's father ran a string of movie theaters in San Francisco, and for a time Oppen had worked in one of them) and with the concept of the montage. Speaking about another of the poems (*NCP* 14), Oppen described it as "a sort of 'montage,' . . . I'm jumping around like the fashionable camera of that time" (Dembo 201).

The poem Oppen was talking about is the one whose first image, of a steam-shovel operator "shot" (to use cinematic terminology) from below, gives way abruptly to "The asphalt edge" and then to a horse, "Loose on the plateau, / Horse's classic height cartless," by which, as he explained later, "I just meant, and imagine on the prairie a horse, not a horse pulling a cart" (Hatlen 200).

Arriving in France in late 1929, George and Mary had immediately decided that, rather than rush from Le Havre to Paris, they would allow themselves to "look, gape, gawk, to dawdle—to try to comprehend what was before our eyes" (*ML* 120). And so they purchased a horse, Pom-Pon, and a cart. With this conveyance (and companion), they spent many weeks on the road, traveling across France to Paris and then, eventually, south to Le Beausset. "We traveled thirty or forty kilometers a day, stopping over a day and a night after every five days of travel, for Pom-Pon needed to rest and to eat more than he had time for while traveling. The slow progress suited us, and we found the long stop-overs a time for talking to people, wandering and observing. Pom-Pon's needs gave us a long lunch-time too. We unharnessed him beside the road, gave him his hay and threw down straw for him to stale; he was such a polite little horse that in harness he was inhibited. He munched his hay and switched his tail in contentment" (*ML* 121).

Over the course of the next two to three years, George's involvements with writing and writers deepened, as did his social awareness. Witnessing poverty in France, reading about poverty in the United States, George and Mary were also receiving a political education. "We were shocked and aghast at the schemes carried out in the last year of Hoover's administration—food was being dumped while people starved. Although we were far from the United States, we had perhaps the advantage of that distance, and our friends the butcher and the hotel-keeper had been educating us. We were innocent of preconceived views, and we looked on at poverty in France, at children so thin and tubercular that they were almost transparent, and our minds began to dwell on politics. . . . Sylvia Beach's book store in Paris had a lending library, and I borrowed Trotsky's History of the Soviet Union, which George and I both read [. . . and] with the Jewish refugees pouring into Paris from Germany in 1932, I could not help seeing their distress and feeling the threat to us, too" (*ML* 136–137).

The threat that George and Mary Oppen perceived was not just to their own future but to that of the larger reality that George came to think of as "humanity." Humanity, for Oppen, had to be more concrete than conceptual, as it has a deeply material as well as historical character; to care about humanity was to "care about the idea of what's going to *happen* to humanity" (Dembo 166; my italics). The meaning of history is entirely dependent on the viability of our "faith" (as Oppen put it) that things have a future. We "would not be willing to live, would find it impossible to live, without some concept of sharing in history or humanity—something which is happening after [our] death" (Dembo 166); "we cannot exist, however mothers may feel, without a sense of depth in the past and expectation in the future" (*SL* 72).

In this context, Oppen seems to have found the temporal dimension of the Poundian image adequate only up to a point. As Pound saw it, "An 'image' is that which presents an intellectual and emotional complex in an instant of time" (Pound 32), but for Oppen that instant is an indexical event, and like the light that features so prominently in *Discrete Series*, it functions not as a container but as action whose movements discover (or create) events. It has to have the capacity to project itself (and also to alter). Indexicality is, as Mary Ann Doane points out, "the imprint of a once-present and unique moment"; it is "the signature of temporality" precisely because the once-present and unique instant of time is a past one being presently pointed out and thereby given a future (Doane 16). It is an image/instant that belongs to all three temporalities; it is a point, but a contrapuntal one functioning as a paradoxical element, ceaselessly circulating through and as the *Discrete Series*.[5]

In the interview that Louis Dembo conducted with him, Oppen acknowledges the influence of Pound's Imagist project on *Discrete Series*; the poem, he says, is "the attempt to construct meaning, to construct a method of thought from the imagist technique of poetry—from the imagist intensity of vision" (Dembo 161). But while this description may account for signal features within the poem and explain the compelling nature of its discrete parts, it does not account for its most notable feature—namely, the seriality. Oppen may be alert to the Imagist program set out by Pound, but he nonetheless opts not for a collection of individual poems but, rather, for a "discrete series." Why?

Part of the answer to that question must be that, from Oppen's point of view, his exegetical impulse, his desire to undertake "a test of truth" or "a test of sincerity" (Dembo 161), demanded a *dialectical* process; only such a process could accommodate the antinomies he perceived in (and as) reality and be true, too, to his own ambivalences. Though his later masterpiece, "Of Being Numerous," may give a fuller representation of the dilemma that good thinking (and Oppen spent many hours of the day engaged in thinking) always discloses, it is *in* this great early work that Oppen most formidably utilizes seriality, both technically and thematically. Oppen quite rightly sees dialectics precisely as a serial unfolding, and the emphasis in the poem lies on it as such; he foregrounds the phenomenal proceeding that constitutes both the cinematic (sometimes almost frame-by-frame) series of "successive happenings" and the "flâneur series" that, initiated by boredom, sets perceiver, perception, and thought wandering, on the streets and/or at sea.

What's under review through the sequence of displacements that result in the process are not only things. It is true that, in "the attempt to construct meaning, to construct a method of thought from [. . .] the imagist intensity of vision," Oppen inevitably turned to the visible, to things. But, like Heidegger (from whose writings Oppen had yet to read but who was already, albeit subliminally, an influence) and like Marx (from whose writings Oppen was then reading), Oppen had ultimately to address himself to the problem of time.

Like Heidegger, Oppen intuited that being is always a being-in-time, that things are always things-of-time: "Her ankles are watches" (*NCP* 9), says Oppen, offering a case in point. But it is important to remember also that Oppen was writing his *Discrete Series* at a period when the large-scale, invasive, and ruthless character of capitalist modernity was becoming suddenly and ubiquitously obvious: he was working in "Bad times" (*NCP* 30). Indeed, among the things most affected by capitalist modernity was (and is) the perception of time itself, and one of the most alarming results of this was the increasing awareness of time, as measured in the form of *recurrent shocks*. As Mary Ann Doane argues, during the period in question "time [had become] palpable in a quite different way—one specific to modernity and intimately allied with its new technologies of representation (photography, film, phonography). Time was indeed *felt*—as a weight, as a source of anxiety, and as an acutely pressing problem of representation. Modernity was perceived as a temporal demand" (Doane 4).

Time, then, is the principle continuum through which Oppen's *Discrete Series* pass, "the continuum par excellence," as Charles Sanders Peirce once noted, "through the spectacles of which we encounter every other continuum." This continuum is inherently paradoxical in character, however; though it "consists in a binding together of things that are different and remain different, so that they are in a measure dependent on one another," it assures that at the same time they remain "in a measure independent," because "time has a point of discontinuity at the present." The indexically at hand, present, palpable instant—this one—in being immediately available to sensuous experience, "differs from all other instants absolutely," while all others, either flowing together into what we know of the past or into what we expect of the future, "only differ in degree" (Peirce 65–66). Oppen set us this paradox in the very title of his poem, Discrete Series.

Over the years, Oppen offered several, very similar, explanations for the title, all of them emphasizing the phenomenological (and empirical) interests he was attempting to satisfy. Of the *Discrete Series* to L. S. Dembo he said, "That's a phrase in mathematics. A pure mathematical series would be one in which each term is derived from the preceding term by a rule. A discrete series is a series of terms each of which is empirically derived, each one of which is empirically true. And this is the reason for the fragmentary character of those poems. I was attempting to construct a meaning by empirical statements, by imagist statements. . . . The poems are a series, yet each is separate, and it's true that they are discrete in that sense; but I had in mind specifically the meaning to the mathematician—a series of empirically true terms" (Dembo 161). And in a letter to Rachel Blau DuPlessis, he defined it thus:

> Discrete Series—a series in which each term is empirically justified rather than derived from the preceding term. Which is what the expression means to a mathematician, as I gather you know.
>
> (I thought too late—30 years too late—that the flyleaf should have carried the inscription 13, 28, 32, 42 which is a discrete series: the names of the stations on the east side subway. (*SL* 122)

But while these explanations appear at first glance to emphasize the grounds for the discreteness of the poems, what is important to Oppen is not the autonomy of the images but their "truth," and that is a temporal matter. The image/instants are recognized as they appear; they constitute events or, as for the Situationists three to four decades later, they are taken as situations, suffused with contingency and transience—that is, with time, passing through the flow of whatever happens at any given moment to bear the truth that this is real.

Notes

1. The term "series" occurs in no form but the plural, and although this may be a grammatical superficiality, Oppen's series should be felt as such; they are constellating, dilemmatic, the mark of the existential condition (to use Oppen's later term) "of being numerous."

2. There is a slight bit of confusion regarding the dating of the composition of *Discrete Series*. Writing in 1973 to John Crawford, Oppen notes, "some poems of Discrete written 1928" (*SL* 254), but three years later, in a letter to Serge Fauchereau, Oppen tells him, "I think the date of the *Discrete Series* poems had better be indicated (1929–1933)" (*SL* 329), and on March 6, 1930, Zukofsky, in a letter to Pound, speaks of a manuscript of thirty-two pages of poetry, which would be exactly the length of *Discrete Series* and suggests that a version, at least, of the work was finished by then (*SL* 371 n. 6). Based on internal evidence, it would seem that at least a few of the poems might have been written in the context of George and Mary's travels in 1928–29, and presumably, stimulated by the forthcoming publication of the book; some writing and revision as well as the arrangement of the poems into the series went on into 1933.

3. This is not to suggest that Oppen's approach is similar to Eisenstein's; quite the opposite is true. Where Oppen resists adding interpretation to image and maintains an almost austere reticence, Eisenstein regarded his films not as "'film eyes' but always 'film fists.' I never make films in which the camera is an 'objective witness,' to be watched by an impassive eye of glass. I prefer to hit people hard on the nose"; Norman Swallow, *Eisenstein: A Documentary Portrait*, 46–47.

4. Kemp, *Oxford Companion*, s.v. "boatswain" and "boatswain's chair."

5. I am freely, but not I hope irresponsibly, borrowing the notion of the "paradoxical element" from Gilles Deleuze, who describes it as that which allows two (or more) series to relate to each other. "This element belongs to no series; or rather, it belongs to both series at once and never ceases to circulate throughout them. [. . .] It has the function of articulating the two series to one another, of reflecting them in one another, of making them communicate, coexist, and be ramified. Again, it has the function of joining the singularities which correspond to the

two series in a 'tangled tale,' of assuring the passage from one distribution of singularities to the next" (Deleuze, *The Logic of Sense* 51).

Works Cited

Deleuze, Gilles. *The Logic of Sense.* Trans. Mark Lester with Charles Stivale. New York: Columbia University Press, 1990.

Dembo, L. S. "The 'Objectivist' Poet: Four Interviews." *Contemporary Literature* 10, 2 (Spring 1979).

Doane, Mary Ann. *The Emergence of Cinematic Time.* Cambridge, MA: Harvard University Press, 2002.

DuPlessis, Rachel Blau. "George Oppen: The Anthropologist of Myself: A Selection from Working Papers." *Sulfur* 26 (Spring 1990).

Heidegger, Martin. "What is Metaphysics?" In *Basic Writings,* ed. David Farrell Krell. San Francisco: HarperSanFrancisco, 1993.

James, Henry. *Complete Stories 1898–1910.* New York: Library of America, 1996.

Kemp, Peter, ed. *The Oxford Companion to Ships and the Sea*. Oxford: Oxford University Press, 1976.

Marx, Karl. "Theses on Feuerbach." In *Karl Marx: Selected Writings,* ed. David McLellan. Oxford: Oxford University Press, 1977.

Oppen, George. *George Oppen: New Collected Poems.* Ed. Michael Davidson. New York: New Directions, 2002.

———. *The Selected Letters of George Oppen.* Ed. Rachel Blau DuPlessis. Durham, NC: Duke University Press, 1990.

———. "The Mind's Own Place." *Kulchur* 3, 10 (Summer 1963).

Oppen, Mary. *Meaning a Life: An Autobiography.* Santa Barbara, CA: Black Sparrow Press, 1978.

Peirce, Charles S. *Collected Papers of Charles Sanders Peirce.* Ed. Charles Hartshorne and Paul Weiss, vol. 6. *Scientific Metaphysics.* Cambridge, MA: Harvard University Press, 1935.

Pound, Ezra. "A Retrospect." In *Modern Poetics,* ed. James Scully. New York: McGraw-Hill, 1965.

Swallow, Norman. *Eisenstein: A Documentary Portrait.* New York: E. P. Dutton, 1977.

Zukofsky, Louis. "An Objective." In *Prepositions.* London: Rapp & Carroll, 1967.

3
Discrete Series and the Posthuman City

Steve Shoemaker

First-generation modernists like Ezra Pound, William Carlos Williams, and Marianne Moore had confronted in the teens and twenties the twentieth century's first bursts of raw technological power—of speed, movement, and Einsteinian dislocations. By the time George Oppen started working on his first book, *Discrete Series,* in the late 1920s and early 1930s, that power had begun to assume more sophisticated forms. Where the early products of the machine age had laid bare their mechanisms in a harsh, solid bristling of gears and girders, the products of the thirties were increasingly cloaked beneath opaque exteriors and polished surfaces. As technology transformed the culture and saturated people's lives, industrial and commercial design was characterized more and more by the smooth suavity of a new array of synthetic materials.[1] In this age of the "streamline," of smooth, forbidding exteriors, the opacities and obscurities of the modern cityscape represented a challenge for both everyday living and poetic perception. Oppen responded to this challenge with what we might call a poetics of *translucence,* a *shining through* that seeks clarity but registers the difficulties of seeing. The slickness of the modern "environment," with its pervasive, machined surfaces, was designed to facilitate speedy acts of perception/consumption, the dazzled and deflected eye turning continually to the next surface. Alongside this modern style, Oppen developed his own poetry of density and resistance—of arduous appearances, strange absences, and unexpected interpositions—designed to add depth to the picture, to slow down and thicken the act of perception in order to achieve what Oppen would call "disclosure." The term is Heideggerian, and like Heidegger's "unconcealment," it suggests a process whereby things that are hidden are brought, sometimes with considerable difficulty, to light. By drawing attention to what is there *and* what is missing, to surface and depth, to hidden parts and disguised pruderies, Oppen's poems, of the thirties and beyond, seek to penetrate the gloss of the commodified, technologized forms comprising so much of the modern (and postmodern) cityscape. In doing so, these poems tenaciously address the problem of what Oppen called "obscured / origin[s]," and insistently raise the "spectre" of "those inexplicable crowds," those human bodies almost lost in the giant machine.

Contemplating Oppen's poetic project at the start of the twenty-first century, we might see *Discrete Series* as an early attempt to register the shift toward what Katherine Hayles, among others, has labeled a "posthuman" order. For Hayles, one of the central features of this new order is the privileging of "informational pattern over material instantiation" (2). The crisis of dis/embodiment that results from this state of affairs has profound implications for the fate of the human subject. According to Jean Baudrillard, writing from a perspective similar to Hayles's on this point, the shiny surfaces of modernity, their refusal of depth, can be seen as part of the play of a "system of objects": "The system of [human] needs has become less integrated than the system of objects; the latter imposes its own coherence and thus acquires the capacity to fashion an entire society" (14–15). This ascendancy of objects over human needs is certainly part of what Hayles would characterize as the move toward the posthuman, and her account goes on to trace this development from a certain angle, emphasizing the trends in thinking that have led us toward current research programs in the development of intelligent machines and artificial life, as well as toward the broader reengineering of the human body and brain. In my own use of the term posthuman, I'd like to mix and match, assimilating Hayles's approach to other critiques of modernity by Baudrillard, Heidegger, Benjamin, and Haraway, among others. Using this framework, we can see Oppen's *Discrete Series* as mapping an early moment in our evolution toward the posthuman condition, by means of a poetic strategy that is thoroughly grounded in an engagement with the urban modernity of the 1930s. Under Oppen's investigative eye, this modern landscape is subjected to an act of dis/closure, revealing itself as a vanguard site of the posthuman order of things, a technologically and socially constructed "reality" placing great demands on human adaptivity.

George Oppen's poetic series would attempt to locate the new technologies, the new visions of a modernized environment, within a human frame of understanding. Or if unable to provide such a frame, given the disorientations of the modern scene, it would be concerned with at least pointing to the human element (or its absence) in the "thingy" realm of the "mechanical-industrial landscape."[2] At times, the result of this attempt is a technomorphic interpenetration or entanglement of human and machine, flesh and steel.[3] As Oppen's poems seek to sort out, or simply register, these entanglements, they are consistently attuned to the dilemma posed by the posthuman crisis of embodiment. The serial nature of these cultural topographies operates in conjunction with an Objectivist commitment to history, registering the entangled singularities of "historic and contemporary particulars," while trying to suggest by means of a thick, bumpy, embodied poetry the awkward movements of history and the jagged lineaments of an age.

The Poetics of Serial Topography

As it was originally printed by the Objectivist Press in 1934, *Discrete Series* consisted of thirty-two brief poems, one poem per page.[4] In an interview with L. S. Dembo, Oppen explained that a "discrete series is a series of terms each of which is empirically derived, each one of which is empirically true" (Dembo 174). My reading of Oppen's use of serial form will emphasize the "empirical" grounding of each "term," or poem, of the series, and speculate on the ways in which Oppen's seriality sets his poems straining toward an engagement with the world-historical transformations of the twenties and thirties. But in Oppen's definition of the "discrete series" there is an inherent tension between the "pure" realm of *mathemata* and that muddied arena of human action, "the empirical." In a letter to a professor of mathematics written in 1967, Oppen discusses the conflict between those "two levels of reality," the mathematical and the empirical, "which perhaps attack each other?" (letter to Sherman Stein, *Selected Letters [SL]* 157). For Oppen, the primary danger in such a conflict was that the mathematical would completely obliterate the empirical; indeed, the threat of mathematical abstraction seemed to him sufficiently serious that one might speak of "the demonic universe of mathematics" (158). In this demonic universe, mathematical thinking rises up in the figure of Ouroboros, "the snake with his tail in his mouth" (158). Oppen wonders if the real danger represented by this figure is not that the mathematical snake is disappearing in an act of self-consumption, but that it is "creating itself," that "the serpent [is] *coming out* of his own mouth?" (158). If the danger of poetry is that one risks the "terror" of confronting the empirical, mathematics confronts one with "the danger of nothing-at-all" (158). Whether self-consuming or self-creating or both, the mathematical Ouroboros needs nothing outside of itself. The snake never ultimately disappears, but "grows and displaces the empirical, or what one thought was the empirical" (158).

So why, then, does Oppen conjure visions of this mathematical demon with his title, *Discrete Series?* For one, because it is simply impossible to elude the mathematical monster in the modern period, which Oppen's fellow "Objectivist" Louis Zukofsky called the Gas Age, the vaporous age of "intellect" and abstraction ("About the Gas Age" 169). As Oppen says in the same letter quoted above: "I fought him [the demon of abstract thinking] down the days and down the nights, from Discrete Series on" (159). And for a further indication of what Oppen is likely to have in mind here, we might turn to a description of what Heidegger calls the state of "mathematical projection" characterizing the modern world: "All bodies are alike. No motion is special. Every place is like every other, each moment like any other. Every force becomes determinable only by the change of motion which it causes—this change in motion being understood as a change of place. All determinations of bodies have one basic blueprint, according to which the natural process is nothing but the space-time determination of the motion of points of mass" ("Modern Science, Metaphysics and Mathematics" 267). In the modern age, the empirical world is in danger of being reduced to, and even *supplanted* by, an abstract system, a grid of coordinates in which all "bodies" can be accounted for by "one basic blueprint." Indeed, Heidegger's description is very close to Hayles's account of the shift away from a "material" understanding of the world and toward an age of disembodied information. Oppen's use of the poetic series, I would argue, acknowledges the power of "mathematical projection" in the modern world, but counters this tendency with an emphasis on the material ground of existence, or what he calls, following Heidegger, "substance" (*SL* 159). The grounding in substance, "which has been the subject of all our planning" (*NCP* 201), draws us out of the "man-made universe" of the mathematical and into "history" (*SL* 159), the arena of human action. The notion of what I will call *serial topography* is crucial here, enacting a kind of writing that performs precise acts of poetic *location* to mediate between "two levels of reality," the abstract and the concrete. As a result of the kind of embodied poetic thinking that Oppen's poems perform, the separation of these "two levels" is ultimately questioned, broken down, by the very form the poetry takes. The "man-made universe" of the mind refuses to disengage itself from the events of history.

In another letter from the 1960s, Oppen wrote that it occurred to him "30 years too late" that "the flyleaf [of *Discrete Series*] should have carried the inscription 14, 28, 32, 42 which is a discrete series: the names of the stations on the east side subway" (letter to Rachel Blau DuPlessis, October 4, 1965, *SL* 122). Here Oppen links his poems directly to the modern urban landscape of New York City, and provides a figure, the subway, for the sort of living and moving negotiation of abstract planning and human use that informs his deployment of the series as writing. Taking Oppen's hint, I would like to propose approaching *Discrete Series* by means of a method of reading-in-motion, or reading-*as*-motion, that should reveal some things about the way the series is put together, the way it works.

Famously (at least among readers of Oppen) the first poem of *Discrete Series* invokes a scene of boredom that ends up leading to a movement outward. The Jamsesian protagonist, Maud/e Blessingbourne, bored denizen of a protected interior, makes an "approach" to a window, "as if to see / what was really going on," and the resultant act of vision propels her, and us, into "the world, weather-swept, with which / one shares the century."[5] As has often been discussed, Oppen came in later years to associate the state of boredom invoked here with Heidegger's treatment of the "mood of boredom" as a philosophical concept, involving awareness of "what *is*" (Dembo 182). According to Heidegger, the experience of "real boredom" (as opposed to the experience of "this book or that play, this activity or that stretch of idleness [which] merely bores us") opens us up to an awareness of "what-is-in-totality" ("What is Metaphysics?" 247), which is close to what Oppen has described as a sense of "awe" before the brute fact of existence (Dembo 177). The question for Maud/e, and for Oppen as he begins his poetic series, is whether s/he will achieve this state of awareness and arrive, despite all obstacles, at a genuine awareness of "what was really going on." The poem stages a prototypical scene of the fundamental search for knowledge, which will be figured in just this way—as an approach to a window—again and again in Oppen's poems. Oppen opens James's story up from a romantic "love triangle" (Maud/e is looking out, at least partly, for the approach of the man she loves) to the larger configurations of the historical world. The poem enacts a shift from a highly mediated and "literary" presentation of Oppen's concerns—especially the search for knowledge and the necessity of making contact with "the world"—to a more experientially grounded encounter with those same difficulties. This opening poem of the series in some sense *enables* the poems that follow—as if, walking to the window with Maud/e, the rest of the series is what Oppen saw.

As the first poem of *Discrete Series* closes with its broad gesture toward the weather-swept historical world, the eye runs over the white space filling the rest of the page and the hand turns the leaf to reach the second poem of the series. The sense of distance traversed, as if one had traveled a very long way indeed between subway stops, is striking:

White. From the
Under arm of T
The red globe.
Up
Down. Round
Shiny fixed
Alternatives
From the quiet
Stone floor . . .
(*NCP* 6)

This brief and enigmatic poem has confounded many readers over the years since its appearance in *Discrete Series* in 1934, standing out as an especially intransigent specimen in Oppen's difficult body of work. But as others have pointed out, a little digging can make short work of the mystery of the "scene" under description. In a letter written to Charles Tomlinson in 1963, Oppen provided a retrospective and explicit account of the poem's referent, complete with a hand-drawn sketch "of an elevator door with . . . two globes over it, one indicating up, the other, down" (editor's note, DuPlessis, *SL* 90). In this same letter, Oppen explains that the "contrivance" had been "so familiar at the time that I don't think anyone was puzzled" (90). He then goes on to comment with wry amusement that the original image had been "lost—it so happens—in the mists of architectural history" and could not "be restored to the consciousness of any reader without a red crayon. And a two-color print job, which is prohibitively expensive" (90). As Joseph Conte convincingly argues, though, a method of reading that contents itself with this information "reduces the poem to a riddle that one declares satisfactorily 'solved' when one has 'discovered' the referent" (297n). For his part, Conte dispenses with Oppen's "elevator" entirely, presenting his own analysis of the poem's "mechanical structure."[6] In Conte's view, the poem's complex internal relations, its mechanisms, have to be taken on their own terms, and "cannot assume a secondary, representational relationship with the world" (125). To assume such a relation would be to betray the Objectivist ambition, expressed by Williams, that "the poem should *be* an object among other objects of the empirical world" (Conte 125). But as I will argue here, this reading of the Objectivist credo fails to take into account the full range of its meanings. The powerful Objectivist concern with the formal workings of the "poem as object" exists *in conjunction with* a historical impulse committing the poem to a full engagement with its sociohistorical context. Williams wrote not only that the poet must create a poem that is itself an object, but also that it should be an object "consonant with his day" (*Autobiography* 265). Similarly, Williams wrote in his review of *Discrete Series* that the poem must face "the dialectical necessities of its day" ("The New Poetical Economy" 269). George Oppen, in his own parlance, pointed out that the poem must always be concerned with "a fact which it did not create," the world.[7] One cannot "solve" the poem by discovering its referent, but neither, the Objectivists suggest, can one isolate its existence in language from the larger world in which it took shape.

We shouldn't bring our reading practice to a halt with the discovery of Oppen's "elevator," then, but neither should we ignore the discovery altogether. Both of these approaches fail to ask *why* Oppen chose to write a poem that takes this urban artifact as its point of departure. Since this question seems to me important, I'd like to begin to indicate another mode of reading. First, we can recover some important contextual cues by looking at the poem's *first* appearance in print, in Louis Zukofsky's *An "Objectivists" Anthology* (1932), where Zukofsky published it under the title "1930'S." Zukofsky's "lost" title preserves some of the sense of historical expectancy established by the opening poem of *Discrete Series,* echoing Maud/e Blessingbourne's approach to "the world, weather-swept, with which / one shares the century." The portentousness of "1930'S" points us to the poem's contemporary context, its modernity, while simultaneously insisting on the historicity of that modern moment, which must take its place in the march of "decades." The title is a useful reminder of the historical impulse that permeated the "Objectivist" originary moment and exercised a constant influence on the formulation of its poetics. And in a letter written to Carl Rakosi in 1931, as he was editing *An "Objectivists" An-*

thology, Zukofsky provided a still more specific scene of interpretation, locating Oppen's poem in relation to the modern interior of a 1930s office building, whose "quiet / stone floor" might ground, as it were, our subsequent readings.[8]

As Williams might have described it, Oppen's poem is "a small . . . machine made of words" (*Selected Essays* 256).[9] It suggests a structural and dialectical interplay of oppositions and contrasts (white/red; up/down) and its suggestions of structure and motion are strikingly prepositional (note the heavy burden borne by *from,* which appears twice).[10] But it is important to see that the poem's delicate structural tensions are not *only* a matter of linguistic play. They are also directly related to the experiential frame the poem invokes—specifically, the experience of the human subject amid the objects of the urban cityscape. As Zukofsky was keen to point out in his own editorial "reading," the poem is particularly concerned to engage one aspect of the "world" in which Oppen lived, to provide a sort of poetic topography of that portion of the modern "mechanical-industrial landscape" epitomized by the "skyscrapers" of New York City. If the typical suburban house was reimagined in the 1930s as "a machine for living in" (Le Corbusier 10), then the New York skyscraper was dramatically more than that, a "giant machine" (Alfred Stieglitz, quoted in Wilson et al. 34), looming on the horizon as the "most important architectural achievement in America" (Wilson et al. 30), the very emblem of modern technology's transformation of the human environment. And it is worth pointing out here that the first "Objectivist" anthology and the Empire State Building appeared on the scene in the same year, 1931. But if painting after modernist painting, and photograph after photograph, capture panoramic visions of the glittering towers comprising New York's famous "skyline," treating them as symbols of the modern, Oppen's poem approaches the city from a different, more *pedestrian* angle, asking us to step *inside* the "giant machine" of one of those skyscrapers.[11]

What is it like to be inside the machine? One answer, Oppen suggests, is that it is boring. Just as Maud/e Blessingbourne's "approach to the window" was motivated by a sort of boredom, boredom is also an emotion typically associated with the scene "waiting for the elevator." The experience of boredom provides an unstated link between the first poem of the series, with its Jamesian setting, and this second poem, with its dramatic change of scene. But as in the first poem, we are not dealing with boredom as we usually think of it, but with an experience that is revelatory of our modes of being in the world. The mundane experience of "waiting for the elevator" is, Oppen's poem seems to suggest, a kind of primal scene of human/machine interface. In terms of "architectural history," the modern skyscraper/machine would not have been possible without the invention of the passenger elevator. The elevator is what makes the skyscraper work. It is an intimate form of those technologies of motion (planes, trains, and automobiles) more commonly evoked as representative of the transformations of the modern period, asking us, strangely, to be a "passenger" within the confines of a stationary dwelling, a structure of human habitation. The elevator is a small machine negotiating between the larger machine that is the building and the human body, resolving dilemmas of size and scale at the cost of a sort of blind absorption. It is appropriate, then, that "we never *get* the referential, substantive noun" (Conte 125) in reading the poem "1930'S," because absence itself is an important element of the experience in question. From a design standpoint, those red and white indicators are a display offered in partial redress of the elevator car's radical absence, an assurance not only that the wait won't be too long but that the car has only momentarily disappeared, not vanished once and for all in the bowels of the machine. The display assures us that the elevator's movements, and so the fate of its human passengers, can be charted, a correspondence established between inside and out.

As Oppen claims the (shaky) ground of everyday urban experience for the poem, he is concerned not with presenting conventionally lyrical or aesthetic responses but with investigating the "unseen" realm of the ordinary. In the process, he reveals that the "boring" domain of everyday responses, usually taken for granted, is in fact subject to intense pressures, full of unstated fears and uncertainties, haunted by strange absences. Apparently with this poem in mind, Oppen once observed that people "are upset and distracted if you ask them to realize not how they feel about a rose, but how they feel waiting for an elevator" (*SL* 24). It is difficult, according to Oppen, to evoke specific reactions concerning a "rose" in poetry "because the sentiment has been generalized to include too much" (24). He wanted his poetry to eschew such generalized sentiment in order to make us *notice our emotional response* (23). For Oppen, Heideggerian "boredom" implies at least the potential for a kind of receptivity. The first two poems of *Discrete Series* suggest acts of "bored" observation, attempts to find out "what was really going on," to transform experience into knowledge. In our "elevator" poem, however, the act of attention is circumscribed by the "fixed / Alternatives" of a culture, and deflected by the slick surfaces of a "Shiny" modernity. Further, an image like "from the / Under arm of T" subjects us to a weird state of dis/embodiment; since "under arms" are usually associated with people, rather than with elevator indicators, we arrive at a kind of subject/object confusion—an experience that will recur as we continue to read the series.

Oppen's poetic attention to "architecture" and "the feel of its interiors" has something in common, I would argue, with Walter Benjamin's treatment of architecture as "the prototype of a work of art the reception of which is consummated by a collectivity in a state of distraction" (239). Benjamin took architecture as an "instructive" example, given that the "state of distraction" was becoming more and more central to modern aesthetic experience (239).[12] Moreover, architecture was interesting to Benjamin because "buildings are appropriated" partly by means of "habit" (240), which must always contribute to mastery of "the tasks which face the human apparatus of perception at the turning points of history" (240). In other words, an attention to people's (distracted and habitual) reactions to the public spaces of architecture can tell us things about modern experience, aesthetic and otherwise, that "contemplation" of the isolated artwork cannot. In the poem "1930'S," George Oppen held up for scrutiny just the sort of quintessentially modern experience described by Benjamin, an experience symptomatic of the profound "changes in the human apparatus of perception," which must take place as the human body learns to adapt itself to the modern world. A hidden repertoire of adaptations required of the body as it negotiates the "fixed / Alternatives" of a machined environment—adaptations of perception, proprioception, cognition—lurks within the experiential frame summoned by Oppen's poem.

In Oppen's poetry, Heideggerian boredom and Benjaminian distraction intersect in the demands made on the perceiver by the modern urban landscape. The bored impetus to vision is deflected by the distracted nature of urban perception. As Michael Taussig usefully elaborates, Benjamin's model of individual contemplation of the isolated artwork giving way to "distracted" patterns of attention involves: "a very different apperceptive mode, the type of flitting and barely conscious peripheral vision perception unleashed with vigor by modern life at the crossroads of the city, the capitalist market, and modern technology" (143). For Taussig, awareness of this sort of distracted experience pushes Benjamin to try to formulate a new mode of response in his writing, to move away from an understanding of meaning that presupposes a contemplative individual and toward a "a distracted collective reading with a tactile eye" (147).

We come to know something like a modern building "through usage, meaning, to some crucial extent, through touch, or better still, we might want to say, by proprioception" (144). I would argue that the implication of this "everyday tactility of knowing" (144) for poetry, and specifically for Oppen's poetry, is that the individual lyric poem, isolated and auratic, is not an entirely adequate medium for registering the "distracted" intensities of modern experience. As Theodor Adorno writes, the traditional lyric poem tends to exhibit a quality of "non-materiality," opposing itself to "the collective and the realm of objectivity" (59).[13] In contrast, Oppen's serial topographies, substituting contiguity and dispersion for auratic autonomy, seem to work with the explicit intention of breaking open the lyric, exposing poetry to the thick and tactile materiality of life among modern "things."

That "quiet, stone floor" in Oppen's "elevator" poem is not an image but a base, a ground of perception that calls attention to the entire proprioceptive experience of the scene, not just an ocular and distanced reading of it. Both poet and reader move in and through a terrain that is at once graphical, devoted to writing and its linguistic imperatives, and immanent, a close engagement with a material world. But in each case, each poem, the "ground" traversed by this double movement is somewhat shaky, the perspective unsteady and occluded. The poem and the series as a whole are full of *dis*orienting cues so the perceiver/reader has difficulty finding his or her bearings. Continuing the process of reading/moving to the next poem of *Discrete Series* the experience is one of tracing a certain continuity across a skewed perceptual framework, of leaping across gaps to find oneself (still) on *un*familiar territory.

The movement from the second to the third poem of the series is in a way a movement from one topographical location to another within the frame "1930'S." Indeed, it is precisely this in one textual sense, since Zukofsky used the title "1930'S" for Oppen's work on two different occasions: in *An "Objectivists" Anthology*, as we have seen; and also in the "Objectivist" number of *Poetry*, where it was applied to an entirely different poem.[14] This other poem, as we are about to see, is the third poem of *Discrete Series*. In this volume both "1930'S" poems are untitled, but they are joined together as a numbered pair. As we move to the second poem of this pair—or following Zukofsky, from one "1930'S" to another—this is what we encounter:

> Thus
> Hides the
>
> Parts—the prudery
> Of Frigidaire, of
> Soda-jerking ——
>
> Thus
>
> Above the
> Plane of lunch, of wives
> Removes itself
> (As soda-jerking from
> the private act
>
> Of
> Cracking eggs);
>
> big-Business[15]

Like the "elevator" poem, this one is concerned with absences, with the hidden dimensions of the urban everyday. The poem begins off-balance, with a space or gap followed by an ambiguous pointer ("Thus") either deferring a statement of subject or constituting an unlikely one.[16] By the third line ("Parts—the prudery"), however, we are signaled that these dislocations are not arbitrary, that some kind of decorum of omission is at work here. The poem's gaps seem to be involved in a kind of "prudery," but what kind of prudery is a prudery "Of Frigidaire"?[17] In a marvelous bit of detective work, Marjorie Perloff juxtaposes Oppen's poem with a General Electric Refrigerator advertisement from a 1927 *Saturday Evening Post*. As Perloff points out, the ad makes a point of what is hidden, leading with the caption "All the mechanism is in here." And as Perloff also notes, the white walls and door of the refrigerator hide both the motor inside and the food items that refrigerator contains. But what I want to draw attention to here is the way the poem's insistence on the hidden, on a logic of "removal," coexists uneasily with a messy entanglement of human and technological frames, of body and machine. Just as one frame is receding another is looming queasily into view.

The (halting and enjambed) movement from line 4 to line 5 (Of Frigidaire, of / Soda-jerking—) rather "jerkily" extends the "prudery" of hidden "Parts," to the act of "Soda-jerking." In lines 9–13, the public, if somehow obscured, realm of "Frigidaire" and "soda-jerking," further "Removes it-self" from the "private," and oddly sexualized, "act / Of Cracking eggs." Both "soda-jerking" and egg-cracking are implicated in the "prudery" at work here, and both are perversely eroticized by the implication. This is an eroticism that arises at the (confused) boundaries of public and private spaces, of what is on display and what is hidden. The poem's logic of removal, of progressively (or regressively) distanced acts, is juxtaposed to the spatial removal of (male) "big-Business" from the (female) "Plane of lunch, of wives," from the "domestic" and biological realities of eating, sex, and reproduction. When "big-Business," which might be considered the referent of the entire poem, eventually makes its delayed appearance in the fourteenth and final line, that appearance has been prepared for by an odd chain of partially obscured acts, half in and half out of the realm of perception. Along this chain, we are moved by strange linkages from one "level of reality" to another, from the concrete if obscure realm of power's worldly manifestations to the abstraction of "big-Business," the capitalist phantasm lurking behind the scene's ordering, one of the prime movers (and re/movers) of the spectral thirties.

The poem's emphasis on "hiddenness" and "removal" again signals a larger crisis of subject and object, of the relation of the perceiver to what is perceived. Concentrating on exactly that "crossroads of the city, the capitalist market, and modern technology" to which Taussig draws our attention in his reading of Benjamin, Oppen gives us a sort of grotesque strip-tease of the forms of power as they rather slyly manifest themselves in the urban everyday. For Oppen, power always "hides what it can" (*NCP* 205); here, the "city of the corporations" (114) exerts itself as an enigmatic presence pierced by strange absences, open to human negotiation only in halting and oblique movements. Since Oppen's poetry is often heavily nounal, or as he puts it, "substantive," the complicated placement of verbs ("Hides," "Removes,") within this nounal frame serves a dramatic purpose.[18] In this case, the poem's verbs call attention to an action of displacement that might easily be disguised by adjectival (e.g., "hidden") or nominal (e.g., "removal") states. The poem's action, its *enactment*, draws attention to the visceral import of the architectural logic of the high-rise office building, to the enforcement of power relations in its hierarchical ordering of stacked "planes."

As I've already suggested, the Objectivist engagement with modernity has moved beyond the modernist focus on brute power and speed. Objectivist poems—and this is especially true of Oppen's work—often ask how the technological transformations of our environment come to structure our thoughts and emotions. Whereas the Futurists made of that prime modern symbol the Eiffel Tower a sort of abstraction, an "empty signifier" open to almost any interpretation, Oppen takes a rather different approach to the office buildings of New York City.[19] For Oppen, the modern artifact is never a "pure signifier," empty or otherwise, as it could be for the Futurists. Instead, it remains stubbornly embodied, stuck in a nexus of social and material relations. The building gets built, is literally shaped by, corporate money ("big-Business")—and however strange or marvelous its architectural innovations, people still have to eat ("the plane of lunch"), or work ("Soda-jerking"), in its environs.

To put it another way: Oppen's "plane of lunch" may momentarily conjure images of sandwiches lined up on one of Picasso's or Braque's flying wedges, but despite the fractures and dislocations of his work, he was adamant that nothing interested him less than "imaginary geometries" (*SL* 56). In his poetry, those fractures and dislocations always remain grounded in "reality," or in what he sometimes refers to as "the onta," meaning "the things that exist."[20] To understand Oppen's quarrel with "imaginary geometries," we might turn to the American scene and the Precisionist painters. Though the Objectivists have often been linked to the Precisionists, Oppen took care to distance himself from their project.[21] In an interview with Kevin Power, George and Mary point out that although Williams did indeed have an affinity with Charles Sheeler and the other Precisionists, they themselves had had a "different viewpoint" based on their "practical experience" of "working in factories" (189). As Mary (herself a painter) elaborates, they felt that Sheeler's techniques for handling the industrial landscape lacked sufficient "solidity," that there was no "third dimension" to his painting and that it was deficient in "strength" and "emotional content" (190).

The terms of this critique are telling. As Oppen explains elsewhere, his own sense of "precision" involves not surfaces but "depth" and "distance": "the need to be able to shift focus, depth of focus, with precision, to control distance, real distance, I mean visual distance and audible distance and get at the crucial moments right on top of the thing" (*SL* 144). Again, Oppen's emphasis falls on the empirical, on the need to grapple with "the thing." The "imaginary geometries" of a too abstract, too "flat" aesthetic call up that "demonic universe of mathematics" which is always threatening to annihilate the world of things. As Oppen wrote in a notebook entry capturing his sense of urgency: "WE HAVE A LONG TRADITION

OF CONTEMPT FOR MATTER, AND HAVE CEASED TO NO-
TICE THAT ITS EXISTENCE—AND ONLY *ITS* EXISTENCE—
REMAINS ABSOLUTELY UNEXPLAINED" ("An Adequate Vision"
17). Oppen's aesthetic of serial topography represents a commitment to this
world of matter and carries out a strategy of tracking the per/mutations to
which it is subjected by the operations of technology.

Such tracking is, again, a function of what Oppen referred to as the
need for disclosure or revelation in poetry. According to Oppen's definition, "a poem, if it is indeed poetry, is always revelatory" (*SL* 139–140). Of
his own prosody, Oppen wrote that "the line sense, the line breaks, and the
syntax are intended to control the order of disclosure upon which the poem
depends" (*SL* 141).[22] Oppen's prosody operates as a specific kind of writing technology matching wits, as it were, with the pervasive technologies
of the urban scene, working its way through layers of disguise, slowly and
painfully turning opacity to translucence. Heidegger is again relevant here,
writing in his essay "The Question Concerning Technology" of the conflict between the two different kinds of potentiality evidenced by the technological world. If poeisis is a kind of "bringing-forth" in which "something concealed comes into unconcealment" (293), technology can also be
a useful "way of revealing"; it can be "something poetic" in itself (294). The
nature of modern technology is such that it often "challenges" nature, subjecting it to "unreasonable demand[s]" (296). This "challenging-forth" or
"setting upon" turns nature into what Heidegger calls "standing-reserve,"
so that: "Everywhere everything is ordered to stand by, to be immediately
on hand, indeed to stand there just so that it may be on call for a further
ordering" (298). In this ordering, things lose their objecthood: "Whatever
stands by in the sense of standing-reserve no longer stands over against
us as object" (298). Heidegger elaborates, using the example of an airliner
waiting on a runway: "Yet an airliner standing on a runway is surely an object. Certainly. We can represent the machine so. But then it conceals itself as to what and how it is. Revealed, it stands on the taxi strip only
as standing-reserve, inasmuch as it is ordered to insure the possibility of
transportation. For this it must be in its whole structure and in every one
of its constituent parts itself on call for duty, i.e., ready for takeoff" (298).
There are times in Oppen's poetry when we do indeed glimpse "the object disappear[ing] into the objectlessness of standing-reserve" (300). But
where Heidegger maintains that "the machine," governed entirely by the
logic of standing-reserve, is "completely unautonomous" (299), I would

argue that in Oppen's poetry the system of technological relations gives rise to a more complex crisis of subject/object relations. The elevator waits for us but we also wait for it (and who hasn't waited for an airplane?); it carries us where we want to go, but within strict limits, and only after we surrender ourselves to its interior. Under examination, the office building reveals order after order of spatial logic to which we must accommodate ourselves. Like the elevator, the "Frigidaire" is a "shiny" modern sort of puzzle box, an enclosure of machined space—into which things disappear from view. And by a modern modular logic, both the lunch counter and the "giant machine" of the office building as a whole are ordered on the same principles, and constructed using the same techniques. The Frigidaire and the lunch counter "enclose" food, food for the human bodies that are in turn enclosed by elevators and office buildings. By eroticizing the scene's partially obscured "Parts" while making visible the mechanical and commercial act of "removal" or dis/appearance, an act which paradoxically both hides and displays power, Oppen's poem calls attention to the persistent traces of the bodies (almost) lost in the machine.[23] In this urban terrain subjects and objects threaten to exchange places; the elevator's red and white indicators stare back at us like glass eyes.

What does this crisis of subject and object mean for the poetic act of seeing? In Perloff's reading, Oppen implicitly "deconstructs" the "visual cliché" of the General Electric refrigerator advertisement, "not by writing a critique of the consumer culture that produces Frigidaires—that would be much too easy and uninteresting—but by rupturing the very sentence and phrasal units in which the image appears" (80). Again, according to Perloff: "[Oppen's] interest is not to produce a clear visual image of a particular scene, a description of lunch at the office building soda fountain, but, on the contrary, to see how *words*, taken out of their normal syntactical contexts, can assume new meanings" (82). Like Conte, Perloff refers us usefully to the importance of the "word as such" in Oppen's poems, and to his refusal of any simple notions of "imagism" or reductive referentiality; but just as valuable is Perloff's gesture outward, through the General Electric advertisement, to the material culture of the 1930s and its commercial representations. Oppen's poetry is always keenly aware of its own linguistic resources, but it also seeks to use those resources to cleanse the doors of perception, to return our attention to a world seen differently, and more sharply. Acknowledging the "Objectivist" debt to an Imagist aesthetic, Oppen wrote that "the strength of Imagism [is] its demand that one actually *look*" ("Three Oppen Letters and a Note" 85). Oppen's poetry struggles with the difficulty and seriousness of this demand, as vision grapples with what Heidegger calls "the arduous path of appearance."

Oppen used that phrase as an epigraph in one volume of poetry, and it pairs neatly with an epigraph from Jacques Maritain he used in another: "We awake in the same moment to ourselves and to things."[24] This "moment" of awakening, the moment of Maud/e's approach to the window, is the occasion of much of Oppen's poetry, and its complexities do much to account for the "arduousness"—the involutions of syntax and complexities of elision—of the small poems making up *Discrete Series*. As we have already seen, Oppen found Heideggerian "boredom" interesting for the insight it might provide into the existence of things, the glimpse it might offer of "what-is-in-totality." Again and again, Oppen's poetry concerns itself with the state of "awe," which he discussed as follows in an interview with Louis Dembo: "I mean the awareness . . . I suppose it's nearly a sense of awe, simply to feel that the thing is there and that it's quite something to see. It's an awareness of the world, a lyric reaction to the world."[25] This sense "that the thing is there and it's quite something to see" asserts itself throughout Oppen's work, often as a kind of celebration of the "pure joy / Of the mineral fact" (*NCP* 114).

But as we have also seen, in the techno-commercial scene of urban America, this solidity is always threatening to give way to "objectlessness," or is it "subjectlessness"? The disorienting interpenetrations of subject and object to be found in the poems of *Discrete Series,* the sense of perception sometimes losing itself amid unreal vistas, are the poetic signs of Oppen's grappling with Baudrillard's "system of objects." This system of objects seems to offer "an immediately legible, universal structure of signification" (20), but in fact one is confronted with: "the image of a false transparency, of a false legibility of social relations, behind which the real structures of production and social relations remain illegible" (21). It is precisely this false "image," this pervasive opacity, that Oppen's own post-Imagist intensity of vision is attempting to penetrate in order to make contact with the "social facts," with the "real structures of production and social relations." Such contact demands the ardors and arduousness of an "Objectivist" prosody.

Again and again in Oppen's series, the human presence is nearly overwhelmed by the machined environment, but the poems remain dedicated to giving meticulous accounts of the transformations, conflicts, and confusions engendered by the dynamics of various sorts of urban encounters.

Authorized by the recombinant nature of Oppen's serial form, we'll jump now to the tenth poem of the book:

Who comes is occupied
Toward the chest (in the crowd moving
       opposite
Grasp of me)
         In firm overalls
The middle-aged man sliding
Levers in the steam-shovel cab, ——
Lift (running cable) and swung, back
Remotely respond to the gesture before last
Of his arms fingers continually ——
Turned with the cab. But if I (how
       goes it?) ——
            The asphalt edge
Loose on the plateau,
Horse's classic height cartless
See electric flash of streetcar,
The fall is falling from electric burst.
(10)

Here the series has moved outside the interiors of "big-Business," perhaps observing an early stage of the labor by which one of those towering office buildings is constructed. But still, as with the elevator or the Frigidaire, we have a scene of technological enclosure. As the man sits "sliding / Levers in the steam-shovel cab," body and machinery are out of sync. The mechanism that contains him responds "Remotely . . . to the gesture before last" of his arms and fingers, and he is "Turned with the cab" (*NCP* 14). When the human, "the living," does assert itself, it is often the case, as this same poem has it, that "Who comes is occupied / Toward the chest (in the crowd moving / opposite / Grasp of me)" (*NCP* 14), that one body is cut off from another.

As in Oppen's other poems of the techno-commercial landscape, attention is drawn to the unnaturalness, the unreality, of the scene by means of unusual syntactic constructions ("who comes is occupied") and intentionally skewed cadences (". . . moving / opposite / Grasp of me"). As Oppen himself has commented, the poems of *Discrete Series* often "tak[e] the city for granted" (McAleavey 66) as the scene from which they arise, but if the scene of urban hyperreality is one Oppen knows well, and with which he is to a certain extent at home, he also keeps continually before us the "strangeness" (McAleavey 63) of the city. In the present poem, the human subject is again nearly eclipsed, swamped by the technologies and materials of the city (steam shovel, streetcar, asphalt), and immersed in the distracted flow of the moving crowd. But this poem also provides a special perspective by juxtaposing the jostle of the urban scene to the preexistent reality of the "plateau"—an effect reinforced by the somewhat surprising presence of the horse, which is characterized as both "classic" and "cartless," as if to gesture toward an order of existence different from that of the urban everyday. Even if the poem is not literally located at the city's outskirts, a metaphorical city limit, "the asphalt edge / loose on the plateau," is revealed. The experience of urban distraction seems to compete with the state of metaphysical awe before the totality-of-what-is, but the two experiences are also weirdly intertwined as well. In this poetic topography, the "giant machine" of the city, with all its fantastic mechanisms, assumes the aspect of a thin shell that can be peeled back, laying bare the more solid and primal substratum of "the mineral fact" of the world.

This kind of "removal," manifesting an aesthetic of exposure, is repeated often in Oppen's poetry, moving in a direction opposite from the removals of "big-Business," leading toward disclosure and revelation rather than obscurity and mystique. Edges, with their threatened unravelings, are important sites in such a poetics of disclosure, and this accounts partly for Oppen's fascination with New York's harbor. The harbor, one of the city's powerfully liminal presences, appears in many of Oppen's poems, including "Party on Shipboard," which is the last poem he wrote for *Discrete Series* (though it is placed after the poem just discussed, eleventh in the series of thirty-two):

Wave in the round of the port-hole
Springs, passing,—arm waved,
Shrieks, unbalanced by the motion ——
Like the sea incapable of contact
Save in incidents (the sea is not
    water)
Homogeneously automatic—a green capped
    white is momentarily a half mile
    out ——
The shallow surface of the sea, this,

Numerously—the first drinks ——
The sea is a constant weight
In its bed. They pass, however, the sea
Freely tumultuous.
(*NCP* 15)

Like the previous poem, this one pulls back from the urban scene, from the "city of corporations," juxtaposing it with the primordial sea, which "is a constant weight / In its bed." Its first two lines suggest that shifting of perspectives between inside and out—the ocean "wave" seen through "the round of the port-hole" (another window) echoed by the "arm waved" inside the ship—that we have already pointed to in Oppen's poetry. As the poem goes on, the waves separate themselves "numerously" from the great weight of the sea, just as individuals loom up from the depths of a crowd. The people, like the sea, are "incapable of contact / Save in incidents"; here, Oppen looks forward to the investigation of human "contact" that will consume much of his later poetry. The keyword "numerously" points forward, in Oppen's poetry of recurrences, to his major series "Of Being Numerous" (1968), which takes as its subject the social forms of human existence.

〜

In all their complicated and various mechanisms, the machines in Oppen's poetry are not mere emblems of brute power. Instead, they are treated as something like prosthetic devices for human thinking and feeling, externalizations of our desires and extensions of our acts of cognition; but the paradox here, as we have seen, is that as we channel more and more of our desires into the machined environment, this environment, this system, grows so extensive and sophisticated that it begins to develop needs of its own. In her "Cyborg Manifesto," Donna Haraway writes of the postmodern shift to a "polymorphous, information society" in terms that are of special interest in thinking about Oppen's use of an aesthetic of serial topography (161). For Haraway, the late twentieth century is a time in which "we are all chimeras, theorized and fabricated hybrids of machine and organism; in short we are cyborgs" (150). Haraway examines the cyborgian reality of the postmodern condition with an emphasis on "communications sciences and modern biologies," which are in her reading, "constructed by a common move—*the translation of the world into a problem of coding,* a search for a common language in which all resistance to instrumental control disappears and all heterogeneity can be submitted to disassembly, reassembly, investment, and exchange" (164). As systems theories are applied to "telephone technology, computer design, weapons deployment, or data base construction and maintenance" the "key operation" is "determining rates, directions, and probabilities of flow of a quantity called information" (164).

In the 1930s, on the verge of this shift into an information society, Oppen's serial topographies arise at the juncture of "poetry" and "information" as competing genres or systems, guided by conflicting strategies of organization.[26] In the characteristic discourses of an information society, "seriality" is often just another name for alienation, as when Baudrillard writes of the "serial production" that results in "an immense combinatorial matrix of types and models," by means of which "needs disappear into products which have a greater degree of coherence [than the needs themselves]" (15). But Oppen's use of the series—with its topographical commitment to "the empirical" and to its own sort of "combinatorial matrix"—seeks to block this disappearance, to preserve or recover those original "needs" and perhaps to hint at the structures to which they might give rise if allowed the opportunity. While reminding us that the opacities of the techno-commercial surround can signal occlusions of thought and deletions of feeling, Oppen's serial topographies enact an alternative, recombinant play, asking us to attend to dynamics of urban experience that normally unfold just beneath the notice of consciousness, and to imagine our way toward an understanding of an emergent (and as Hayles would say, post-human) order of existence.

Haraway's postmodern vision is predicated on the technology of microelectronics, which is "the technical basis of the simulacra" (165). According to her reading, in the information age "our best machines are made of sunshine; they are all light and clean because they are nothing but signals, electromagnetic waves, a section of a spectrum" (153). But as other critics have shown, the "construction of sociotechnical systems" was well advanced as early as the nineteenth century and the work of Charles Babbage, which was revealingly divided between the pragmatic rationalizations of the factory system and the speculative potentiality of his mechanical proto-computer, the "difference engine."[27] The poetry of *Discrete Series* is poised between Haraway's "light and clean" world of microelectronics and the dirty, heavy world of "gear-and-girder" technology, between the personal computer and the steam shovel. The elevator and the Frigidaire, both powered by quiet, electric motors and hidden mechanisms, mediate between these two worlds, prefiguring the technologies to come. Further, Oppen's method of embodied poetic thinking, of "thinking with the things as they exist" (to use Louis Zukofsky's phrase), shows us that the "system of objects" is at once abstract and concrete, participating equally in each of the "two levels of reality" that his series sets out to investigate.[28] All those moving "objects" whose trajectories are traced in Oppen's poetry are both thingily present and just one abstracted step away from taking their places among the bits and bytes flowing through the circuits of the information age.

The network of trains, elevators, steam shovels, telephones, and other machines negotiated by Oppen's poems is something like what Michel Callon and John Law describe as a "hybrid *collectif*," meaning "an emergent effect created by the interaction of the heterogeneous parts that make it up" (485). This description represents an attempt by Callon and Law to think beyond the habit of identifying *agency* exclusively with human decision making. In their scheme, "things" do not act by themselves: "instead there are relations, relations which (sometimes) make things" (485). Accordingly, "it's the *relations*—and their heterogeneity—that are important. Relations which *perform*" (485). Machine networks and human networks entangle and interpenetrate in a skein of furious activity, and this interpenetration gives another dimension to Oppen's exploration of "the meaning / Of being numerous." What did George/Maude see when s/he approached the window? According to the "view" put forward here the poems of *Discrete Series* are moving graphs of the human body subjected to terrific demands on its adaptive capacities. They are elegies to a human world—and, perhaps, small parables (from *parabola,* or juxtaposition) for a cybernetic future.

Notes

1. For accounts of industrial design in the thirties, see, for example, Martin Greif, *Depression Modern*; Miles Orvell, *The Real Thing*; Cecilia Tichi, *Shifting Gears*; and Richard Guy Wilson, Diane H. Pilgrim, and Dickran Tashjian, *The Machine Age in America*.

2. I take the phrase "mechanical-industrial landscape" from Sayre's useful discussion of "Objectivist" poetics in relation to Precisionism ("American Vernacular" 319).

3. I use the term technomorphic to designate the complement of what Wilson calls biomorphism.

4. This scheme was not followed when Oppen's *Collected Poems* were printed by New Directions in 1975, making for a good deal of confusion about when poems begin and end. Michael Davidson's edition, *New Collected Poems,* rectifies the matter.

5. Maud Blessingbourne is the heroine of Henry James's tale "The Story In It." Oppen adds an "e" to her first name.

6. On the "mechanical structure" of the poem, Conte is quoting Williams's 1934 review of *Discrete Series* (124–125). Conte sets out to show us how the poem "works" by paying particular attention to its "syntactical impulse," which, in the absence of a verb, "depends almost entirely on prepositional phrases" (*Unending Design* 125).

7. See "Three Oppen Letters with a Note" (80). Oppen links the phrase to his sense of the word "realism": "It is true I speak of a Realist poetry! Realist in that it is concerned with a fact which it did not create" (80).

8. Zukofsky collection, Harry Ransom Center, folder 2.

9. As I discuss in the preface to this book, however, Oppen had significant reservations about this formulation. It is difficult to determine exactly when these reservations developed.

10. Note Oppen's distrust of predication, as expressed in the Dembo interview, in *The Contemporary Writer.*

11. This reference to the "glittering towers" of the New York skyline was originally written before the events of 9/11/01. Those events have horrifically dramatized the symbolic and political functions of the cityscape.

12. Architecture provides a useful exemplum because, in some form or another, "buildings have been man's companions since primeval times" (239). But the best and most extreme example of modern "reception in a state of distraction" (240) was provided by the cinema, with its "constant, sudden change" constituting a "shock effect" (238).

13. Adorno is himself interested in exposing the limits of this traditional conception of the lyric. In my reading, Oppen's sense of these limits drives him toward the investigation of serial form.

14. The titular repetition lends credence to the suggestion that Zukofsky saw Oppen's work as peculiarly representative of the historical moment. Further supporting this suggestion is the fact that Oppen's contribution to An *"Objectivists" Anthology,* brief as it is, appears in the "epic" section of the volume.

15. I am using the version from Oppen's *Collected Poems.* The *Poetry* version does not capitalize "Business" in the poem's last line.

16. Marjorie Perloff observes of the poem's beginning ("Thus / Hides the / Parts") that "characteristically," Oppen "omits the subject noun or pronoun" (*Radical Artifice* 80).

17. "Frigidaire": The word is another example of technology-and-advertising-inspired neologism, like the materials names surveyed by Greif. By the time Op-

pen wrote this poem, it had already graced the canon of modern poetry at least once before, entering by way of Pound's wittily anachronistic verbal layerings in "Homage to Sextus Propertius" (1919), where the Augustan poet/speaker's cellar does not bristle with wine jars, "nor is it equipped with a frigidaire patent" (*Selected Poems* 80). If the refrigerator suggests affluence in Pound's poem of 1919, it may have been more a symbol of middle-class prosperity by the early thirties—a tribute to its success at becoming what Perloff calls "a secular icon" (Perloff, *Radical Artifice* 80).

18. "I'm really concerned with the substantive, with the subject of the sentence, with what we are talking about, and not rushing over the subject-matter in order to make a comment about it. It is still a principle with me, of more than poetry, to notice, to state, to lay down the substantive for its own sake" (Dembo interview 174).

19. On the Eiffel Tower as "empty signifier," see Perloff, *The Futurist Moment,* 205.

20. These quotations come from a letter not included in the *Selected Letters,* but cited by DuPlessis 379n.

21. For attempts to link the Objectivists to the Precisionists, see especially Sayre, "American Vernacular." The link makes more sense for Williams than for the other Objectivists.

22. These letters were written in response to queries from Fauchereau, who was translating some of Oppen's poetry into French. They were printed in "Three Oppen Letters and a Note."

23. In this light, Schimmel's desire to read the first "1930'S" poem (our "elevator" poem) as a representation of "a Bonnard nude" is particularly interesting. Harold Schimmel, "Zuk. Yehoash David Rex."

24. The phrase from Heidegger serves as one of the epigraphs to Oppen's third volume of poetry, *This in Which* (1965). The sentence from Maritain is used in Oppen's second volume, *The Materials* (1962).

25. This description is actually used in the interview to define what Oppen meant by another phrase, "the life of the mind" (Dembo 177), but I give priority here to his use of the term "awe."

26. This is an argument I hope to make at greater length at a future date, but what I have in mind is that poetry is more resistant to "dematerialization" than information is; poetry insists on having a body. One of the main narrative threads of Hayles's book is the story of "*how information lost its body,* that is, how it came to be conceptualized as an entity separate from the material forms in which it is thought to be embedded" (2). But Hayles does not discuss poetry. For a stimulating account of the role of literature, and specifically poetry, in a digital culture, see McGann's *Radiant Textuality.*

27. See Simon Schaffer, "Babbage's Intelligence."

28. For Zukofsky's phrase, see his essay "Sincerity and Objectification," which

prefaced the "Objectivist" number of *Poetry*. "Writing occurs which is the detail, not mirage, of seeing, of thinking with the things as they exist, and of directing them along a line of melody" (273).

Works Cited

Adorno, Theodor. "Lyric Poetry and Society." *Telos* 2 (1974): 57–71.

Baudrillard, Jean. "The System of Objects." *Selected Writings*. Ed. Mark Poster. Stanford: Stanford University Press, 1988.

Benjamin, Walter. "The Work of Art in the Age of Mechanical Reproduction." *Illuminations*. New York: Shocken Books, 1985. 217–252.

Callon, Michel, and John Law. "Agency and the Hybrid Collectif." *South Atlantic Quarterly* 94, 2 (1995): 481–508.

Conte, Joseph. *Unending Design: The Forms of Postmodern Poetry*. Ithaca, NY: Cornell University Press, 1991.

Greif, Martin. *Depression Modern: The Thirties Style in America*. New York: Universe Books, 1975.

Haraway, Donna. "A Cyborg Manifesto." *Simian, Cyborgs and Women: The Reinvention of Nature*. New York: Routledge, 1991. 149–182.

Hayles, Katherine. *How We Became Posthuman: Virtual Bodies in Cybernetics, Literature and Informatics*. Chicago: University of Chicago Press, 1999.

Heidegger, Martin. *Basic Writings*. Ed. David Farrell Krell. San Francisco: Harper & Row, 1977.

———. "Modern Science, Metaphysics, and Mathematics." In *Basic Writings*, 247–283.

———. "The Question Concerning Technology." In *Basic Writings*, 287–317.

———. "What is Metaphysics?" In *Basic Writings*, 95–112.

James, Henry. "The Story in It." *Daisy Miller, Pandora, the Patagonia, and Other Tales*. New York: Charles Scribner's Sons, 1909. 409–435.

Le Corbusier. *Towards a New Architecture*. New York: Praeger, 1927.

McGann, Jerome. *Radiant Textuality: Literature after the World Wide Web*. New York: Palgrove, 2001.

Oppen, George. "An Adequate Vision: A George Oppen Daybook." *Ironwood* 26 (1985): 5–31.

———. *Discrete Series*. New York: Objectivist Press, 1934.

———. Interview with Kevin Power. *Montemora* 4 (1975): 186–203.

———. Interview with L. S. Dembo. *The Contemporary Writer*. Ed. L. S. Dembo. Madison: University of Wisconsin Press, 1972.

———. "Oppen on Oppen: Extracts from Interviews," conducted by David McAleavey. *Sagetrieb* 5, 1 (Spring 1986): 59–93.

———. *New Collected Poems*. Ed. Michael Davidson. New York: New Directions, 2002.

———. "Three Oppen Letters and a Note." *Ironwood* 5 (1975): 78–85.

————. *The Selected Letters of George Oppen.* Ed. Rachel Blau DuPlessis. Durham, NC: Duke University Press, 1990.

Orvell, Miles. *The Real Thing: Imitation and Authenticity in American Culture, 1880–1940.* Chapel Hill: University of North Carolina Press, 1989.

Perloff, Marjorie. *The Futurist Moment: Avant-Garde, Avant Guerre, and the Language of Rupture.* Chicago: University of Chicago Press, 1986.

————. *Radical Artifice in the Age of Media.* Chicago: University of Chicago Press, 1991.

Sayre, Henry M. "American Vernacular: Objectivism, Precisionism and the Aesthetics of the Machine." *Twentieth Century Literature* 35, 3 (1989): 310–342.

Schaffer, Simon. "Babbage's Intelligence: Calculating Engines and the Factory System." *Critical Inquiry* 21, 4 (1994): 203–227.

Schimmel, Harold. "Zuk. Yehoash David Rex." *Louis Zukofsky: Man and Poet,* ed. Carroll F. Terrell, 235–245. Orono, ME: National Poetry Foundation, 1979.

Taussig, Michael. *The Nervous System.* New York: Routledge, 1992.

Tichi, Cecelia. *Shifting Gears: Technology, Literature, Culture in Modernist America.* Chapel Hill: University of North Carolina Press, 1987.

Williams, William Carlos. *Autobiography.* New York: New Directions, 1948.

————. "The New Poetical Economy." Reprinted in *George Oppen: Man and Poet,* ed. Burton Hatlen. Orono, ME: National Poetry Foundation, 1981.

Wilson, Richard Guy, Diane H. Pilgrim, and Dickran Tashjian. *The Machine Age in America 1918–1941.* New York: Brooklyn Museum, 1986.

Zukofsky, Louis. "About the Gas Age." In *Prepositions: The Critical Essays of Louis Zukofsky.* Berkeley and Los Angeles: University of California Press, 1981. 169–172.

————, ed. *An "Objectivists" Anthology.* Var, France: To Publishers, 1932.

III
Among the Philosophers

4
Oppen's Heidegger

Peter Nicholls

I

In 1960, after almost ten years of political exile in Mexico, George and Mary Oppen were finally able to return to New York City.[1] Oppen was writing again and reading voraciously. One of his new excitements was the work of Heidegger which was now beginning to appear in English translation.[2] In a late interview, Mary Oppen recalled that the couple "read a great deal of Heidegger" at this time, partly encouraged by their new son-in-law, Alexander Mourelatos, a philosopher specializing in the texts of the pre-Socratics. Mourelatos, who married the Oppens' daughter Linda in 1962, "began to give us whatever new translations were around," recalled Mary.[3]

What had prepared Oppen for this sudden excursion into European philosophy? There are few clues to his intellectual interests during the Mexico years, but it is perhaps not fortuitous that the one work we know him definitely to have read was Jacques Maritain's *Creative Intuition in Art and Poetry* (1954). Oppen's interest in Maritain is known mainly from his adaptation of a passage from it for an epigraph to his 1962 collection *The Materials*: "We awake in the same moment to ourselves and to things." The source is as follows:

> Now if it is true that *creative subjectivity awakens to itself only by simultaneously awakening to Things,* in a single process which is po-

etic knowledge; and that the way by which the free creativity of the spirit enters into act is essentially poetic intuition, and that poetic intuition is nothing but the grasping of Things and the Self together through connaturality and intentional emotion—then it must be said that in breaking away from the existential world of Nature, from Things and the grasping of Things, nonrepresentative art, by this very fact, condemns itself to fall short of its own dearest purposes and the very ends for the sake of which it came to life. (my emphasis)[4]

Maritain's idea of "awakening" was rich in implication for Oppen at the time he discovered it. First, it proposed poetry as a special kind of "knowledge," one for which, as Maritain put it, "there is no goal, no specifying end" (131) and which aspires to the condition of 'ontological simplicity," following the example of the child "who seems simply astonished *to be,* and condemns all our interests and their futility" (267). Second, it offered some kind of analogy with Oppen's own reawakening to poetry, and with his own engrained sense of the self's imaginative sympathy and involvement with the things of the world. And, third, Maritain's book might well have seemed to Oppen to promise an "awakening" from what he would increasingly come to see as the bad dream of a type of modernism he now identified primarily with Ezra Pound. Pound, of course, had written a commendatory preface for *Discrete Series,* and it may have seemed in 1934 that Objectivism was to be an orderly development from the older poet's imagism. Yet the twenty-five-year "gap" in Oppen's career had also seen the unfolding of a truly disastrous global history, a history marked by the trauma of mass slaughter and suffering. We must remember, too, that Oppen was returning to poetry in a period over which the invention of the atom bomb cast *its* long shadow. Insofar as his poetry was witness to past and present terrors, so it accepted—as a fundamental obligation—the need to, as it were, rewrite that earlier modernism which had shown itself so inadequate to the challenge of modern barbarism.

    Oppen may have been grateful at the time for Pound's endorsement, but now he was constantly interrogating the older poet's errors, the failure of his economic and political theories and the apparent futility of a poetry committed to an ideology of "knowledge." "Pound," he remarked, "never freed himself from argument, the moving of chess pieces" (Young, "Conversation" 5), and, again, "Pound's ego system, Pound's organisation of the world around a character, a kind of masculine energy, is extremely foreign to me" (Dembo 170). This type of modernism Oppen now saw as characterized by "ego," by an agonistic relation of subject and object, and by a masculinist sense of aesthetic form as something won from struggle with a recalcitrant "other." It was not surprising that Maritain's idea of "connatural knowing," of subjectivity awakening to itself only by simultaneously awakening to things, gestured in the direction of a fundamental recasting of a modernism that now seemed disastrously complicit in the waves of violence that had engulfed the twentieth century.[5]

For Oppen, reviving his poetic ambitions in the early sixties, the work of Heidegger must have seemed to offer a complex development and intensification of some of the ideas he had already absorbed from Maritain. Above all, it was Heidegger's elaboration of a philosophical poetics that seemed to him to provide an alternative to the political entailments of Poundian modernism. Interestingly, although Mary, in the interview just cited, remarked that Heidegger's controversial politics presented "a real problem," there is little evidence, published or unpublished, that Oppen himself was much concerned on this score.[6] I have found only one passage in his notes where he confronts the issue. Here he seems to refer to a study of Heidegger by Laszlo Versényi, who, he says, "feels that H[eidgger] may lead to rather bad things—One is aware of that danger. It is not possible to read H without experiencing some fear. Still, H's awareness of the world is among the most vivid, the most poignant in literature—We almost have to agree to take a chance on that. There is an extreme rawness, like a raw sun. My feeling is that we should risk it" (UCSD 16, 15, 7).[7] Oppen certainly took that "risk," assuming perhaps that his own inherent skepticism about mystical ideas of "folk," "nation," and the agrarian "idyll" would insulate him from the dubious charms of Heidegger's "ontological pastorale" (Lacoue-Labarthe, "In the Name of . . ." 62). The "risk" was worth taking because Heidegger offered a response to those terrors of the new atomic age that had haunted *The Materials*, and he did so by making the retrieval of a certain poetic or "meditative" thinking a pressing necessity. Here in short was a development of that poetics of being that Oppen had already discovered in Maritain and that would now allow him to move on from the dark perspectives of *The Materials* to that sense of the "miraculous" that is so distinctive a feature of *This in Which*. The association of the latter volume with Heidegger is further supported by the recent discovery of the poet's paperback copy of *Introduction to Metaphysics*, the title page of which bears the annotation "'This in which' all truth is contained—the universe contains all truth—[illegible]."[8]

Oppen's interest in Heidegger was a sustained and surprisingly systematic one. In a 1973 interview with Charles Tomlinson, in fact, he claimed to have read the philosopher as early as 1950 (UCSD 16, 34, 4). The reference would be to the first English translation of Heidegger's work, *Existence and Being*, which made available four essays: "Remembrance of the Poet," "Hölderlin and the Essence of Poetry," "On the Essence of Truth," and "What is Metaphysics" (the essay that includes Heidegger's account of "boredom" that Oppen associated with the first poem of *Discrete Series*). The collection was edited by Werner Brock, who also supplied long and detailed accounts of *Being and Time* and of the four essays. Oppen doesn't seem to quote from or allude to particular passages in *Being and Time*, and his copy (held in the Mandeville Special Collections) is unmarked and shows—unusually—little indication of extensive use. When asked in an interview in 1980 whether it was this work in particular that influenced him, Oppen replied, "Yes, in particular" (Hatlen and Mandel 34), but it is likely that his knowledge of the text came mainly from Brock's essay.[9] *Existence and Being* remained an important collection for him and there is some evidence that he returned to it in the early sixties.[10] Rachel Blau DuPlessis has suggested that it is this volume along with *Being and Time* that Oppen loaned to Robert Duncan in 1969.[11]

During the sixties and into the seventies, Oppen seems to have kept up with translations of Heidegger as they appeared. A passage in the 1963 "Pipe-Stem Cleaner Daybook" (UCSD 16, 19, 6), for example, shows his familiarity with *What Is Philosophy?* (translation 1958),[12] and an important letter from 1966 records his reading of the 1960 translation *Essays in Metaphysics: Identity and Difference* (SL 136). Additionally, in a 1978 interview with David McAleavey, Oppen recalled reading Heidegger's "Conversation on a Country Path," one of two short pieces that comprise *Discourse on Thinking*, which appeared in translation in 1966 (McAleavey, "Oppen on Literature" 118). It is likely that his reference to "indwelling" in a letter to John Crawford was a result of his reading this text.[13]

Oppen also read Heidegger's *Introduction to Metaphysics* (translation 1959), which provided an epigraph for *This in Which* ("the arduous path of appearance"),[14] and the account in that volume of Parmenides's Fragment #3 ("The same is to think and to be") stimulated his interest in the pre-Socratic thinkers.[15] Of other texts by Heidegger alluded to by Oppen there is *On the Way to Language* (1971), a line from which—Stefan George's "No thing may be where words break off"—apparently concludes an uncollected poem called "Words."[16] In the McAleavey interview, Oppen recalled his enthusiasm for "A Dialogue on Language" included in that volume (McAleavey, "Oppen on Literature" 117). A quotation from Heidegger's *The Question of Being* (translation 1959) in Oppen's notes indicates his acquaintance with that text,[17] and another page of quotations and jottings shows that he read *Poetry, Language, Thought* soon after the translation appeared in 1971.[18] Among several Heidegger texts owned by the Oppens, Alexander Mourelatos notes the presence also of *Kant and the Problem of Metaphysics* (translation 1962).[19]

This outline should give us a clearer sense of the intensity and persistence of Oppen's interest in Heidegger. Indeed, the 1980 interview intimates that he was still reading Heidegger in his final years (Hatlen and Mandel 34), though Mary Oppen carefully corrects this by remarking that "those were ideas that were digested. . . . Heidegger somehow isn't there any more. We seem to have taken it. We look at it again and somehow it doesn't have that freshness or [of?] discovery that it did have." By 1980, Oppen was almost certainly too ill to wrestle with the intricacies of Heidegger's works, though the presence of one of them in his room at the time of this interview testifies, perhaps, to the symbolic significance that the philosopher's work still held for him.

One key to that significance lies in the powerful distinction Heidegger draws between "calculative" and "meditative" thinking—the former is rooted in the will and sees the world as nothing more than a resource to be exploited. In *Discourse on Thinking,* for example, which Oppen read soon after its publication in 1966, Heidegger says famously that nature has become "a gigantic gasoline station, an energy source for modern technology and industry" (50). Against which, "meditative thinking" offers a radically different way of being, which Heidegger calls, after the early German mystic Meister Eckhart, "releasement," "letting go" (*Gelassenheit*) (54). In the essay "On the Essence of Truth," Heidegger proposes that "The freedom to reveal something overt lets whatever 'is' at the moment *be* what it is. Freedom reveals itself as the 'letting-be' of what-is" (*Existence and Being* 333). Heidegger defines this "overtness" as the Greek *aletheia,* "unconcealment," thus contrasting "our ordinary idea of truth in the sense of propositional correctitude" with "that still uncomprehended quality: the revealedness (*Entborgenheit*) and revelation (*Entbergung*) of what-is" (*Existence and Being* 306). In a marginal comment on the essay, Oppen observed similarly that "*Truth* is not a statement, not a thing,"[20] and in his notes (UCSD 16, 13, 2), he transcribed the following passage: "The initial revelation of what-is-in-totality, the quest for what-is-as-such, and the beginning of the history of the West, are one and the same thing and are contemporaneous in a 'time' which, itself immeasurable, alone opens the Manifest to every kind of measurement" (*Existence and Being* 336).

That temporal perspective is further elaborated in Heidegger's discussion of Parmenides in *An Introduction to Metaphysics*. There he argues that with the Sophists and Plato a cleavage opened up between thinking and being, with the latter term assimilated to the "suprasensory realm" of the idea (89). "Truth" then became not disclosure of being, but "the correctness of the logos. With this the logos has departed from its original inclusion in the happening of unconcealment" (156). "This differentiation," argues Heidegger, "is a name for the fundamental attitude of the Western spirit. In accordance with this attitude, being is defined from the standpoint of thinking and reason" (122)—or "argument," to use the word Oppen applied critically to Pound. As one commentator notes, the "enframing" of the modern world by technology "drives out our ability even to *see* the whatness, objectness, the in-itselfness of beings" (Young, "Conversation" 53; his emphasis). Instead, we are enmeshed in the representational thinking of logic, which, says Heidegger, entails *"letting something take up a position opposite to us, as an object"* (*Existence and Being* 328; original in italics). The subject-object relation that has dominated Western thinking thus entails a fundamental violence to the world: "To re-present here means to bring what is present before one as something confronting oneself, to relate it to oneself, the person representing it, and to force it back into this relation to oneself as the normative area" ("The Age of the World View" 11). For Heidegger, then, experience is not to be considered as something distinct from thinking (its content or raw material); rather, as Krzysztof Ziarek explains, "experience, refigured as event, is a form of thinking which acts upon reality and effects it, 'lets it be' through the act of transposing it into language. . . . For Heidegger being means participating in the linguistic event (*Ereignis*) which opens a world and history" (*The Historicity of Experience* 52). This opening of a world situates man not as a distanced observer, but as one being among others ("being" thus denoting a "being-with").[21] "Letting be" means allowing other beings to disclose or present themselves rather than conforming them to external judgment and interpretation: "The *Being-true* (*truth*) of the assertion must be understood as *Being-uncovering*," as Heidegger puts it in *Being and Time* (261).

Here we can begin to see how Oppen found in Heidegger an authoritative development of the "ontological simplicity" celebrated by Maritain. For Heidegger, Greek philosophy originated in "astonishment" before the question of Being and the relation of the one (Being) to the all (being).[22] This wonder in face of existence leads to a view of the world to which Oppen was instinctively responsive. In Julian Young's words, with Heidegger, "one understands the world as something contingent, fragile, precious, something which far from being *of course* there, *might not have existed at all*" (*Heidegger's Later Philosophy* 60; emphases in original). This fragility and sense of possibility are reflected in the play of disclosure and concealment that, for Heidegger, characterizes our grasp of Being. For Being as the condition for entities to be is not something about which we can speak: "Being lies in the fact that something is, and in its Being as it is; in Reality; in presence-at-hand; in subsistence; in validity; in Dasein; in the there is" (*Being and Time* 26, and see the discussion in Naylor). Since "no thing corresponds to the word and the meaning 'being'" (*An Introduction* 73), Being is "neither a subject of predication nor a predicate" (Mulhall, *Heidegger* 9). As soon as we refer in language to the being of an entity, Being withdraws into this particular being, so while naming or "saying" discloses beings, it simultaneously registers the absence of Being from language.[23] How then are we to talk about "the marvel of all marvels: that what-is *is?*" (*Existence and Being* 386). "The little word 'is,'" as Heidegger calls it in *Identity and Difference* (66), quickly lost its primal force: "In the form of statement logos itself became something already-there. It became something handy that one handles in order to gain and secure the truth as correctness" (*An Introduction* 157). This "already-there" measures knowledge by its conformity with fact, whereas "the unconcealedness of beings—this is never a merely existent state, but a happening" (*Poetry, Language, Thought [PLT]* 54). Oppen follows Heidegger closely in his conviction that "if we still possessed the word 'is,' there would be no need to write poems" (*SL* 249).

But of course we do not possess the word "is" in the full plenitude of presence, and we are in that sense plagued forever by a lingering sense of anteriority, of perceiving what-is not in the splendor of its disclosure but in a degraded state of already-having-been. Yet while this recognition might seem to promise nothing but a thoroughgoing pessimism, Oppen shares Heidegger's view that poetry is the privileged means by which we might recover our sense of being. The following passage from "Hölderlin and the Essence of Poetry," is duly transcribed in Oppen's notes (UCSD 16, 22, 58): "poetry is the inaugural naming of being and of the essence of all things—not just any speech, but that particular kind which for the first time brings into the open all that which we then discuss and deal with in everyday language. Hence poetry never takes language as a raw material ready to hand, rather it is poetry which first makes language possible. Poetry is the primitive language of a historical people" (*Existence and Being* 307). The primacy assigned to poetry is closely connected, for Oppen, with, as he puts it in another of his notes, "The idea, in Heidegger, that man may have to discard humanity in order to live" (UCSD 16, 19, 7).[24] Oppen gives no source for this idea, but it is likely that he is alluding again to Heidegger's essay "What is Metaphysics?" There we find an elaboration of what is called "essential thinking." Whereas calculative thinking "uses everything that 'is' as units of computation," essential thinking "expends itself in Being for the truth of Being": "The need is: to preserve the truth of Being no matter what may happen to man and everything that 'is'" (*Existence and Being* 388, 389). Heidegger thus argues that "this sacrifice is the *expense of our human being* for the preservation of the truth of Being in respect of what-is" (389; my emphasis).[25]

Heidegger's distinction sheds some light on Oppen's later feeling that the full impact of his own work had been missed: "I begin to understand that the earlier books have been taken to be a simple realism—I was in these books speaking of Being: I had thought I could arrive at the concept of Being from an account of experience as it presents itself in its own terms" (*SL* 410 n. 29). Such comments point up the inadequacy of any view of Objectivism which simply situates it in a smooth line of development from Imagism (Hugh Kenner's *A Homemade World* is one example).[26] For whereas Imagism was absolutely founded on a subject-object dualism, what Oppen now saw himself attempting entailed a much more fundamental reaction to customary modes of thinking, and it was here that his earlier poems seemed to him to resonate with Heidegger's systematic critique of modern subjectivity and the technology that "enframes" it. Against the idea of a "distanced" subject, aloof from the world in its objectivity and intent on manipulating and judging what is before it, Heidegger—and Oppen with him—seeks an elision of thinking with being.[27] We are dealing, then, not with "representation," with "letting something take up a position opposite to us, as an object" (*Existence and Being* 328), but with an event—the emergence of a "world"—in which things come into their own as beings rather than simply presenting themselves as available for human ends. In the wake of Objectivism, Oppen does, of course, speak of "objects," but he does so with a particular Heideggerian inflection. Heidegger, for example, writes: "It is through the work of art as *essent being* that everything else appears and is to be found is first confirmed and made accessible, explicable, and understandable as being or not being" (*Introduction to Metaphysics* 134; my emphasis). In his copy, Oppen rings the words I have italicized and writes "I.e. as an object," thus linking objectness to the disclosive force of being rather than making it a condition of subservience to subjectivity. Several pages later, in another passage marked by Oppen, Heidegger speaks of "the preponderant power of being [which] bursts in its appearing" (137), a phrase which may have suggested the idea in the poem "Leviathan" that "What is inexplicable / Is the preponderance of objects" (*New Collected Poems [NCP]* 89).

Here, perhaps, we might also understand Oppen's departure from the emphasis placed on the verb as transfer of energy by Pound and Ernest Fenollosa, for that syntactical model can only endlessly reaffirm the subject-object dualism which, in Oppen's view, it is poetry's function to overcome.[28] So he notes to himself: "The fact that things and people BE. This is the major subject of thought and feeling. It is almost impossible to say to most readers. They regard the verb as all but meaningless, perhaps because it is intransitive: it is not an action of one thing on another" (UCSD 16, 16, 8). What Oppen seeks is, as he puts it, "The fusion of subject and object where all is acted upon" (UCSD 16, 17, 1), which is perhaps one way of denying the primacy of self-consciousness and of making the poem not so much an expressive act as a medium of confluence and receptivity. Once Oppen had begun to read Heidegger, his idea of "the objectification of the poem" increasingly entailed not just the displacement of the subject, but a definition of thinking as a process inevitably *missing* its object as it sought disclosure rather than knowledge. Hence the limitations of propositional discourse, for "The 'is' in a proposition has nothing to do with real existence . . . , but with 'being valid for,' 'holding good for'" (Caputo 146). As Heidegger put it in "What is Metaphysics?" "Being is not a product of thinking. It is more likely that essential thinking is an occurrence of Being" (*Existence and Being* 387). By not operating within the constraints of logic or representation, poetry has the capacity to release its objects from instrumentality, instigating instead what Oppen calls "a new cadence of disclosure" (*SL* 97). That "cadence" carries, for him, an explicitly Heideggerian charge: "Prosody: the pulse of thought, of consciousness, therefore, in Heidegger's word, of human *Dasein*, human 'being there'" (UCSD 16, 14, 3).

Poetic thinking thus conceived is not a matter of articulating a thought already had, but rather of deploying the resources of writing to disclose the texture of thinking as it takes shape. "I write in order to know," says Oppen, "As action and process" (UCSD 16, 16, 4). The aim, however, is not some kind of spontaneous production or automatic writing; rather, it is to reveal thought as embodied in the irreducible spatiotemporal "thereness" of the poem, with its phonic echoes and silences, its syntactical shape and typographical layout.[29] Hence, as critics have observed, Oppen's fascination with the "little words," not only with nouns but with deictics, words which show "that this in which the thing takes place, this thing is here, and that these things do take place" (Dembo 163).[30] And, of course, that "taking place" is itself the event (or advent) of the poem: "I do not mean to prescribe an opinion or an idea, but to record the experience of thinking it," writes Oppen (UCSD 16, 19, 4). This, finally, is the objectification of the poem, as thought becomes present to itself as "being." Yet it is, by its nature, an avowedly strange sort of thinking, one conditioned by the possibilities of poetic form and open to the "accidents" of emerging rhythmic contour and lineation. "I am concerned," Oppen writes in his *Daybook*, "with 'thinking' (involuntary thoughts) that requires the poem, the verse" (Young, "Selections" 2). And just as such thinking is not settled in advance and can even seem to the thinker "involuntary," so the world it creates is one of openness and possibility.

Not surprisingly, perhaps, the poems that most successfully enact this event of incipience are those in which a jubilant seeing comes to the fore, as in the poem cited by Oppen to characterize the new collection, "Psalm":

In the small beauty of the forest
The wild deer are bedding down—
That they are there!
(*NCP* 99)

The poem's epigraph, "Veritas sequitur . . . ,""Truth follows from the being of things," is taken from Aquinas; Oppen probably came upon it in Maritain's *Existence and the Existent*, where it provides the epigraph to chapter 1, "Being" (20).[31] Maritain's introduction to that chapter perfectly describes the overall focus of *This in Which*: "It is that existent universe, set firmly upon primary facts, which we are required to discover, not deduce"

(Maritain, *Existence and the Existent* 20). So in "Psalm" the wild deer are discovered "bedding down," and the crux of the poem lies in the absolutely simple recognition of the "primary fact" "That they are there!"

The deer may recall those of Williams's *Spring and All* ("the imagination strains / after deer / going by fields of goldenrod" [218]) or of Stevens's "Sunday Morning" ("Deer walk upon our mountains" [56]), but more suggestive is the possible allusion to Rilke's "Eighth Elegy":

> With all its eyes the creature-world beholds
> the open. But our eyes, as though reversed, encircle it on every side,
> like traps
> set round its unobstructed path to freedom.
> What *is* outside, we know from the brute's face
> alone; . . .
> (Rilke, *Selected Works* 242)[32]

Discussing the poem in a letter, Rilke observed that 'the animal is *in* the world' whereas "we stand *before it* by virtue of that peculiar turn and intensification which our consciousness has taken" (quoted in Heidegger, *PLT* 108). Oppen's deer are similarly figures for a nonsymbolizing, nonappropriative approach to the world. As he puts it in "The Building of the Skyscraper," this is to discover "Not a declaration which is truth / but a thing /Which is" (*NCP* 149), and this emphasis upon being produces a language which not only intimates a certain irreducibility—"The small nouns / Crying faith / In this in which the wild deer / Startle, and stare out" ("Psalm," *NCP* 99)—but which does so through an insistent use of what in linguistics are termed shifters or deictics, those "little words" that derive their meaning purely from the occasion in which they are uttered: "They who are there," "this in which," and so on. As Oppen put it in a late interview, "what I'm doing is making that Heideggerian gesture of 'pointing'" (Power, "Interview" 195), an allusion, perhaps, to the account of "saying" given in *On the Way to Language*: "we understand saying in terms of showing, pointing out, signalling. . . . *The essential being of language is Saying as Showing*" (123). This "pointing" is not even primarily to objects designated by words but to the event of language itself. As Giorgio Agamben puts it, "The opening of the *ontological* dimension (being, the world) corresponds to the pure taking place of language as an originary event, while the *ontic* dimension (entities, things) corresponds to that which, in this opening, is said and signified" (*Language and Death* 26).[33] Oppen's "point-ing," his way of shifting emphasis from the content of his words to the pure fact of their utterance, implies a poetics of being that does not now require the impacted syntax of *Discrete Series* and can thus produce more fluent and expanded structures.

A passionate revelation of "place" points to a more certain recognition that "This is our home, the planets / Move in it / Or seem to, / It is our home" ("A Narrative," *NCP* 152). Oppen is reclaiming "the childish here" ("Philai Te Kou Philai," *NCP* 97) and the poems seek to make their own spatiotemporal occasion equivalent to the disclosure of this world of be-ing, presenting themselves as singular moments of what is called in "The Occurrences" "the creating / *Now*" (*NCP* 144). Even the "stone" universe of *The Materials* is somehow redeemed, with Oppen able to celebrate "the pure joy / Of the mineral fact // tho it is impenetrable / As the world, if it is matter // Is impenetrable" ("A Language of New York," *NCP* 114). Here Maritain's awakening "to ourselves and to things" produces forms of ecstatic perception expressive of a love powerful enough to overcome "a ruined ethic // Bursting with ourselves" ("Philai Te Kou Philai," *NCP* 97) and to realize the sense of "home" in "The act of being, the act of being / More than oneself" ("World, World—," *NCP* 159). In "A Narrative," for example:

> River of our substance
> Flowing
> With the rest. River of the substance
> Of the earth's curve, river of the substance
> Of the sunrise, river of silt, of erosion, flowing
> To no imaginable sea. But the mind rises
>
> Into happiness, rising
>
> Into what is there. I know of no other happiness
> Nor have I ever witnessed it. . . .
> (*NCP* 155; ellipses in original)

The "act of being" reveals itself as a "being / More than oneself," with the mind "rising" with the sun, its momentary perception caught up in the all-bounding "earth's curve."

As the last lines of the poem put it, this is "the open / Miracle // Of place":

... I thought that even if there were nothing

The possibility of being would exist;
I thought I had encountered

Permanence; thought leaped on us in that sea
For in that sea we breathe the open
Miracle

Of place, and speak
If we would rescue
Love to the ice-lit

Upper World a substantial language
Of clarity and respect.
(*NCP* 156)

Oppen's "ice-lit / Upper World" may recall the allegory of the cave in Book VII of Plato's *Republic* where the prisoners ascending to the upper world are suddenly able to "gaze upon the light of the moon and the stars and the spangled heaven" and to find a new "clarity" after the "false notions" and the darkness of the cave (*The Republic* 216). The odd phrase "thought leaped on us in that sea," which is picked up again as a quotation in "World, World—," "'Thought leaps on us' because we are here" (*NCP* 159), may echo a passage in Heidegger's essay "What is Metaphysics." There we are told that "Philosophy is only set in motion by leaping with all its being, as only it can, into the ground-possibilities of being as a whole" (*Existence and Being* 380). The first lines of the passage quoted from "A Narrative"—"I thought that even if there were nothing / The possibility of being would exist"—also seem to find a context in Heidegger's essay as an answer to the famous question posed on the same page: "Why is there any Being at all—why not far rather Nothing?" And Oppen's "I thought I had encountered // Permanence" becomes clearer in the light of a much later comment: "I begin to understand that the earlier books have been taken to be a simple realism—I was in these books speaking of Being: I had thought I could arrive at the concept of Being from an account of experience as it presents itself in its own terms" (*SL* 410 n. 29).

II

There would be no new English translations of Heidegger's work until the appearance of *Poetry, Language, Thought* and *On the Way to Language* in 1971. Oppen's next volume, *Of Being Numerous* (1968) deliberately forsook "the light of the miraculous" for the plight of "Man embedded in the sensory and the historic" (UCSD 16, 16, 2). The long title poem evoked the streets of New York City where "The roots of words" have become "Dim in the subways"; here "the open / Miracle // Of place" (*NCP* 156) glimpsed in *This in Which* is extinguished by "A ferocious mumbling, in public / Of rootless speech" (*NCP* 173). Is a poetics of being a possibility in a world of mere "chatter" (*Gerede*), as Heidegger had called it in *Being and Time*? Here the rush of the subway and the "madness in the number of the living" testify to "A state of matter," which, in contrast to the illuminations of *This in Which*, bluntly defines modernity as "Anti-ontology" (*NCP* 172). In "Of Being Numerous," it is Heidegger's attack on inauthenticity that Oppen echoes:

> Unable to begin
> At the beginning, the fortunate
> Find everything already here. They are shoppers,
> Choosers, judges; . . . And here the brutal
> Is without issue, a dead end.
> They develop
> Argument in order to speak, they become
> unreal, unreal, life loses
> solidity, loses extent, baseball's their game. . . .
> (*NCP* 170)

The strongly repudiated "they" of this passage recalls the "they" of *Being and Time* where Heidegger speaks of "an impassioned freedom toward death—a freedom which has been released from the Illusions of the 'they,' and which is factical, certain of itself, and anxious" (*Being and Time* 311). Oppen's shoppers, choosers, and judges, however, are still caught up in the unreality of the "they," where everything is "already here" and the hopes of any authentic new beginning already dashed. As I've suggested elsewhere (Nicholls, *George Oppen*), Oppen rigorously tests various political possibilities in this poem, but his thinking is now shadowed throughout by Heidegger's notion of "being-towards-death" ("death is a way to be, which Dasein takes over as soon as it is" [*Being and Time* 289]). In section 26 of the poem, for example, "We stand on // That denial of death that paved the cities / . . . and that pavement // Is filthy as the corridors / Of the police" (*NCP* 178). In the three collections to follow, it was Oppen's growing sense of his own mortality that would create rich but troubling inflections of his poetics.

In February 1967, the Oppens moved back to San Francisco, the city of George's adolescence. It was a significant move for many reasons, not least for the memories of youthful times it brought into play. Most important, though, was the ocean itself and the intimations of what Oppen called "a metaphysical edge" that the horizon seemed to imply (UCSD 16, 34, 4). An elegiac tone and a sense of ending pervade this collection: "We have begun to say good bye / To each other / And cannot say it" "Some San Francisco Poems," *NCP* 227) and "We have gone / As far as is possible" ("Some San Francisco Poems," *NCP* 233). And yet this pathos of ending is derived from the quite opposite and tremendous power of the world to endure, to renew itself. This power acquires various shapes in Oppen's late poetry, including the blazing forth of the image that is frequently associated with Blake's "Tyger." Where death and ending are more traditionally associated with darkness, Oppen finds everywhere a brightness and energy which are at once miraculous and terrifying. Late in *Seascape,* for example, he notes that "One had not thought / To be afraid // Not of shadow but of light" ("Some San Francisco Poems," *NCP* 233).

In the next collection, *Myth of the Blaze* (written 1972–75, but not published as a separate volume) the "burning" radiance of Blake's vision is once again the force that discloses the real.[34] It was while composing these poems that Oppen read Heidegger's *Poetry, Language, Thought* (1971). We can be certain about this because a short page of notes relating to this text is filed with drafts of poems from *Myth of the Blaze* (UCSD 16, 24, 11). The notes begin by quoting Heidegger: "the saying of the unconcealedness of what is." The relevant passage from "The Origin of the Work of Art" is as follows: "Projective saying is poetry: the saying of world and earth, the saying of the arena of their conflict and thus of the place of all nearness and remoteness of the gods. Poetry is the saying of the unconcealedness of what is" (*PLT* 74).[35] In contrast to the "rootless speech" evoked in "Of Being Numerous," Heidegger's "saying" brings things into being by naming them and thus drawing them into what he calls (after Rilke) the "open" or the "clearing." Oppen picks up on this terminology in his notes: "Truth," he writes, "it is an open clearing / simply, an open clearing," while Heidegger explains (*PLT* 72) that it is "the Open which lets poetry happen, and indeed in such a way that only now, in the midst of beings, the Open brings beings to shine and ring out." Yet—here we might recall Oppen's lines about fearing not the shadow but the light—"The clearing in which beings stand is in itself at the same time concealment" (*PLT* 53), so the light of disclosure is also a withholding of something. This, as Gerald Bruns puts it, is the "self-concealment in which the work closes in upon itself, refuses to give itself up to our penetrative gaze" (Bruns, *Estrangements* 40). Poetry, continues Bruns, is in this sense 'a *listening* to the otherness of language, that is to its strangeness or nonhumanness, its indifference to our linguistic competence, its uncontainability within the structures of communicability, its resistance to sense' (Bruns, *Estrangements* 25, his emphasis). In his notes, Oppen emphasizes this point: "Truth," he writes, "Not a statement: an open clearing. / Poetry is not *statement* but, to use Heidegger's word, 'unconcealedness,'" and underneath "Poetry" he has written in parentheses "the image." We know, of course, that Heidegger's theory of language in this essay is intimately bound up with his "turn" from human being to Being, so that we now have to consider language not as "the voicing of the inner man" (*PLT* 229) but as a "peal of stillness" (*PLT* 228) that "sounds" in the speaking of mortals. As Heidegger puts it in *On the Way to Language,* "Everything spoken stems in a variety of ways from the unspoken, whether this be something not yet spoken, or whether it be what must remain unspoken in the sense that it is beyond the reach of speaking. Thus, that which is spoken in various ways begins to appear as if it were cut off from speaking and the speakers, and did not belong to them, while in fact it alone offers to speaking and to the speakers whatever it is they attend to, no matter in what way they stay within what is spoken of the unspoken" (120). This is one meaning of Heidegger's difficult word *Ereignis,* usually translated as "appropriation," that we are "caught up by language" and somehow taken out of our selves (Bruns, "Disappeared" 128). Oppen's late work is powerfully informed by this sense of the "otherness" of language. "No longer writing out of the past, no longer searching my knowledge," he remarks, "I discover the thing by writing it as if I were swept on some current around a bend——" (UCSD 16, 24, 11). But where Heidegger in his thoughts on language sometimes veers toward a complacent fantasy of tranquil "dwelling" (see Stoekl 40-41), Oppen's sense of the externality of language was, on the one hand, a fulfilment of all his earlier calls for "silence" and "transparency," and on the other a register of his slide into the "strangeness" of Alzheimers. "The word in one's mouth becomes as strange as infinity," he wrote in his notes (UCSD 16, 26, 8), and this "strangeness" colors many of the poems in *Myth of the Blaze.* In "Confession," for example:

as all this becomes strange
enough
I come to know it is home a groping

down a going
down middle-voice. . . .
(*NCP* 258)

These lines catch exactly Oppen's sense of fading linguistic agency, for
the middle voice form "differs from the reflexive in that the subject is
not the actor but is nevertheless involved in the outcome of the action"
(Moran 467). The same anxiety is there in *Primitive*, in "The Tongues,"
for example:

     the words
out of that whirlwind his
and not his strange
words surround him
(*NCP* 275)

"His / and not his," it is an unresolvable contradiction that emerges in
many forms in these late poems and we can perhaps see why by returning
to Oppen's notes on *Poetry, Language, Thought*. At the bottom of the page
we find the following jottings:

           Cleft?
"what unites opposites is the *rift*"   (but they both exist)
((but opposites are not contraries)) (contradictions)
               The pain (?) of the threshold that unites
  images: the word [world?] unified
     by the cleft, the gap: "the world" extant
         in the gap
(UCSD 16, 24, 11) (see figure 3)

Again the references are to "The Origin of the Work of Art" and specifically to the passage in which Heidegger develops his idea of the "rift"
(*Riss*) between world and earth: "The world grounds itself on the earth,
the earth juts through the world" (*PLT* 49). Now if there seems to be, as

3. Manuscript page reproduced by permission of the Estate of George Oppen. © Linda Oppen. Used with permission. From the George Oppen Papers at the Mandeville Special Collections, University of California at San Diego. The sheet is located at UCSD collection 16, box 24, file 11.

Alan Stoekl argues, "a drift, in Heidegger, from a thinking of Being as divisiveness and duality to a thinking of Being as unity" (Stoekl 41), in the "Origin" essay the emphasis is still clearly on the conflictual nature of the relationship: "In essential striving . . . the opponents raise each other into the self-assertion of their natures" and "The work-being of the work [of art] consists in the fighting of the battle between world and earth" (*PLT* 49). The poem, we can conclude, is caught within just this tension: while, as Oppen puts it, "The poem must conceive the world or it is 'a thought[,]' a remark" (UCSD 16, 14, 7), the language the poet uses can never lose its 'earthy character' (*PLT* 69).[36] The tensions here between language and reality, between thinking and poetry, are not ones that can be canceled by some appeal to ultimate harmony. Earth and world are unified only in their constant struggle and individual self-assertion, hence the rift also rends and causes pain ("Pain is the joining agent in the rending that divides and gathers" [*PLT* 204]). The rift, then, tells us that "Truth establishes itself as a strife within being" (*PLT* 63), so that "as a world opens itself the earth comes to rise up."[37] That same ascent is figured in Oppen's late poem "Semite":

> the proofs
> are the images the images
> overwhelming earth
>
> rises up in its light
> (*NCP* 251)

The image now becomes the rift itself in which, as he puts it in his notes, "the world [is] extant" or, literally, "stands out," discloses itself.[38] But the "rising up" here should counsel caution when handling this word "image," for, like Heidegger, Oppen is not thinking of it in a representational sense, as the secondary presentation of an object. Indeed, on a number of occasions in the late poems we have an insistence on the word "image" (several times as "image image") and that act of pure nomination is also a withholding of what we would normally think of as the function of the image (to be an image *of* something).

Maurice Blanchot is helpful here: "In literature," he writes, "doesn't language itself become altogether image? We do not mean a language containing images or one that casts reality in figures, but one which is its own image, an image of language (and not a figurative language), or yet again, an imaginary language, one which no one speaks" (Blanchot, *Space* 34).[39] It is not, then, a matter of "cast[ing] reality in figures" but of seeing "figures" (Oppen's "image," Heidegger's *Gestalt*) as the opening of a world ("extant in the gap"). "The nature of the image," writes Heidegger, "is to let something be seen" (*PLT* 226), and one can imagine how readily Oppen would have concurred with the claim several lines later, that "poetic images are not mere fancies and illusions but imaginings that are visible inclusions of the alien in the sight of the familiar" (*PLT* 226).[40] In Oppen's previously unpublished poem "The Extreme," "Light grows, place becomes larger or deepens, the familiar / Becomes extreme" (*NCP* 332), and here, as so often in the late poems, Heidegger's vision seems to bring within one focus that "miraculous" world encountered in *This in Which* and the frighteningly intense world with which Oppen was struggling in his illness. That this was indeed a component of the late poems, though one perhaps now deeply laid, is demonstrated by the lines that describe the "morning's force" that is unleashed by the murder of Mickey Schwerner and his friends in "The Book of Job and a Draft of a Poem to Praise the Paths of the Living":

> children rose in the dark
> to their work there grows
> there builds there is written
> a vividness   there is rawness
> like a new sun the flames
> tremendous. . . .
> (*NCP* 241)

In an early version of these lines, Oppen had written:

> Not our children
> Who rose in the dark
> To their work there grows
> There builds there is written
> A vividness there is rawness
> Like a sun that flames
> Tremendous the sun
> Itself, I would say we must risk this. . . .
> (UCSD 16, 24, 6)

The vision here is Heidegger's, as we can see by recalling some remarks by Oppen quoted at the beginning of this essay: "Still, H[eidegger]'s awareness of the world is among the most vivid, the most poignant in literature. We almost have to agree to take a chance on that. There is an extreme rawness, like a raw sun. My feeling is that we should risk it" (UCSD 16, 15, 7). It is this "vividness" that blazes forth in so many of Oppen's late poems; and if Heidegger could be charged with "complacency" in his later fantasies of "dwelling," in passages like the following Oppen could still grasp the essential "rawness" of a vision embracing "*both* gentleness *and* destructiveness" (*OTW* 179):

> "What, then, is the spirit? In his last poem, 'Grodek,' [Georg] Trakl speaks of the 'hot flame of the spirit.' The spirit is flaming, and only in this sense perhaps is it something flickering in the air. Trakl sees spirit not primarily as *pneuma,* something ethereal, but as a flame that inflames, startles, horrifies, and shatters us. Flame is growing lumination. What flame is the *ek-stasis* which lightens and calls forth radiance, but which may also go on consuming and reduce all to white ashes" (*OTW* 179).

Notes

1. I am grateful to Linda Oppen for permission to quote from published and unpublished material by George Oppen. I would also like to thank Alexander Mourelatos for generously responding to my questions.

The following abbreviations are used in the text: UCSD, Oppen Papers in the Archive for New Poetry, Mandeville Special Collections of the University of California at San Diego (cited by collection number [16], box and file number; *SL,* Oppen, *The Selected Letters*; *NCP,* Oppen, *New Collected Poems*; *PLT,* Heidegger, *Poetry Language Thought*; *OTW,* Heidegger, *On the Way to Language*.

2. Oppen's interest in Heidegger has frequently been noted but rarely discussed in the detail it deserves. The best accounts are Randolph Chilton, "The Place of Being in the Poetry of George Oppen," Burton Hatlen, "'Not Altogether Alone in a Lone Universe': George Oppen's *The Materials*," Paul Naylor, "The Pre-Position of Being, Seeing and Knowing in George Oppen's Poetry," Susan Thackrey, *George Oppen: A Radical Practice,* 33–45, and Forrest Gander, "Finding the Phenomenal Oppen," *No: A Journal of the Arts,* 1 (nd).

3. Dennis Young, "Conversation with Mary Oppen," 23. See also the discussion of Heidegger in David McAleavey, "Oppen on Literature and Literary Figures and Issues," 117–120. Mary remarks that "Our son-in-law gets these books for us, every time he sees a Heidegger quote he usually sends it to us" (118). In a communication to me (July 8, 2003), however, Mourelatos says that "I have no such recollection myself, and find no evidence of it in copies of letters I sent them."

4. Jacques Maritain, *Creative Intuition in Art and Poetry* (1954; New York: Meridian Books, 1955), 159–160 (this is the edition used by Oppen). In McAleavey, "Oppen on Literature," 117, Oppen claims that his epigraph is "a deliberate misquotation" from Maritain, though it is not clear why. Michael Davidson is the only

critic to have ventured a location for the passage (*NCP* 362], and his proposal is, I think, incorrect. For some brief but pertinent reflections on the relevance of Maritain to Oppen, see Burton Hatlen, "Not Altogether Alone in a Lone Universe," 332–333. The phrase of Maritain's that I have italicized provides the closest source of Oppen's epigraph, but in the prelims of his own copy (held in the Mandeville Special Collections) he writes: "source of my misquotation: page 83" and then quotes and encircles the following italicized passage on that page: "The poet does not know himself in the light of his own essence. Since man perceives himself only through a repercussion of his knowledge of the world of things, and *remains empty to himself if he does not fill himself with the universe,* the poet knows himself only on the condition that things resound in him, and that in him, at a single wakening, they and he come forth out of sleep." On the page facing the title page, Oppen has also written: "Things: that things resound in him and he and they come forth together out of sleep." For a more detailed consideration of Maritain's importance for Oppen, see my "George Oppen in Exile: Mexico and Maritain."

5. For the concept of "connatural knowing" in Maritain, see John P. Hittinger, *Liberty, Wisdom, and Grace* 203–212.

6. See Young, "Conversation with Mary Oppen," 23. Young asks: "Did you ever reconcile Heidegger's politics," and Mary replies, "No. That was a real problem."

7. According to Mourelatos (personal communication), Oppen owned a copy of Laszlo Versényi, *Heidegger, Being and Truth.* In the passage quoted, Versényi is referred to simply as "V." Versényi remarks on various negative implications of Heidegger's philosophy: "Man is no longer in possession, in control, of himself, let alone of beings and Being. He is possessed by Being for its disclosure" (127).

8. Oppen's copy of *An Introduction to Metaphysics,* trans. Ralph Manheim (New York: Anchor Books, 1961), was among books recently found by Lauren Holden at the house on Eagle Island, Maine, in which the Oppens used to stay during their sailing holidays. It will be deposited in the Mandeville Special Collections at UCSD. (Information from Linda Oppen.)

9. Oppen owned the paperback edition of Heidegger, *Existence and Being,* which is paginated differently from the hardback published at the same time. My citations are of this edition. Brock's "An Account of 'Being and Time'" occupies, pages 11–116. Most of Oppen's markings are of passages in Brock's introduction. In a letter to John Crawford (UCSD 16, 3, 44), Oppen refers to a passage "from Heidegger—or, for brevity, Werner Brock commenting on and partly quoting from Heidegger." The volume is referred to in David McAleavey's interview, "Oppen on Literature and Literary Figures," 120, where Mary also confesses, "I got nowhere with *Being and Time,* I had to give it up."

10. A marginal annotation in Oppen's copy compares a passage from Heidegger to a view held by William Bronk, whose manuscript of *The World, Worldless* Oppen was reading in January 1963. Heidegger's quotation of Hölderlin's line

"Foolish is my speech" (260) provokes the marginal comment: "cf. Bronk: The center of things as 'To not know.'"

11. See *Selected Letters* 182: "lending you a selection of Heidegger 'early' and 'Late' periods, if it matters." Oppen had also loaned Charles Tomlinson a work by Heidegger in 1964—see *Selected Letters* 386 n. 8.

12. In a passage from the *Daybook,* Oppen quotes from Heidegger's *What is Philosophy?* 29: "We have uttered the word 'philosophy' often enough. If, however, we use the word 'philosophy' no longer like a wornout title, if, instead, we hear the word 'philosophy' coming from its source, then it sounds thus: *philosophia.* Now the word 'philosophy' is speaking Greek. The word, as a Greek word, is a path" (UCSD 16, 19, 6).

13. *Selected Letters* 115: "That which exists of itself cannot be explained it cannot be analysed. It is the object of contemplative thought, it is known by 'indwelling.'" The letter is dated June 1965 in *Selected Letters,* but the original carries no date. It is therefore tempting to think that Oppen's sudden use of "indwelling," a word not found elsewhere in the Heidegger texts he was reading, makes the date of this letter some time in 1966. Heidegger develops the term in *Discourse on Thinking* 82ff. The German *In-Sein* is rendered "Being-in" in the translation of *Being and Time* (see, for example, 79). See also Versény, *Heidegger, Being, and Truth* 11 on "Being-in" or "in-dwelling": "In Heidegger's use the term (*In-Sein*) refers to Dasein's intentionality, its interest in, awareness of, openness toward, familiarity and involvement with the beings in its world."

14. See Heidegger, *An Introduction to Metaphysics* 113. In his notes (UCSD 16, 19, 7), Oppen also gives an elliptical version of the following from *An Introduction* 197: "because being is initially *physis,* the power that emerges and discloses, it discloses itself as *eidos* and *idea.*"

15. See *Selected Letters* 133, and the discussion with Alexander Mourelatos about the translation of fragment 14 (*SL* 165–167). There is also a brief discussion of Parmenides's fragment 3 in Heidegger's *Identity and Difference* 17ff.

16. See Burt Kimmelman, *The "Winter Mind"* 90. The line is apparently quoted in a 1971 letter from Cid Corman to William Bronk (Columbia University Archives). This poem, which differs from an unpublished one with the same title in the UCSD archive, was, says Kimmelman, "published at the time in a magazine." I have not so far been able to locate it.

17. See UCSD 16, 17, 6 where Oppen quotes the following from *The Question of Being* 43: "For it is a part of the essence of the will to power not to permit the reality which it has power over to appear in that reality in which it itself exists."

18. For the notes on *Poetry, Language, Thought* 63–64 (discussed below), see UCSD 16, 24, 11. A reference in a letter of 1973 to "the predominance of objects["] (*SL* 254) may recall Heidegger's talk of "the predominance of objectness" in his account of Rilke there (130).

19. Alexander Mourelatos, personal communication. A reference in a letter

of 1973 to "the predominance of objects["] (*SL* 254) may recall Heidegger's talk of "the predominance of objectness" in his account of Rilke there (130). Oppen quotes from *The Question of Being* 43, in his notes: "For it is a part of the essence of the will to power not to permit the reality which it has power over to appear in that reality in which it itself exists" (UCSD 16, 17, 6).

20. Oppen's copy of *Existence and Being* 302. He is commenting on the following passage: "But if rightness (truth) of statement is only made possible by the overt character of behaviour, then it follows that the thing that makes rightness possible in the first place must have a more original claim to be regarded as the essence of truth."

21. See, for example, *Being and Time* 161: "because Dasein's Being is Being-with, its understanding of Being already implies the understanding of Others."

22. See, for example, *What is Philosophy?* 81ff. Cf. Dembo 172–173 where Oppen says, "The sense of awe, I suppose, is all I manage to talk about."

23. See, for example, White, *Heidegger* 86. Cf. Ziarek, "The Reception of Heidegger's Thought," 119: "It would seem that Heidegger does not advocate the unity of Being and word, since the word points to Being as already withdrawn, concealed, other. The word is not a meaning added to a thing; it lets the thing be, in the sense that it relates it to the self-withdrawing clearing of Being." King 137 observes that "Heidegger thinks that meaningful tautology is the only way in which we can express that being is not something, but the sheer 'other' to all beings."

24. Compare *Selected Letters* 395 n. 8: "Heidegger I think does not assume the permanence of man, and indeed, how can we? This is the difficult thing to confront: we begin to confront it in that word." See also UCSD 16, 19, 7 where Oppen quotes the following from *An Introduction* 118: "The question of what man is must always be taken in its essential bond with how it stands with being."

25. Cf. *Identity and Difference* 30-31: "Hence facing the present squarely, it [thought] gets a glimpse—beyond the human situation—of the pattern of Being and Man in what is befitting both, that is, con-cern."

26. See Kenner, *A Homemade World* 169 for the view that the Objectivists "seem to have been born mature, not to say middle-aged. The quality of their very youthful work is that of men who have inherited a formed tradition: the tradition over the cradle of which, less than twenty years previously, Ezra Pound had hoped to have Henry James, O.M., speak a few words." For a discussion of this claim, see Nicholls, "A Homemade World?"

27. For an extended discussion of this kind of 'distancing' as a recurrent feature of Western thought, see Kolb.

28. See also Nicholls, "George Oppen and 'That Primitive, Hegel,'" 353–354.

29. For some suggestive remarks on poetic "thereness," see Wardi 4. Oppen brings these elements together in his comment (*SL* 97) that "A new syntax is a new cadence of disclosure, a new cadence of logic, a new musical cadence. A new 'structure of space.'"

30. The phrasing here takes us, of course, to the title of Oppen's 1965 volume, *This in Which*. The studied repetition of "this" also points up that word's status as the "canonical deictic"—see Bennington 290: "'This' can refer to itself as word or utterance or token or event, whereas 'I,' 'here' and 'now' can only refer to the agent of the saying, and the place or time in which what is said is said." Heidegger had remarked similarly in *Being and Time* 262 that "the ultimate business of philosophy is to preserve the *force of the most elemental words* in which Dasein expresses itself." For a helpful account of the importance of deictic markers to Oppen, see Naylor.

31. In "Interview with George Oppen," 20, Reinhold Schiffer asked Oppen, "Do you think you got to Aquinas through Maritain?"; Oppen replied, "Yes, very definitely, very definitely."

32. Oppen owned this volume. See also "Quotations," *NCP* 140: "The infants and the animals / And the insects / 'stare at the open'" and the uncollected poem "[Sympathy]," *NCP* 301: "Rilke's 'the animals and the insects / stare at the open.'"

33. See also Giorgio Agamden, *Language and Death* 25: "The sphere of the utterance thus includes that which, in every speech act, refers exclusively to its taking place, to its instance, independently and prior to what is said and meant in it. Pronouns and other indicators of the utterance, before they designate real objects, indicate precisely *that language takes place*. In this way, still prior to the world of meanings, they permit the reference to the very *event of language*, the only context in which something can be signified" (emphases in original).

34. Cf., for example, Young, "Selections," 3: "Blake's Tyger in the small words, They burn. The nouns are the visible universe, the night sky burning."

35. Oppen's next note reads, "so purely spoken," probably a reference to a much later passage in the volume where Heidegger writes, "The opposite of what is purely spoken, the opposite of the poem, is not prose" (*PLT* 208).

36. Cf. *On the Way* 101: "The sound of language, its earthness is held with the harmony that attunes the regions of the world's structure, playing them in chorus."

37. Cf. *On the Way* 39, on the "sound of language rising from the earth."

38. Cf. Heidegger, *Poetry, Language, Thought* 64, on the "figure" (*Gestalt*) which provides the structure in whose shape the rift composes and submits itself.

39. Note also the preference in Oppen's late poems for what Michael Hamburger called in *The Truth of Poetry* the "generic image" (stone, earth, sea, etc.).

40. In the poem which opens *Poetry, Language, Thought*, Heidegger also writes: "The splendour of the simple. // Only image formed keeps the vision. / Yet images formed rests in the poem" (7).

Works Cited

Adorno, Theodor W. *Notes to Literature*. 2 vols. Trans. Shierry Weber Nicholsen. New York: Columbia University Press, 1992.

Bennington, Geoffrey. *Legislations: The Politics of Deconstruction.* London: Verso, 1994.

Blanchot, Maurice. *The Space of Literature.* Trans and introd. Ann Smock. Lincoln: University of Nebraska Press, 1982.

Bruns, Gerald. "Disappeared: Heidegger and the Emancipation of Language." In *Languages of the Unsayable: The Play of Negativity in Literature and Literary Theory,* ed. Sanford Budick and Wolfgang Iser. Stanford, CA: Stanford University Press, 1987.

———. *Heidegger's Estrangements: Language, Truth, and Poetry in the Later Writings.* New Haven, CT: Yale University Press, 1989.

Caputo, John D. *The Mystical Element in Heidegger's Thought.* Athens: Ohio University Press, 1978.

Chilton, Randolph. "The Place of Being in the Poetry of George Oppen." *George Oppen: Man and Poet.* Orono, ME: National Poetry Foundation, 1981: 89–112.

Corman, Cid. *William Bronk: An Essay.* Carrboro: Truck Press, 1976.

Davidson, Michael. "An Adequate Vision: From the Daybooks." *Ironwood* 26 (Fall 1985): 5–31.

Dembo, L. S. "The 'Objectivist' Poet: George Oppen." *Contemporary Literature* 10 (1969): 159–177.

DuPlessis, Rachel Blau. "The Anthropologist of Myself: A Selection from Working Papers." *Sulfur* 26 (Spring 1990): 135–164.

Gander, Forrest. "Finding the Phenomenal Oppen." *No: A Journal of the Arts,* 1 (n.d., n.p.).

Groth, Miles. *Translating Heidegger.* New York: Humanity Books, 2004.

Halliburton, David. *Poetic Thinking: An Approach to Heidegger.* Chicago: University of Chicago Press, 1981.

Hamburger, Michael. *The Truth of Poetry.* 1969. Harmondsworth: Penguin Books, 1972.

Harries, Karsten. "Language and Silence: Heidegger's Dialogue with Georg Trakl." In *Martin Heidegger and the Question of Literature: Toward a Postmodern Literary Hermeneutics,* ed. William V. Spanos, 155–171. Bloomington: Indiana University Press, 1976.

Hatlen, Burton. *George Oppen: Man and Poet.* Orono, ME: National Poetry Foundation, 1981.

———. "Not Altogether Alone in a Lone Universe." *George Oppen: Man and Poet,* ed. Burton Hatlen, 325–357. Orono, ME: National Poetry Foundation, 1981.

———, and Tom Mandel. "Poetry and Politics: A Conversation with George and Mary Oppen." *George Oppen: Man and Poet,* ed. Burton Hatlen, 23–50.

Heidegger, Martin. "The Age of the World View." *Martin Heidegger and the Question of Literature: Toward a Postmodern Literary Hermeneutics.* Bloomington: Indiana University Press, 1976.

———. *Being and Time.* Trans. John Macquarrie and Edward Robinson. Oxford: Blackwell, 1962.

———. *Discourse on Thinking.* Trans. John M. Anderson and E. Hans Freund. New York: Harper & Row, 1966.

———. *Essays in Metaphysics: Identity and Difference.* Trans. Kurt F. Leidecker. New York: Philosophical Library, 1960.

———. *Existence and Being.* Ed. and introd. Werner Brock. Chicago: Henry Regnery Company, 1949.

———. *Identity and Difference.* Trans. Joan Stambaugh. New York: Harper & Row, 1969.

———. *An Introduction to Metaphysics.* Trans. Ralph Manheim. New York: Anchor Books, 1961.

———. *Kant and the Problem of Metaphysics.* Bloomington: Indiana University Press, 1962.

———. *On the Way to Language.* Trans. Peter D. Hertz. New York: Harper & Row, 1971.

———. *Poetry, Language, Thought.* Trans. Albert Hofstadter. New York: Harper & Row, 1971.

———. *The Question of Being.* New York: Twayne, 1958.

———. *What is Philosophy?* Trans. William Kluback and Jean T. Wilde. London: Vision Press, 1958.

Heller, Michael. "'Knowledge is Loneliness Turning': Oppen Going Down Middle-Voice." *Ironwood* 26 (Fall 1985): 51–61.

Hittinger, John P. *Liberty, Wisdom, and Grace: Thomism and Democratic Political Theory.* Lanham, MD: Lexington Books, 2002.

Kenner, Hugh. *A Homemade World: The American Modernist Writers.* 1975; London: Marion Boyars, 1977.

Kimmelman, Burt. *The "Winter Mind": William Bronk and American Letters.* Madison, WI: Farleigh Dickinson University Press, 1998.

King, Magda. *A Guide to Heidegger's* Being and Time. New York: SUNY Press, 2001.

Kolb, David. *The Critique of Pure Modernity: Hegel, Heidegger, and After.* Chicago: University of Chicago, 1986.

Lacoue-Labarthe, Philippe. "In the Name of . . ." In *Retreating the Political,* ed. Philippe Lacoue-Labarte and Jean Luc-Nancy, trans. Simon Sparks, 55–86. London: Routledge, 1997.

McAleavey, David. "Oppen on Literature and Literary Figures and Issues." *Sagetrieb* 6 (1987): 109–135.

Mallarmé, Stéphane. *Selected Prose Poems, Essays and Letters.* Trans. Bradford Cook. Baltimore: Johns Hopkins University Press, 1956.

Maritain, Jacques. *Creative Intuition in Art and Poetry.* New York: Meridian Books, 1955.

Moran, Dermot. *Introduction to Phenomenology*. London and New York: Routledge, 2000.

Mourelatos, Alexander. Letter to the author. July 8, 2003.

Mulhall, Stephen. *Heidegger and* Being and Time. London: Routledge, 1996.

Naylor, Paul. "The Pre-Position of Being, Seeing and Knowing in George Oppen's Poetry." *Contemporary Literature* 32 (1991): 100–115.

Nicholls, Peter. "A Homemade World? America, Europe and Objectivist Poetry." *The Idea and the Thing in Modernist American Poetry*. Ed. Cristina Giorcelli. Palermo: Ila Palma, 2001.

———. "George Oppen in Exile: Mexico and Maritain." *Journal of American Studies* 39, 1 (April 2005): 1–18.

———. "George Oppen and 'that primitive, Hegel.'" *Paideuma* 32, 1–3 (Spring, Fall, Winter 2003): 351–376.

———. *George Oppen and the Fate of Modernism*. Oxford: Oxford University Press, 2007.

Oppen, George. "'Disasters': Versions and Notes." Ed. Cynthia Anderson. *Ironwood* 26 (Fall 1985): 146–152.

———. *New Collected Poems*. Ed. Michael Davidson. New York: New Directions, 2002.

———. Papers in the Archive for New Poetry, Mandeville Department of Special Collections of the University of California at San Diego. Collection no. 16.

———. *The Selected Letters*. Ed. Rachel Blau DuPlessis. Durham, NC: Duke University Press, 1990.

Plato. *The Republic*. Trans. Benjamin Jowett. Oxford: Clarendon Press, 1888.

Power, Kevin. "An Interview with George and Mary Oppen." *Montemora* 4 (1978): 187–203.

Rilke, Rainer Maria. *Selected Works: Volume II Poetry*. Trans. J. B. Leishman. London: Hogarth Press, 1960.

Safranski, Rudiger. *Martin Heidegger: Between Good and Evil*. Cambridge, MA: Harvard University Press, 1998.

Schiffer, Reinhold. "Interview with George Oppen." *Sagetrieb* 3, 3 (Winter 1984): 9–27.

Stevens, Wallace. *Collected Poetry and Prose*. New York: Library of America, 1997.

Stoekl, Allan. "De Man and the Dialectic of Being." *Diacritics* 15, 3 (Autumn 1985): 36–45.

Thackrey, Susan. *George Oppen: A Radical Practice*. San Francisco, CA: O Books, 2001.

Versényi, Laszlo. *Heidegger, Being, and Truth*. New Haven, CT: Yale University Press, 1965.

Wardi, Eynel. *Once Below a Time: Dylan Thomas, Julia Kristeva, and Other Speaking Subjects*. Albany, NY: SUNY Press, 2000.

White, David A. *Heidegger and the Language of Poetry.* Lincoln: University of Nebraska Press, 2001.

Will, Frederic. *Literature Inside Out: Ten Speculative Essays.* Cleveland, OH: Press of Western Reserve University, 1966.

Williams, William Carlos. *The Collected Poems 1909–1939.* Ed. A. Walton Litz and Christopher MacGowan. Manchester: Carcanet Press, 1986.

Young, Dennis. "Conversation with Mary Oppen." *Iowa Review* 18 (1987): 18–47.

———. "Selections from George Oppen's *Daybook*." *Iowa Review* 18 (1988): 1–17.

Young, Julian. *Heidegger's Later Philosophy.* Cambridge: Cambridge University Press, 2002.

Ziarek, Krzysztof. *The Historicity of Experience: Modernity, the Avant-Garde, and the Event.* Evanston, IL: Northwestern University Press, 2001.

———. "The Reception of Heidegger's Thought in American Literary Criticism." *Diacritics* 19 (1989): 114–127.

Zukofsky, Louis. "Program: 'Objectivists,' 1931." *Poetry* 37 (February 1931): 268–272.

———. "Recencies." *An "Objectivists" Anthology.* Le Beausset: To Publishers, 1932): 9–25.

5
Finding the Phenomenal Oppen

Forrest Gander

It is in his attitude, his attitude toward words, that George Oppen finds the ground for being and so creates poetry that is, for me, a source for a richer and more communal life. In "World, World—" he goes so far as to say,

> The self is no mystery, the mystery is
> That there is something for us to stand on.
>
> We want to be here.
>
> The act of being, the act of being
> More than oneself.
> (*New Collected Poems [NCP]* 159)

In 1927, Heidegger's *Being and Time* was published in Germany. At about the same time, Oppen began *Discrete Series,* cribbing some phrases from a speech Heidegger gave in 1929 and "consciously attempting to trace," he would later note, "the act of the world upon the consciousness" (*Ironwood* 14). Much later, as translations became available in the 1960s, Oppen read Heidegger extensively and recognized many convergences in their thinking. He wrote the poem "Route" in *Of Being Numerous* after wrestling with Heidegger's essay "Identity and Difference." And in his notebooks, Oppen scrawled: "Heidegger's statement that in the mood of boredom the existence of what-is is disclosed, is my Maude Blessingbourne in *Discrete Se-*

ries who in 'boredom' looks out the window and sees 'the world, weather-swept, with which/ one shares the century'" (*Ironwood* 14). Both Oppen's and Heidegger's descriptions of experience are characterized by a world-directed intentionality. And both men were drawn to the pre-Socratic philosophers. For each of them, too, *awe* is a critical word.

Heidegger wanted to overturn Platonism, to crack the frame of constraining metaphysical oppositions. But in his work after *Being and Time*, he concentrates on fundamental ontology, the inquiry into Being, at the expense, arguably, of examining other kinds of perception. It might be said that he becomes more absorbed with Being, capitalized, than with beings in particular. But in Oppen's oeuvre, *being* remains writ insistently small. It is evidenced in small words, in the small marvels of the commonplace. Oppen is less interested in the edifice than in the way the eye selects a single brick. If he worries that as the clarity of seeing increases, his distance from others also increases, he nevertheless identifies himself as an ordinary person touched by the grasses. Oppen takes his stand on the mineral fact of the world where, mediated by language, he coexists with objects and others. He writes in his notebooks. "THE SUBJECTIVE IS NOT OUTSIDE OF NATURE, IT IS INCLUDED IN NATURE, IT IS INCLUDED IN THE WORLD" (*Sulfur* 26 154).

Even so, Oppen's phenomenological sensibility shifts between *Discrete Series*, with its confederation of syntaxes and its helical mix of observations, and *Of Being Numerous*, with its more meditative investigation into intersubjectivity, with its query into how it might be possible to come to terms with existence among others, human and inhuman, in a place awash with preconceptions and logocentrism. In many of the poems after *Of Being Numerous*, Oppen turns his attention to a less urban landscape and to the act of writing. Yet book by book, Oppen's words continue to emerge from a stance that acknowledges perception as the product of a participatory relationship with the world, a relationship that closely aligns his poetics with the phenomenology of Maurice Merleau-Ponty (MP).

In those sections of his notebooks published so far,[1] Oppen mentions Heidegger, Maritain, Schelling, Wittgenstein, and a few pre-Socratic philosophers, but not Merleau-Ponty, whose book *The Phenomenology of Perception* was published in English in the same year (1962) as the English version of Heidegger's *Being in Time*. We know, though, from his correspondence with Michael Heller, who recommends MP's *The Visible and the Invisible* to him, that Oppen "read quite a bit of Merleau-Ponty" (*SL* 310–311). Certainly Oppen, himself, focuses on connecting the visible and the invisible—the "Bolt / In the frame / Of the building" (*NCP* 23) as he writes in *Discrete Series*—and in his notebooks he refers to "The seen and the unseen" in connection with his own work. Oppen and MP equally insist that Being-in-the-world means *bodily being*. Likewise, the experience of *silence* is critical to both men; each uses the word talismanically. They share other key terms as well. In *The Visible and the Invisible*, MP asserts "We are not co-eval" (184) and explains that time must constitute itself, must always be seen from the point of view of someone who is in it. Oppen, in *Of Being Numerous*, claims, "We are not coeval / With a locality / But we imagine others are" (*NCP* 164).

Repeatedly, in salient themes and in strikingly comparable phrases their critical thinking intersects. To highlight the affinity between MP and Oppen is to open up fruitful ways to read the poems and see more clearly, in both poetic structures and concerns, in the angular syntax and in the angle of inquiry, those specifically phenomenological aspects of Oppen's poetics.

~

What MP proposes, essentially, is that the sensory-motor act of perception constitutes consciousness. We can't be satisfied to say *I think, therefore I am*. Our bodies, in dialogue with world from the get-go, shape our thinking. As our perceptual habits narrow that primary, bodily relation with the world into more rigid and predictable patterns, we see the things of the world as familiar objects isolated from us but subject to our control. We find ourselves caught in a dialectical world of subject and object where everyone and everything is independent, disconnected. But, MP exclaims, "The momentum of existence towards others, towards the future, towards the world can be restored as a river unfreezes (*Phenomenology* 165).

Our bodies, which evolution on earth has coaxed into the upright, bipedal shapes we recognize on the subway absently paging the *New York Times* with nimble fingers and opposable thumbs, these bodies, fashioned by the world and always present in a world, affect what and how we perceive and so influence the modes of our consciousness. With the bodies of staghorn flies, we would experience an utterly different reality. It is the human body, says MP, located in the context of the world, which provides a means for our relation with everything else.

He goes on to point out that no thing is utterly inert, no thing can be seen in only one way. In fact, our seeing is never complete since there is always more to an object than we can possibly make out. Instead, we might say that phenomena unfold, they draw us into relationship, they disclose themselves to our perceptions. Oppen, who writes, "The play begins with the world" (*NCP* 222), would certainly concur.

Both writers were reacting against rationalism and calling for a pre-reflective engagement with alterity. This imagination of a *first vision* MP calls the *primordial*. Oppen uses the word *primitive* in a remarkably similar way, linking it to *first things*. Meditating on *Primitive,* the title he gives to his last book, Oppen comments: "The Primitive fact: *the existence of the world* and that the light of the world is our humanity (our humanity is the light of the world . . . 'Primitive' i.e.: first things" (*Sulfur* 26 162–163). Like MP, Oppen nourishes a faith in a primary perception, one that is pre-linguistic, an urge, as he writes, "To feel oneself at the very beginning of language" (*Sulfur* 27 212).

Whether one ever can climb out of language to see the world as it really is or map some realm of reality that is language-independent are questions I will not argue here. As for MP and Oppen, the condition they describe is not unlike the Zen Buddhist state of No-Mind, an epistemological nakedness. In sloughing presumptions that circumscribe our thinking, both writers suggest we might step from the ruts of a conditioned perception into the clarity that each prizes. "It is absolutely necessary," Oppen advises, "to be able to forget what one knows of 'the act'; to be able to begin each poem from the beginning" (*Iowa Review* 5). Even as MP argues that intellectualism fails to "give us any account of the human experience of the world" (*Phenomenology* 255), that we need to make ourselves ignorant of what we are looking for, Oppen, on a parallel path, writes, "I THINK THAT IF WE FOLLOW VERY SCRUPULOUSLY THINGS AS WE FIND THEM, WE ARE DRAWN BEYOND OLD CONCEPTS AND, PERHAPS, BEYOND THE POSSIBILITIES OF CONCEPTS" (*Iowa Review* 17).

For both writers, perception is initial and reciprocal. Oppen believes that "Poetry has to be protean; the meaning must begin there. With the perception" (*SL* 22). In his notebooks he says that "the present, the sense of the present arrives before the words—and independent of them" (*Sulfur* 26 149). He paraphrases Jacques Maritain: "we awake in the same moment to ourselves and to things" (*Iowa Review* 17). But even as he recognizes that neither the self nor the objects of the world can be seen apart from the world that contains them, Oppen does not obliterate their differences. He avows, "a blurring of the distinction between subjective and objective—There has been no instant in my life when such a blurring was possible for me / for one thing: too much a carpenter: I know what a blue guitar is made *of*" (*Sulfur* 27 209). In *The Phenomenology of Perception*, MP similarly notes how, even though we may incorporate them, even for instance when the steering wheel, as we drive, seems to become an extension of our body, objects and subjectivities are distinct, however mutually implicative. MP speaks of a *coexistence* or *coincidence* of embodied subject and world. And Oppen writes: "'one's soul': it means the image of the world, the image of the world in yourself" (*Conjunctions* 188).

Given their experiential grounding, it is no wonder that they both loved Cézanne's work. In his essay on "Cézanne's Doubt," MP rehearses the painter's break with Impressionism, Cézanne's quickening desire to recover the density of *things,* their tangible presence, from the fuzzy dissolve of the Impressionistic style. He suggests Cézanne was driven to recuperate black and earth tones in order to "represent the object, to find it again behind the atmosphere" (*Sense and Nonsense* 12). Oppen makes an analogous distinction, albeit in different terms. He writes in his notebooks that surrealism, its influence extending to most of modern art, "means to produce art not out of the experience of things, but out of the subjectivity of the artist" (*Iowa Review* 1). His own way of making poetry, Oppen remarks, is atypical. "My work," he emphasizes, "is produced from the experience of things" (*Iowa Review* 1). Oppen even quotes Cézanne, who held that "Painting from nature is not copying the object. It is materializing one's sensations" (*Iowa Review*). And in his contemplation of Thomas Hardy, Oppen reconfigures Cézanne's dictum. He writes: "As to Hardy's 'realism'/ phenomenology—I carry the matter considerably further I would not say that a landscape is dour—I cannot imagine myself saying that, I would say that we feel it so—" (*Sulfur* 26 158). When Oppen writes, "THE THOUGHT. IT IS NOT / IN US, WE ARE IN IT" (*Conjunctions* 202) or it is "not that the world is meaningless but that all meaning means the world" (*Sulfur* 26 154), he fashions corollaries to Cézanne's famous assertion that "Nature is on the inside."

To look at the poem "Psalm" from *This in Which* or "A Theological Definition" from *Of Being Numerous* is to recognize a subjectivity opening out onto otherness, the draw into relationship with things, the bouleversement of "in" and "out," and the mingling of language (even letters) with emotion-laden experience. Oppen remains astounded to find that his "Self=presence," as MP has it, "is presence to a differentiated world" (*The Visible and the Invisible* 191) of beings and things. Astonished simply "That they are there!," Oppen places his faith in words, "the small nouns," that they might communicate something of the feeling of being present to "what is," the worldly THIS "in which the wild deer / Startle, and stare out" (*NCP* 99).

In "If It All Went Up In Smoke" (*NCP* 274) printed below, meanings are figured in the play of closeness and distance, in the shift of pronouns from *one* to *us* to *I*. Notice the contention that the poem begins in a pre-linguistic, selved world, the emphasis on small things, the Whitmanesque identification with grass blades and touch. Is "savage" another word for primitive, the world burned clear of preconception? Is the object of the verb "praise" the distant clause "all // that is strange"? Is the sudden cry of "help me" an acknowledgment of the poet's vulnerability or is it a solicitation of the reader to help make the poem, to participate in its experience, to bring the poem to its beginning in the reader?

If It All Went Up In Smoke
that smoke
would remain

the forever
savage country poem's light borrowed

light of the landscape and one's footprints praise

from distance
in the close
crowd all

that is strange the sources

the wells the poem begins

neither in word
nor meaning but the small
selves haunting

us in the stones and is less

always than that help me I am
of that people the grass

blades touch

and touch in their small

distances the poem
begins

Oppen writes in his notebooks, "I choose to believe in the natural consciousness, I see what the deer see, the desire NOT TO is the desire to be alone in fear of equality / I see what the grass (blade) would see if it had eyes" (*Iowa Review* 14).

Instead of the traditional Western account of a consciousness that digests the external world, Oppen honors a consciousness interwoven with the world of objects, a consciousness that is nothing if not a collaboration with the world.

~

For me, bolting from college in 1978 with a degree in geology, Oppen's phenomenological poetics was revelatory. Engineering sciences had given me an analogy for understanding some of his syntactical strategies. I knew that unlike thermodynamic entropy, which measures loss, informational entropy measures the *richness* of possible messages carried by a channel. A channel that carries one single message, newspaper language one might contend, has the lowest informational entropy. But the messages channeled through Oppen's syntax are rich and allow for alternative readings, many kinds of information. Instead of developing from subject to verb to object and resolving logically, Oppen's sentences sanction a syntactical flexibility that promotes simultaneous, collaborative meanings. His poems, frequently enjambed and eschewing periods, are characterized by their high informational entropy.

I came to San Francisco from Virginia in 1979 and met him that summer. He was already suffering from Alzheimer's, although no one used that word, and Mary, his wife, protected him from strangers. When I visited, I came with Michael Cuddihy, the editor of the literary magazine *Ironwood.* Cuddihy, in fact, had begun the magazine by soliciting work first from Oppen, who sent, according to the editor, a minor poem. Although Oppen was his hero in many ways, Cuddihy rejected the poem and Oppen wrote back to him, "Ahh, a serious editor." Then he sent the new poems with which Michael Cuddihy launched his first issue.

In his poems, George Oppen wanted words to act out *truthful, lived experience.* His poetry is very literally a practice of perception. He even speaks of emotion "as the ability to perceive" (*SL* 40). The syntax of an Oppen poem rivets our attention to both word and world in an enactment of intentional consciousness, the very act of perception and thought coming into being, of language and feeling arising as experience. His poems can be intricate, the syntax polyvalent, the disclosure nonlinear and difficult to render into anything like statement. And as such, his poetry might be considered an expression of life. As the biblical Isaiah reminds us, "it shall be a vexation only to understand." Clarity is not the same thing as simplicity.

Finally, in Oppen's poems I feel the momentum of an existence toward others and toward the world. That is how I found him. And that is how his work finds me.

Note

1. Editor's Note: This essay was written before Stephen Cope's edition of the *Selected Prose, Daybooks, and Papers* was published. But Merleau-Ponty does not appear in the index to that volume.

Works Cited

Merleau-Ponty, Maurice. *The Phenomenology of Perception.* London: Routledge and Kegan Paul, 1962.

———. *Sense and Non-sense.* Chicago, IL: Northwestern University Press, 1964.

———. *The Visible and the Invisible.* Chicago, IL: Northwestern University Press, 1968.

Oppen, George. "An Adequate Vision: A George Oppen Daybook." Ed. Michael Davidson. *Ironwood* 26 (1985): 5–31.

———. *Collected Poems.* New York, New Directions, 1975.

———. "George Oppen, the Anthropologist of Myself: A Selection from the Working Papers." Ed. Rachel Blau DuPlessis. *Sulfur* 26 (Spring 1990): 135–164.

———. "George Oppen, the Philosophy of the Astonished: A Selection from the Working Papers." Ed. Rachel Blau DuPlessis. *Sulfur* 27 (Fall 1990): 202–220.

———. *The Selected Letters of George Oppen.* Ed. Rachel Blau DuPlessis. Durham, NC: Duke University Press, 1990.

———. "Selections from George Oppen's Daybook." Ed. Dennis Young. *Iowa Review* 18, 3 (1988): 1–17.

———. "'Meaning Is to Be Here': A Selection from the Daybook." Ed. Cynthia Anderson. *Conjunctions* 10 (1987): 186–208.

IV
Two Wars

6
One among Rubble
George Oppen and World War II

Kristin Prevallet

I. Backdrop: War Stories

On October 6, 1944, the 411th Battalion (part of the 103rd Division of General Brandenberger's Seventh Army) set out from the Port of New York and landed in Marseilles. This was the first leg of a long journey through Alsace and southern Germany that finally ends in Austria. Moving north through the Vosges mountains, the 411th battalion arrived deep in the heart of German controlled Alsace just as the Germans were heavily attacking the Allied front. The weather was severely cold and the ground was covered with a thick layer of snow—"a battle in snow and ice," as the WWII memoirist Paul Fussell describes it (34). On December 14, in the city of Climbach, the battalion met with direct artillery and heavy mortar fire but managed to push through and repulse the attack. Now nicknamed "the fighting 411th," the battalion crossed over the Maginot Line and became the first group of Brandenberger's Seventh Army to fight in Germany. Facing the German Army's Seigfried Defenses, the battalion suffered heavy casualties when it was forced to fight off the German counteroffensive for twenty-two hours before finally retreating. When Nazi general Von Rundstedt led his offensive against Allied positions in the Ardennes (called "The Battle of the Bulge"), the 411th shifted its position northward to add support for General Patton's Third Army. It wasn't there for long when it was again relocated, this time further south to the

Strasborg-Bitche area where Allied forces were again under heavy attack. The 411th suffered heavy casualties in the town of Sessenheim, which, according to a pamphlet written by members of the 411th after the war, was "a small German-held Alsatian town surrounded by the thick pine forests of Hagenau" (8). Here in the forest, the battalion was surprised by direct fire from German Tiger tanks—a tank that, as the military historian John Keegan writes, was extremely loud and "with its 88-mm gun and 100-mm-thick armor, proved consistently superior . . . to every other tank of the war" (402). Facing defeat, the Seventh Army was ordered to retreat, and withdrew during the night to march, as the battalion writes, "along roads blanketed with swirling snow" (9). Finally, after sixty-seven days of continuous contact with Hitler's army, the "fighting 411th" was granted a reprieve.

On March 15, 1945, the battalion looped back to resume its trek through Alsace and managed to liberate four cities, causing the Germans to withdraw behind the Siegfried line. Crossing into Germany four days later, once again it was the 411th who led the Seventh Army into Germany. On April 3 the battalion arrived at Klingenmunster—a major milestone in the war, as it marked the official breach of the Siegfried Line and opened the Rhine Valley for the entrance of Allied troops. Around the end of April, the 411th reached the city of Landsberg—the site of the prison where Hitler drafted *Mein Kampf.* There they took part in the liberation of the Kaufering concentration camps—a complex of eleven camps where 14,500 Jews were murdered between June 1944 and April 1945. According to its pamphlet, the battalion arranged for the proper burial of 750 victims.

George Oppen, who was a truck driver and later a gunner for the 411th Battalion, was severely wounded approximately one week before the battalion took part in the liberation of the Kaufering camps. On April 22, 1945, somewhere between the southern German cities of Klingenmunster and Albeck, Oppen's truck came under artillery fire and, with two other men, he jumped into a foxhole after an 88 mm shell exploded directly above them. Oppen survived the shelling with wounds to his face, back, and legs (*Meaning a Life* 178). However, the other men with him did not survive, and apparently, with the explosions of enemy artillery all around him, Oppen had little choice but to watch them die. As recounted by David McAleavy, Oppen felt guilty for the rest of his life that he did not attempt to drag the wounded soldiers to safety, even though to do so would have been unjustifiably risky. Oppen remained in the fox-hole with the dead men for several hours until the shooting stopped; it was here that he buried the dogtags that would have incriminated him as being Jewish had the Germans found him. He writes in the poem "Of Hours":

No man
But the fragments of metal
Tho there were men there were men   Fought
No man but the fragments of metal
Burying my dogtag with H
For Hebrew in the rubble of Alsace

Oppen was transported to a medical hospital in Nancy where he stayed for two months. When he was released and went to claim his jacket, the at-tendant thought the serial number must be wrong because, as McAleavy remembers Oppen saying, the jacket was so riddled with holes that it must have "belonged to someone who had died" (310).

II. Rubble and Vertigo

Stories of soldiers trapped and wounded in foxholes during World War II are common. Fussell describes an almost identical scene, hiding in a fox-hole, listening as the shells come closer and closer . . . and then the "red-hot metal tearing into my body." He watches as another soldier "turns from flesh color to white, and then to whitish green as his circulation stopped" (44). But of course each war story is particular to each witness, and each witness has unique memories of the train of thoughts going through his or her mind. In "Of Hours" Oppen writes, "I must get out of here / *Father* he thinks *father*." But aside from panic and prayer, Oppen re-calls that lines of poetry were also running through his mind: Louis Zu-kofsky's, "How shall I — Her soles new as the sunned black of her grave's turf, / With all this material / To what distinction" (Zuk 38); the first line of Sir Thomas Wyatt's lyric, "They Flee from Me, That Sometimes Did Me Seek"; and an amended version of Charles Reznikoff's short poem, "Among the heaps of brick and plaster lies / a girder, still itself among the rubbish" (Reznikoff 107). In a letter to Milton Hindus, Oppen writes that "these poems seemed to fill all the space around me and I wept and wept" (*Selected Letters [SL]* 338). As he writes in "Myth of the Blaze":

because of this   lost to be lost   Wyatt's
lyric and Rezi's
running thru my mind
in the destroyed (and guilty) Theater
of the War

The Reznikoff lyric that Oppen refers to in this poem is the "line about
the girder [which] was with me all through that war and every time I
thought of it I wept and wept, I don't know what about, just that it was
so beautiful" (DuPlessis, "Objectivist Poetics" 44). Oppen returned frequently to this line throughout his writing life, citing it in poems, letters,
and notes as very significant to his own ideas about syntax, line, clarity,
and meaning. It is therefore quite significant that he misquotes this line
of poetry that he loves so much, changing Reznikoff's word "rubbish" to
his word "rubble": "'The girder is still itself among the rubble,' and we cite
that line over and over to ourselves—and we meant to be ourselves among
the rubble—and it was rubble or it was very close to rubble. It was very
close to catastrophe, you know, not only close but was catastrophe because
a world war is catastrophe, after all" (DuPlessis, "Objectivist Poetics" 29).
    This modified line about the girder in the rubble, which Michael
Davidson calls the "governing ethos in Oppen's poetics" came to him during the war (*Ironwood* 5). Although he always attributes it to Reznikoff,
the fact that he changed the line break and the wording transforms it into
his own line of poetry. As Robert Franciosi writes, "He literally re-writes
Reznikoff's girder poem to accommodate his own personal and social
ethos" (393). This rewriting is significant to a poet who, during this time,
was in the midst of a twenty-four-year-long period of silence in which he
did not write any poetry at all because, as he later recounted, "poetry was
not the most important thing in the world at that time" (DuPlessis, "Objectivist Poetics" 24–25). And yet, as is clear from this line, his mind turned
to poetry during what must have been one of the most horrific and fright-
ening experiences of his life. His pen may have been silent, but something
significant was being written in his mind—a line of poetry that would stay
with him for the rest of his life, directly shaping his poetics. Of the girder
line Davidson also writes: "It defines those enduring products of human
labor that exist despite and yet within the 'rubble' of modern history. . . .
It is not the Imagist ideal of a transitory moment caught by the artist between juxtaposed images and removed from time. It is the poem *in time*,
part of the rubble and yet 'still itself,' unchanged by the synthetic imagina-

tion" (*Ironwood* 5). It is also Oppen as a human being *in time*, hiding in the foxhole with a dead body. Both men are part of the rubble, and yet Oppen is "still alive." Oppen is himself the girder which remains in the midst of the rubble, in the midst of the catastrophe of war.

III. The Blaze of Tyger and Tiger

The direct combat Oppen experienced in World War II deeply affected him and consistently made its way into his poetry. It is impossible to speculate how Oppen's poetic project would have changed had he taken part in the liberation of the Kaufering concentration camps. Even without this experience, he writes: "I have written of the war. Painful; very painful to approach, to begin to speak" (*Ironwood* 18). This difficulty in speaking is the ethical precision that guides Oppen's poetics—his desire not to directly represent for fear of misrepresenting; or rather, that "what is important is not the conclusion, but what we are talking about" (*Ironwood* 9). As is clear from Harvey Shapiro's recent anthology, *Poets of World War II*, the way Oppen writes about World War II is not the way that most poets choose to represent it, whether as a means of describing personal experience (as in Karl Shapiro's, "Lost in the vastness of the void Pacific / My thousand days of exile, pain, / Bid me farewell" [83]), a means of asserting manhood (as in Randall Jarrell's, "Men wash their hands in blood, as best they can: / I find no fault in this just man" [87]), a means of conveying the glory and horror of war through precise images (as in James Dickey's, "For the moment when the roofs will connect / Their flames, and make a town burning with all / American fire" [157]). Oppen does not attempt to explicitly represent what is painful; he does not write of war as a revelation of shared or personal experiences. In his poetry, references to it are neither isolated nor intended to be universal. The form of his poems—often serial stanzas connected by fragments—assures that his experience of war is not prioritized over any other events in his life. His near-death scare in the foxhole is no more or less significant than descriptions of his daughter, his home, his aesthetic, philosophical, and political realizations.

And yet, the shocking and emotionally disruptive fact of war comes through in his poetry, sometimes subtly and sometimes overtly. Oppen's poem "Myth of the Blaze" is both explicit and opaque—it includes direct references to the war that break down into disjointed fragments. Beginning with the foxhole story, the words of the poem—like the unspeakable awareness of coming close to dying—break apart and finally disappear. For Oppen, the foxhole story is a dangerous mental place; as such it is the poem's center of gravity, around which language falls like artillery shells. As the poem moves along and the mind remembering can no longer speak of the experience, the lines break apart and the references fragment. The poem begins with the question, "why had they not / killed me why did they fire that warning / wounding cannon only the one round I hold a / superstition." But that which is too "painful to approach" is displaced onto the eyes of Blake's Tyger, and at this point in the poem the syntax completely falls apart and only associations remain behind. The Tyger becomes a Tiger, who becomes a tiger:

> end of the tunnel what are the names
> of the Tyger   to speak
> to the eyes
>
> of the Tiger   blaze
> of the tiger   who moves in the forest leaving
>
> no scent
>
> but the pine needles' his eyes blink

The wavering between the capitalization of Tiger ("the names / of the Tyger / . . . to the eyes / of the Tiger / blaze / of the tiger") indicates that more than the beast is being invoked; it "move[s] in the forest leaving / no scent" much like, in the deep cold forests of Alsace, German Tiger tanks took aim at men hiding in foxholes. Through the pine needles of the dead forest the Tigers move like a tiger, connected homonymously and superstitiously to the Tyger that burns through the forests of the imagination's night. Of course it is only an exercise to read such a focus into this poem—its dwindling away makes locking into a specific interpretation almost impossible. As an experience, the very form of the poem is a body encountering shrapnel. The pain of witness and experience is revealed in this poem as the language is torn apart.

IV. Surviving Rubble

Oppen's experience in the theater of war was ten years into his period of silence, which began in 1934 and would last for twenty-four years. This silence, which DuPlessis describes as his "historic choice" ("The Familiar" 21), was a choosing of political activism and engagement over poetry. As Mary Oppen writes in her autobiography, "Events moved us with them,

and we believed that fascism meant death to us along with other Jews"
(158). She is speaking here of the early 1930s—a time when, "The propaganda of fascism and the authoritarian state appealed to many who saw
no other solution to the economic collapse of the United States" (146–
147). As the war in Europe gathered momentum, the American discourse,
as Studs Terkel writes, changed: "What had been a country physically
as well as geographically isolated had become, with the suddenness of a
blitzkrieg, engaged with distant troubles . . . Our huge industrial machine
shifted gears . . . In the words of President Franklin D. Roosevelt, Dr. New
Deal was replaced by Dr. Win the War" (168).

Oppen was working as a pattern maker in Long Island when, in 1943,
he abruptly moved to Detroit. This, according to DuPlessis, meant instant
induction into the U.S. Army—an induction with which he was eager to
comply. "How does one say he is 'in favor' of a war, meaning he is in favor
of someone else fighting it?" (*SL* 303). As Mary Oppen writes, "George
wanted to go to the war. The enemy was fascism, and we agreed that the
war must be fought. It seemed to us that the lives of all Jews were endangered by fascism; our lives were in danger, and to not fight in the war was
to ask of others what we would not do for ourselves" (173). Despite this initial imperative, the choice to fight in the war was one that Oppen would
come to question, possibly even regret, later in his life. First and foremost there was the stress that his decision put on his family. His daughter Linda was only two years old, and it was extremely difficult for Mary to
raise a child while receiving her husband's letters a month after they were
written, not knowing whether or not he was still alive. Of course, his near
brush with death in the foxhole must have given him tremendous pause.
Mary had been very clear, saying to him, "You must come back alive,
do not throw yourself away in any moment's heroism. I want you to return" (172).

Aside from these personal reasons for regretting his time in the service,
there is the looming fact that this war, as Terkel writes, "warped our view
of how we look at things today . . . [it] encourages the men of my generation to be willing . . . to use military force anywhere in the world" (173).
This was the permission that gave way to Vietnam, to the U.S. imperialism that Oppen called a "dirty secret." As Oppen writes, "The name of
the game is imperialism, and we throw away our lives for it. We can hardly
be said to possess our own lives" (*Ironwood* 25). Fighting *against* fascism
and *for* a better collective future that is known and understood through the
individual is the reason he went to war. His was a moral cause, an ethical

necessity. Possessing one's own life is Oppen's sense that "we meant to be ourselves among the rubble" (DuPlessis, "Objectivist Poetics" 29). And yet to fight for it, he had to participate in the machine, claim loyalty to the U.S. Government.

Regardless of the difficulty in reconciling the individual with the war machine, Oppen refused to be "disengaged" from the experience. It haunted him when he returned to France on a vacation with Mary, sixteen years later. In a letter to his daughter Linda, he writes: "And I had seen the town rubble: they were bulldozing paths thru the rubble. And of course, the rubble was not just stone, you know. There were bodies in it, we damn near died. People bombed and putting the same mess back" (*SL* 50). Oppen sees the piles of stone and bodies superimposed over the reconstructed cities, hears the bulldozers plow through the rubble—and he writes in "Of Being Numerous:"

> I cannot even now
> Altogether disengage myself
> From those men
>
> With whom I stood in emplacements, in mess tents,
> In hospitals and sheds and hid in the gullies
> Of blasted roads in a ruined country

Oppen's refusal for poetry to be disengaged from experience is a poetic synthesis of what DuPlessis calls, "densely inrooted particulars" ("Objectivist Poetics" 132). Included in this dense inrooting are all the men he fought with and almost died with, the people he met along the way, the cities through which he traveled. From these very lived and individual particulars comes the poem, which struggles to make meaning from the singularity of each.

Eliot Weinberger describes Oppen's process of reworking poems as "the struggle itself . . . cutting out and pasting words on top of other words, as though he were a mason building a brick wall" (*New Collected Poems* x). This process indicates that there is an architecture at work in Oppen's poetics. Words in his poems work quite literally as girders, and certain are sporadically repeated throughout his books—including "machines," "the world," "the sea," "ruins," "bricks," "birth," and "rubble." His specific interest in how things are put together and are sustained—related to the time he spent supporting himself and his family as a carpenter—makes the girder words all the more significant. He uses such words as supports that connect poems from various books to his correspondence. All of this comes together in a careful construction of language that is "the business of the poet."

In the poem, "The Building of the Skyscraper," Oppen writes:

There are words that mean nothing
But there is something to mean.
Not a declaration which is truth
But a thing
Which is. It is the business of the poet
'To suffer the things of the world
And to speak them and himself out.'

It is the business of the poet to suffer the "things" of the world by speaking through and about them. Words hold this power, even if we as readers have learned to not always look to them for such substance. But when we do look, there is the danger of falling, like the steel worker on the girder in the first section of the poem who looks down in spite of being trained to work without doing so. The "things of the world" and the words used to describe them are a spiral of both contingency and catastrophe.

At the same time, the vertigo of words can, on the way down, reflect etymological, personal, and historical contexts. Oppen wants to be as material as possible, using words to provoke different definitions and layers of meaning. For instance, "rubble" is a girder word falling in vertigo. As such, it appears over and over again in the poems and letters, revealing a little more about its meaning and significance each time. First, there is the fact that as it moves between Reznikoff and Oppen it wavers between "rubble" and "rubbish." This is perhaps not entirely arbitrary, considering that etymologically the two words are linked. Both words are of obscure origin, though probably derive from ancient French plurals of *robel, rubel*. Because these plural forms are not definitively of French origin, the exact relation is difficult to ascertain. The OED's definition of the word "rubble" as, "Waste fragments of stone, esp. as constituting the rubbish of decayed or demolished buildings" solidifies a connection between the two words, a linkage established in fallen buildings, victims of time, or of war. Despite the etymological uncertainly of their connection, through Oppen they come full circle into themselves.

But what Oppen did in transforming Reznikoff's line was more than an etymological word game—it was the realization of a deeply personal reconciliation between "poetry" and "the world." Oppen made the decision to leave poetry in order to directly confront the reality of his times through lived action. But in spite of this, at some point he had to realize that the two do not need to mutually exclude each other. "Rubbish" was Reznikoff's word—it tied him to his place in time, New York City in the 1930s. "Rubble" was Oppen's word and served the same purpose—to locate him in time. Rubble is the remains of stone, what remains after demolition, before the construction has begun. When demolition is caused by bombs, there are bodies mixed in with the rubble—"To a body anything can happen, / Like a brick" (*Selected Poems [SP]* 53). "Blood from the Stone," the title of the first poem Oppen wrote after his twenty-four years of silence, is a precise image, the horror of which Oppen saw every time his battalion passed through a war-torn city.

"Blood from the Stone" sustains the synthesis between poetry and lived experience—both the larger historical facts of war and the personal realizations of what it meant to be in the midst of it. The poem is Oppen's coming home, both to his family from the war, and to poetry from silence.

O!
Everything I am is
Us. Come home.

"In every street, / In all inexplicable crowds, / what they did then / Is still their lives." Coming home is a deeply conflicted state of mind. The inexplicable is the problem of describing in words all that has happened, and all that has been seen and felt. Coming home to language, Oppen finds his way back to poetry, a state where the fragmented and shocked being can articulate his movements through time:

Sidereal time
Together, and among the others,
The bequeathed pavements, the inherited lit streets:
Among them we were lucky—strangest word.

Oppen was lucky—he willingly took the risk of almost dying and still was able to return home to his family. His regrets and his retrospection are simply put: "So we lived / And chose to live / These were our times" (*SP* 54).

The concept and experience of war itself is a girder that supports and connects many of the poems in Oppen's various writings, though references to it are sporadic and never isolated. War is clearly an organizing— or disorganizing—principle in Oppen's work, given that references to it occur in some of his most significant and critically appreciated poems, namely "Of Hours," "Myth of the Blaze," "Route," "Survival: Infantry," "A Language of New York," and "Of Being Numerous." As he writes, "My work concerned, almost obsessed, with the question of violence. It is not only that large part of my generation that faced the question of revolution, and not only the fact that I faced, like others, some part of the Second World War—it is that art is the most violent of all actions—it means to break thru what has contained us. That which without art would contain us as it contains a plant" (*Ironwood* 19–20).

As a sustaining connective beam, the presence of war, the catastrophe and sadness of it, is central to Oppen's poetics. Breaking through what contained him, Oppen quit writing poetry for twenty-four years in order to fully participate in the urgent political crisis of the 1930s and 1940s. And yet, the violence he witnessed never left him; he broke through the rubble of history to find in poetry a viable and restorative force.

Works Cited

Davidson, Michael. Introduction to "An Adequate Vision: A George Oppen Daybook." *Ironwood* 26 (1985): 5–6.

DuPlessis, Rachel Blau. "Objectivist Poetics and Political Vision: A Study of Oppen and Pound." In *George Oppen: Man and Poet.* Orono, ME: National Poetry Foundation, 1981. 123–148.

———. "'The familiar / becomes extreme': George Oppen and Silence." *North Dakota Quarterly* 55, 4 (1987): 18–36.

Franciosi, Robert. "Reading Reznikoff: Zukofsky and Oppen." *North Dakota Quarterly* (1987): 383–395.

Fussell, Paul. "Doing Battle: The Making of a Skeptic." *The War: Stories of Life and Death from World War II,* ed. Clint Willis. New York: Thunder Mouth Press, 1999.

Hatlen, Burton, and Tom Mandel. "Poetry and Politics: A Conversation with George and Mary Oppen." *George Oppen: Man and Poet.* Orono, ME: National Poetry Foundation, 1981. 24–47.

Keegan, John. *The Second World War.* New York: Penguin, 1989.

Kinlaw, Howard M., et al. *"From Bruyéres to Brenner": The Combat Story of the Fighting 411th*. Innsbruck, Austria, 1945.

McAleavy, David. "The Oppens: Remarks Towards Biography." *Ironwood* 26 (1985): 309–318.

Oppen, George. *New Collected Poems*. Ed. Michael Davidson. New York: New Directions, 2002.

———. *The Selected Letters of George Oppen*. Ed. Rachel Blau DuPlessis. Durham, NC: Duke University Press, 1990.

———. *Selected Poems*. New York: New Directions, 2003.

Oppen, Mary. *Meaning a Life: An Autobiography*. Santa Rosa, CA: Black Sparrow Press, 1990.

Reznikoff, Charles. *The Poems of Charles Reznikoff 1918–1975*. Ed. Seamus Cooney. David R. Godine, 2005.

Shapiro, Harvey, ed. *Poets of World War II*. New York: Library of America, 2003.

Terkel, Studs. *MY American Century*. New York: New Press, 1997.

Weinberger, Eliot. "Preface: Oppen Then." *New Collected Poems*, ed. Michael Davidson. New York: New Directions, 2002.

7
"The Air of Atrocity"
"Of Being Numerous" and the Vietnam War

John Lowney

> I'm finding it difficult to write poetry—An eerie feeling writing poetry
> with the war going on. I don't know if I can. A lot of resistance, a lot of
> doubt, too much as things stand to induce people to throw away a few
> million lives of young men . . . HAVE people recognized the amount
> of lying that has been done?
>   —George Oppen, 1965 Letter to Diane Meyer

In his introduction to *Of Being Numerous* in George Oppen's *New Collected
Poems,* Michael Davidson asserts that the Vietnam War "provides the occasion for numerous poems in the book, as [Oppen] attempted to negoti-
ate his older Marxist views against the claims of the New Left and youth
moments" (379). While there are few direct references to the Vietnam War
in *Of Being Numerous,* Davidson's claims are amply supported by the letters and working papers that Oppen wrote while composing the book. The
sections of the long title poem that reflect on war are not only fundamental to its inquiry into "the concept of humanity," as Oppen wrote, they are
also profound in their interrogation of militaristic language and nationalist ideology. The Vietnam War "air of atrocity" permeates the entire poem
and threatens the very act of writing.[1] It is remarkable, then, that "Of Being Numerous" has received little attention as a war poem or, more specifically, as a Vietnam War poem, even though Oppen's book won the Pulitzer Prize for poetry in 1969.[2] While Oppen was not antagonistic toward
"the claims of the New Left and youth movements" (Davidson, Introduction 379), his identification with the earlier generation of the Depression
and World War II has limited consideration of "Of Being Numerous" as
a "Vietnam era" poem.[3]

   As Oppen's letter to his niece, Diane Meyer, suggests, the Vietnam War
is indeed the occasion for "Of Being Numerous," an occasion that challenged his sense of purpose as a writer almost as acutely as the Great Depression, when he had found it so difficult to reconcile his vocation as a

poet with his commitment to social justice that he stopped writing altogether and dedicated himself to organizational activity with the Communist Party.[4] Oppen wrote most of "Of Being Numerous" in 1965 and 1966, revising and expanding the earlier sequence of poems, "A Language of New York," that he had published in *This in Which* (1965). As he gradually came to realize while composing "Of Being Numerous," the growing revolt against state authority during the Vietnam War recalled the state of social crisis that he had experienced in the 1930s and 1940s. "I perhaps cannot write poetry in war time," he wrote in the working papers for his long poem. "I couldn't before, and perhaps cannot now. I become ashamed, I become sick with shame." In a note dated January 1966 he wrote, "If we launch that 'general war in Asia,' I think I will have to give this up again. What will one do when the troop trains start shipping young men off to their deaths? Shall one write poetry?" (Discussion of *Another Language of New York*). Particularly disturbing to Oppen was the "amount of lying" about the war, the disjunction between official rhetoric and the actual events of the war. Vietnam-era poetry that protested U.S. military policy began with this disjunction as a point of departure, underscoring the power of poetry to counteract the distortion of language that justified the war. Yet, as Cary Nelson has written, the Vietnam War called into question even the Whitmanian tradition of a "compensatory poetic of open forms" (10). As a result of the rhetorical duplicity that rationalized the escalation of military force in Southeast Asia, "the whole medium of public discourse becomes a mode of deception, and not even poetic utterance is innocent" (9). The most ambitious interrogations of the Vietnam War by American poets in the 1960s, such as Allen Ginsberg's "Wichita Vortex Sutra," Denise Levertov's "Staying Alive," or Adrienne Rich's "Shooting Script," reveal the limitations of Whitman's visionary democratic poetics through the rhetorical structure of their poems. Neither the prophetic voice nor the representative stance of Whitman's poetry could adequately express the Vietnam-era betrayal of his mythic vision of American democracy. Nowhere is the question of this legacy addressed more rigorously than in "Of Being Numerous."

The problem of writing poetry in a time of social crisis, specifically wartime, is embedded throughout "Of Being Numerous." Oppen's response to the "eerie feeling" of writing poetry in wartime is to incorporate "resistance" and "doubt" into the syntax and structure of his serial poem. He does so through an intertextual network of voices that share his concern with the act of writing during wartime. This network includes selections from poets whose writing invokes the experience of war, such as Thomas Hardy's lyric poem "The Oxen," written during World War I; William Blake's long prophetic poem *Jerusalem*, written in the midst of the Napoleonic wars and the ensuing period of reaction; and Walt Whitman's Civil War letters. Juxtaposed with these literary allusions are quotations from conversations and correspondence with his contemporaries, especially women, from Mary Oppen and June Oppen Degnan to younger writers such as Rachel Blau DuPlessis and Diane Wakoski. As DuPlessis and Peter Nicholls, among others, have argued, this intertextual dynamic radically decenters the speaking subject of the poem; in doing so, it enacts a critique of the ethics as well as the aesthetics of the "ego system" that structured Pound's *Cantos* and subsequent long poems such as *Paterson* and *The Maximus Poems*.[5] While "Of Being Numerous" posits, at times, an agonistic relation between the poet and the world, it critiques this relation through its dialogic structure, through its rhetorical strategies of self-questioning as well as through its extensive quotation, whether explicit or implicit, of voices and texts. "Of Being Numerous" is composed largely of quotations, beginning with its first section, which concludes by quoting Mary Oppen's discussion of the post–World War II long poem by Yves Bonnefoy, *Du mouvement et de l'immobilité de Douve*.[6] In interweaving male and female voices throughout the poem, Oppen also enacts a critique of the hegemonic masculinist stance of representing war, including the subject positions through which he remembers his own experience of World War II. From the middle sections of the poem (especially 18–20), which situate the U.S. involvement in Vietnam within an inherited history and rhetoric of empire, to the concluding sections, which relate the public discourse of war to the "domestic" social relations of men and women, "Of Being Numerous" destabilizes conventional distinctions between war fronts and home fronts, between masculine public and feminine private spheres, as it enacts a critique of the nationalist ideology that informed American imperialism.

The volume and variety of antiwar poetry written in the United States during the Vietnam War was extraordinary. Poetry played a more prominent role as a mode of protest than in any previous war in American history. The number of popular anthologies of antiwar poetry that coincided with the completion, publication, and initial reception of *Of Being Numerous* testifies to this unprecedented importance of poetry as a mode of protest. Among these anthologies were *A Poetry Reading against the Vietnam War*, edited by Robert Bly and David Ray (1966); *Where Is Vietnam?*

American Poets Respond, edited by Walter Lowenfels (1967); the *1968 Peace Calendar & Appointment Book: Out of the War Shadow,* edited by Denise Levertov (1967); *War Poems,* edited by Diane di Prima (1968); and *Poems of War Resistance,* edited by Scott Bates (1969). While subsequent poetry by Vietnam War veterans would evoke the tropes of World War I and World War II soldier poetry, however ironically, the antiwar poetry contained in these anthologies differed from previous war poetry in several significant ways. Perhaps most important, this poetry responded to mass media coverage that made the Vietnam War more omnipresent in the United States than any previous war: television coverage alone transported the violent and bloody imagery of warfare into millions of living rooms every evening. Secondly, poetry that protested the Vietnam War was variously mediated by the new social movements of the 1960s from the civil rights movement, to the women's and gay rights movements, to the countercultural movements of the Beats and hippies. Finally, because the Vietnam War was understood by its opponents as an unjust act of imperialist aggression, antiwar poetry by American writers expressed both personal and national guilt more insistently than in previous wars.[7] More than any previous military conflict in U.S. history, the Vietnam War was defined by the disjunction between the rhetoric of policy makers and the reality of those who were subject to U.S. military policy. Presidents Kennedy, Johnson, and Nixon each invoked the language that informed U.S. involvement in World War II in their defense of military policy in Vietnam: they variously articulated their commitment to freedom and peace as they ordered the escalation of coercive violence and deadly destruction. As Graham Greene's *The Quiet American* (1955) intimated long before most Americans had ever heard of Vietnam, the U.S. obsession with making the world safe for democracy was hardly as innocent and benevolent as cold war policy makers professed. While U.S. policy and rhetoric appealed to the nationalist mythology of the frontier and manifest destiny in justifying the war, the level of destruction in Vietnam not only belied the professed values of U.S. military policy but also increased awareness of the imperialist history that this nationalist mythology had obscured.

Oppen completed "Of Being Numerous" before the antiwar movement was large enough to generate the national media attention it would later attract. His long poem, then, predates much of the best-known antiwar poetry of the 1960s, and as specific as it is to his own experience as a veteran of World War II as well as of the Communist Left of the 1930s, it anticipates the later inquiry into American imperialism that was compelled by the Vietnam War. The year in which Oppen worked most intensively on "Of Being Numerous," 1965, saw an escalation of U.S. military involvement in Southeast Asia as well as the escalation of duplicitous rhetoric by policy makers, particularly President Johnson. As U.S. bombing of north and south Vietnam intensified, and as the buildup of U.S. ground troops increased, the antiwar movement also grew. Approximately 25,000 people marched in New York City for the First International Days of Protest on October 16, and over 50,000 attended a Washington, D.C., demonstration sponsored by the Committee for a Sane Nuclear Policy (SANE) a month later. Other modes of protest increased in 1965 as well, from campus rallies and teach-ins to individual acts of witness, including suicide and the first public draft-card burnings. A major turning point in the war took place at the end of the year on Christmas Day, when President Johnson announced a thirty-day truce, discontinuing the bombing of north Vietnam as he launched his international diplomatic "peace offensive." At the same time, however, the United States intensified its air war and ground campaign in south Vietnam and increased its practice of chemical warfare, particularly its deadly spraying of napalm. By the end of January in 1966, when Johnson ordered the resumption of bombing in north Vietnam despite public pressure to maintain the pause, it had become clear to many that diplomatic discussions of peace had been disingenuous. The war policy became even clearer to the general population of the United States when Senator William Fulbright, the chair of the Senate Foreign Relations Committee, conducted nationally televised hearings on the Johnson administration's Vietnam policy. The Fulbright hearings had a major impact on public opinion, as many viewers saw for the first time dissent about Johnson's war policy within the realm of established Washington policy makers. While the antiwar movement did not immediately grow as a result, the Second International Days of Protest in New York (March 25–26) exemplified the social broadening of the antiwar movement: leading the march of about 50,000 protesters were veterans of World War I, World War II, and the Korean War.[8]

The sections that address the Vietnam War in "Of Being Numerous" represent the poem's sharpest indictment of the brutal hypocrisy of American hegemony. They also represent a turning point in the poem's struggle to articulate a "language of New York" that can register the contradictions of a divided society. Oppen wrote frequently about the Vietnam War when he was composing "Of Being Numerous," and his response to the war is instructive for understanding the poem's dramatic conflict between the "isolated man" and "the people." Oppen's criticism of U.S. military policy was especially pronounced during the escalation of the war in early 1965, when news of the secret air war in Laos was revealed. His indictment of the deceitfulness of the Johnson administration was uncompromising, as a 1965 letter he sent to his sister, June Oppen Degnan, exemplifies: "As for the *News*—if I should abandon all resolve to be realistic—if I should say what I think we *should* do—I think the people should march on Washington and arrest the president. And I think they should do so immediately—tomorrow. I find I am more devoted to democracy than I had known. I find I am absolutely opposed to secret actions, carried out in pursuit of secret policies and strategies by secret means. These secret procedures seem to me unlimitedly perilous" (*Selected Letters [SL]* 111–112). As adamant as Oppen's criticism of the government was, he was less confident about the public response to such secrecy. On the one hand, he wrote that "99 percent of the people should agree with me, and then they should act in the most rapid possible way to stop all action in Vietnam pending public discussion." But he was not so confident that such public outrage would last, as he added that "on the contrary, they are going to get used to this war. The power of the fait accompli" (*SL* 112). A year later, Oppen was no less skeptical about the prospect of massive protest against the escalation of the war, although he retained hope in the judgment, if not the actions, of "the people." "[M]aybe the 'mass of the people' will surprise us again," he wrote to his sister June in January 1966. "There is—built-in, genetic—a model in family relations, in family love, which is not, it almost never is, *merely* predacious. It's there, it's not an impossibility" (*SL* 130). The translation of this model into mass political resistance to war was unlikely, however, given the coercive rhetoric of government propaganda: "People do want 'the world'—the human world—to continue. They have no particular reason to, but they do. Which provides the possibility of rational argument. It is just that, unfortunately, insanity possesses a tremendous pull, insanity is very infectious" (*SL* 131).

Oppen was compelled enough by the "insanity" of the war to participate in antiwar demonstrations in 1966.[9] He was compelled as well to question the viability of writing poetry when the need for political action was so urgent. As outraged as he was about the war, Oppen persevered in writing "Of Being Numerous." He was defensive about writing poetry, but he was also realistic enough in his analysis of the antiwar movement in 1965–66 to justify writing. In contrast to the angry tone above is the more stoical tone he expressed in the same letter: "I think we must decide to live thru this—the napalm and the rest. Easy enough to throw one-self away with horror but I don't suppose that's really what we want to do. To manage to live with it, to live thru it, if we get to, without however deceiving oneself. To speak calmly and carefully of hell. I have no great knack for it" (*SL* 130). The contrast of this resolution with his contempt for the Johnson administration's secret war policy is striking. While it in-dicates his uncertainty about the appropriate response to the war, it also exemplifies the honesty and rigor of his self-questioning. The problem of the poet's response to the Vietnam War, and to war more generally, recurs throughout "Of Being Numerous" as well. While this conflict is not fully resolved, the sections that address the Vietnam War most directly, 18–20, ultimately confirm the commitment to "live thru it . . . without however deceiving oneself."

Section 18 follows one of the most challenging and discordant sections of the poem. The dialectic of the singular and the numerous that reverber-ates throughout "Of Being Numerous" is informed at times by a profound sense of alienation, an alienation specific to its modernist urban topos, but intensified by the poet's consciousness of time, of age, of change, personal and cultural.[10] And the social differences that complicate a conceptualiza-tion of "the people" are themselves numerous in "Of Being Numerous." Most notable are the divisive differences of class, of generation, and of gender, which coincide with the emerging national conflict about the Vietnam War. Section 17 represents the urban site of the subway, which recalls such modernist poetry as Ezra Pound's "In a Station of the Metro," Hart Crane's *The Bridge,* and Louis Zukofsky's "Mantis." Oppen's sub-way, however, is peculiarly disorienting. Rather than a site in which the poet's consciousness of "the people" is intensified by the enclosed space of the station or the train, this subway is composed of a cacophony of voices whose coexistence seems more coincidental than meaningful. "It is not easy to speak," section 17 concludes, "A ferocious mumbling, in public / Of rootless speech" (*New Collected Poems [NCP]* 173). The distance between this "ferocious mumbling" and "the air of atrocity" that begins section 18 is, however, vast. The seemingly anarchic site of the subway, as incoher-ent and vaguely threatening as it appears, does represent a vital interaction of "the people," where otherness is spontaneously negotiated. The impe-rialist site of the U.S. military in Vietnam, on the other hand, represents mechanical, dehumanizing acts of routine murder, where otherness is in-visible as it is obliterated. Section 18 in fact directly opposes the "air of atrocity" to the unseen people on the ground:

It is the air of atrocity
An event as ordinary
As a President.

A plume of smoke, visible at a distance
In which people burn. (*NCP* 173)

As calmly "distant" as the tone of this section is, there is no mistaking its target. The military "air of atrocity" is identified with the power of the president, whose accountability for the burning "people" is implicit but unquestionable. Yet the act of brutal destruction is itself obscured by its evidence: the "plume of smoke" is "visible at a distance," but it also signifies the distances between those who drop the bombs—and those who authorize the bombing—from the people who burn as a result. The repetition of the generic term "people" is significant here: not only does the poem not distinguish between soldiers and civilians, or adults and children, who burn, it does not define them as others. It instead suggests a continuum of the Vietnamese victims of U.S. bombing and the common "people" who are the subject of the poem.

Section 18 is both matter-of-fact in its statement and oblique in what it is saying; its stance subtly mocks the self-righteous but deceitful rhetoric of U.S. military spokesmen during the war. The more precise meaning of "the air of atrocity" is withheld until the next section: "Now in the helicopters the casual will / Is atrocious" (*NCP* 173). The poem's anger toward the U.S. Government is likewise more explicitly revealed here: "Insanity in high places" (*NCP* 173) conflates the insanity of the soldiers in helicopters with the insanity of those in "high places" who authorize their actions, most notably the president. Following this direct statement is a more obscure image of the soldier in a helicopter: "The fly in the bottle" (*NCP* 173). This phrase stands alone, spatially separated from the rest of the poem and syntactically fragmentary. The image of the "fly in the bottle," although not placed in quotation marks in the poem, is from Wittgenstein's *Philosophical Investigations*: "What is your aim in philosophy?—To shew the fly out of the fly-bottle" (*NCP* 384 n. 19). Oppen attributes this quote to a conversation he had with his son-in-law, the philosopher Alexander Mourelatos: "I think of the phrase . . . as a quotation from you, not as a quotation from Wit[tgenstein] because that was the moment when we understood each other" (*SL* 177). This expression of intergenerational, familial solidarity—"Whatever our differences, we are not those insane flies" (*SL* 178)—suggests the pattern of embedding philosophical discourse within domestic conversation that is initiated in the poem's beginning. This appropriation of Wittgenstein's image evokes the political purpose of Oppen's poem: the isolation of the line itself accentuates the sense of fragmentation and estrangement that results from "insanity in high places." And, as Burton Hatlen has written, this image recalls the problem of separation that recurs throughout "Of Being Numerous" ("Opening Up the Text" 279). The concluding lines of section 19 make this especially clear: "Insane, the insane fly // Which, over the city / Is the bright light of shipwreck" (*NCP* 173). Language is at once a symptom and the only means to counteract "the bright light of shipwreck." The image of the fly in the fly-bottle from *Philosophical Investigations* is moreover concerned with the specific problem of language accentuated by sections 18–19, as it occurs in a long series of meditations on the problem of understanding and communicating pain, of reconciling the experience of bodily pain with the pain of others. The "atrocity" of the war, which takes the problem of separation to a deadly, dehumanizing extreme, is embodied in "the insane fly": "fly" can be read as both verb and a noun, as act and as the reified subject of the act. As this section makes clear, to "speak calmly and carefully of hell," as Oppen wrote to his sister about the Vietnam War, does not shield one from its "bright light."

Only through interrogation of the military "insanity" that perpetuated the Vietnam War can "Of Being Numerous" recognize a meaningful commonality between the poet and the "riders / Of the subway" (*NCP* 174). Paradoxically, the very act of imaginatively inhabiting "the air of atrocity" engenders a distance from this "insanity" but also a more compassionate recognition of its "infectious" power. The section that follows "the bright light of shipwreck" ponders the compelling but deceptive appeal of war, not just the spectacle of Vietnam but the recurring phenomenon of war. And while section 20 begins with an implied opposition of the poet to "They" who "await / War, and the news / Is war // As always," this opposition is temporary. The appeal of war is ideological, the effect of propaganda whose promises are inevitably illusory: "That the juices may flow in them / Tho the juices lie." The "news" of war is furthermore not new; the equation of war narratives with "history" is itself ideological but also ancient. The fascination with war, though, however delusional, is what connects the poet to the subway riders. This shared obsession with war is born of a shared consciousness of mortality. "But who escapes / Death," the poem asks, "Among these riders / Of the subway." Significantly, "they" and "I" become "we" through an allusion to a poem, a poem whose relation to war is neither stated nor direct. "As in Hardy's poem of Christmas," Oppen writes, "We might half-hope to find the animals / In the sheds of a nation / Kneeling at midnight" (*NCP* 174). The metaphorical resonance of these "Draft animals, beasts for slaughter" during the Vietnam War is clear enough without knowledge of "Hardy's poem of Christmas," "The Oxen." It is telling that Oppen refers to a "poem of Christmas" in the aftermath of President Johnson's "peace offensive." The fact that Oppen invokes a poem that was written during World War I, though, makes it an especially significant intertext for "Of Being Numerous." World War I, which Oppen could remember from his childhood, was not only the war between imperialist states that foreshadowed the global conflicts that shaped his life, it was also the war that would redefine the United States as a world power. The World War I years were also the years of Oppen's childhood. "Of Being Numerous" situates its story of "half-hope" not in a specific national site of redemption, however, whether the British site of Hardy's poem or the American site of Oppen's childhood, but in "the sheds of a nation." The generic "nation" where the sheds are located represents the *problem* of nationalism more than the presumably protective shelter of a national identity: the "draft animals" in the sheds, after all, are "beasts for slaughter."

World War I was also the war that established the masculine authority of the modern soldier poet. The testimony of the combatant decrying the horrors of modern trench warfare has resonated beyond World War I: the tropes of British writers such as Wilfred Owen, Siegfried Sassoon, and Robert Graves persisted into World War II and Vietnam War soldier poetry by American writers as well. It is interesting, then, that Oppen recalls a World War I poem as far removed from this site of authority as "The Oxen," which is domestic in its setting and is narrated by an elderly man. "The Oxen" contrasts the distant but compelling memory of the speaker's naïve childhood belief in the "folk" story of the oxen, kneeling on Christmas Eve, with the more skeptical era of his adulthood. "So fair a fancy few would weave / In these years," Hardy writes (*Complete Poetical Works* 206), professing his desire to believe in such "fancy" again. "These years" represent the speaker's old age, and they represent modernity, but they also represent the more immediate, and more ominous, presence of the war that informs the speaker's longing to return to his childhood.[11] While Oppen's allusion to "The Oxen" appeals less to memory than to the present crisis of conscience evoked by "Of Being Numerous," a crisis of conscience that is at once personal and national, Hardy's poem invokes the memory of childhood, and the collective memory of folk wisdom, as a momentary antidote to despair. However fleeting the antidote of memory is in "The Oxen," and however tenuous Oppen's renewal of this antidote is, the allusion to Hardy's poem reaffirms the social power of language to alleviate the pain of "Failure and the guilt / Of failure" (*NCP* 174), to transform experience that is individually felt into a shared perception of this experience. This shared perception is notably *not* defined in opposition to a national other, but it *is* defined in opposition to the "draft animals" themselves. The stark existential statement "that we do not altogether matter" (*NCP* 175) that concludes section 20 intimates how profound the need is for such conciliatory tales "as in Hardy's poem of Christmas."

Sections 18–20 represent the most direct response to the Vietnam War in "Of Being Numerous." Their dramatic significance suggests how important the war is to the entire poem as well. While section 20 confirms Oppen's resolve to "live thru" the Vietnam War rather than "throw oneself away in horror," it also anticipates the return to the idea, and ideology, of the American nation in section 24, where the poem arrives at a resolution that contests the idea of an exclusive national identity. Section 24 returns to the problem of exceptionalism that links the Puritan heritage of the United States to the "air of atrocity" that represents American imperial power in Vietnam. In response to "this nation / Which is in some sense / Our home. Covenant!" the poem proposes an alternative "covenant." This secular lower-case "covenant"—"There shall be peoples"—revises the language of the poem as well as of American national identity (*NCP* 176). In adopting a language of social pluralism, of "peoples" rather than "the people" or "the People," "Of Being Numerous" resolves, however provisionally, the opposition of the poet to the social totality, opening the poem to a less determinate, more permeable "language of New York," a language that suits the city's vibrant social flux. It also undermines not only an exclusionary construct of nationality but the primacy of nationality altogether.

The Vietnam War sections in "Of Being Numerous" furthermore exemplify the poem's resistance to the exclusively masculine authority of the soldier's testimony in representing war. Sections 18–20 not only problematize the gendered distinctions between war front and home front, between the public and the domestic, they foreshadow the poem's increasing attention to intimate relations between men and women. The nostalgic memory of wartime male camaraderie that occurs in section 14, "those men / With whom I stood in emplacements, in mess tents, / In hospitals and sheds" (*NCP* 171), is gradually supplanted by the dialogue of husband and wife, of father and daughter, of brother and sister, and of male and female writers. While this dialogue converges with the discourse of war only obliquely, "Of Being Numerous" concludes with a wartime scene that blurs conventionally male and female subject positions. The poem concludes with three sections that evoke the experience and vision of nurses. The figure of the nurse is perhaps *the* most conventional representation of feminine valor, with its implied ethic of self-sacrifice and unconditional care for those in need. The anonymous encounter between a nurse and a dying old man in sections 38–39, then, seems to contradict the poem's disavowal of restrictive gendered social roles and expectations. The work of nurses is so readily understood as women's work that it is easy to overlook the fact that Oppen does not identify the nurse in the poem by any indication of gender. While the patient is "a very old man," the nurse is identified only as "Nurse."

So what do these questions about the nurse-patient relationship have to do with the last section of the poem, which is comprised of a prose quotation identified in a headnote by "Whitman: April 19, 1864"? Although the addressee of this quotation is not identified, it is taken from a letter Walt Whitman wrote to his mother, Louisa Van Velsor Whitman, during the Civil War. His letter returns us to the public sphere of national politics, as he describes the "great bronze figure, the Genius of Liberty" atop the Capitol in Washington. He notes especially that when the sun is setting it "shines on the headpiece and it dazzles and glistens like a big star: it looks quite // curious" (*NCP* 188). The fact that this understated colloquial description of "the Genius of Liberty" (the "Statue of Freedom") was composed on Patriot's Day, during the most brutal period of the Civil War, is as ironic as it is "curious." The quotation of Whitman's letter situates "Of Being Numerous" within a national historical framework that is implied more than it is stated throughout the poem. The social upheaval of the Vietnam War era is superimposed not only onto Oppen's memory of war and revolutionary struggle but also onto the Civil War and Revolutionary War dates of Whitman's letter. Like the earlier allusion to Hardy, Whitman's letter reminds us that "Of Being Numerous" is very much a war poem.

Whitman's letter is of course also the testimony of a nurse, as he writes from his Washington position of attending to the wounded and dying Union soldiers in military hospitals. Whitman, as his letters to his family reveal, was intensely affected by not only the physical suffering he witnessed but by the deep emotional attachment and painful separation he experienced in ministering to the soldiers. A week after the letter that Oppen quotes he wrote: "Mother, it is serious times—I do not feel to fret or whimper, but in my heart & soul about our country, the army, the forthcoming campaign with all its vicissitudes & the wounded & slain—I dare say, Mother, I feel the reality more than some because I [am] in the midst of its saddest results so much" (Whitman Letter to Louisa Van Velsor Whitman, April 26, 1864, *Correspondence* 213). He was so affected that he himself became seriously ill, as a result of the psychological strain he had experienced as well as exposure to disease, only a month after the letter that Oppen quotes. To recover from his illness he returned to his family home in Brooklyn, not far from Oppen's home during the writing of "Of Being Numerous," where he completed his volume of Civil War poems, *Drum Taps.*

The excerpt from Whitman's letter that Oppen quotes represents a moment of relief from the unbearable burden of war, a moment of calm in a period of intense national and personal trauma. While the excerpt foregrounds Whitman's attention to the "curious" image of the "Genius of Liberty" at sundown, the Civil War is no more a "backdrop" to this passage than the Vietnam War is to "Of Being Numerous." It is the chaos of violent conflict that makes the process of observation a meaningful act of affirmation, an act of resistance to the nihilism of war. Oppen has stated that the "curious" end of his long poem is partly "a joke on Whitman," but that it also signifies "an awareness of the world, a lyric reaction to the world" (Dembo interview 177). This "lyric reaction" is inherently intersubjective— and intertextual—as the epistolary form and Oppen's quotation of Whitman's words underscore. Oppen later wrote in a letter about the quotation that the word "curious" also contains the root "*curia*: care, concern" (*SL* 402–403 n. 6). The implicit figure of the (male) poet as nurse, the figure of "care" and "concern," links the Whitman quotation to the poems that immediately precede it. As incongruous as Whitman's observation of "the Genius of Liberty" appears, though, Oppen's appropriation of his language also responds to contemporaneous invocations of Whitman during the Vietnam War. The exhausted wartime figure of the older poet, immersed in the trauma of damaged lives, is hardly the brashly masculine figure of "Song of Myself." It is far removed from the youthfully optimistic poet whose expansive vision of American democracy was so frequently— and sometimes facilely—invoked by successors who lamented the betrayal of this vision during the Vietnam War. The figure of Whitman that concludes "Of Being Numerous" is instead both curiously touching and curiously absurd. In defamiliarizing the iconic poet of the American "people," Oppen suggests an affinity with the poet transformed by the trauma of war. At the same time he suggests the need to question the cultural mythologies by which war is justified, by which "the air of atrocity" becomes "ordinary." This "curious" critique of American nationalist ideology not only makes "Of Being Numerous" an extra-ordinary poem of the Vietnam era, but also a poem that resonates with renewed significance in the twenty-first century.

Notes

1. *New Collected Poems* 173.

2. Hatlen, Hooker, and McAleavey concentrate most intensively on the poem's engagement with the Vietnam War, but Oppen's readers have not related "Of Being Numerous" to other 1960s antiwar poetry. DuPlessis's notes to Oppen's *Selected Letters* provide the most substantial evidence for the war's impact on his composition of "Of Being Numerous." Oppen himself saw the Pulitzer Prize as an opportunity to take a more prominent public stance against U.S. military policy. After winning the prize, he received a certificate of honor from the Board of Supervisors of the City of San Francisco. In response to this he wrote in a November 2, 1969, letter of acknowledgment that he also sent to the *San Francisco Examiner* and the *San Francisco Chronicle*:

> I thank you for the honor which you have given me, though I receive it at a time when honors may mean little and that little for a very short time. In this year which may present our last opportunity to withdraw from war I urge you to speak for the most crucial interests of the people in this city in asking that our young men be brought home out of Asia, out of Africa, out of Latin America, and that we may lead our lives as a sane people. (*SL* 204)

3. See my chapter on Oppen in *History, Memory, and the Literary Left* (192–229) for a more extensive consideration of Oppen's complicated relation to the 1930s Left.

4. The letter to Diane Meyer is included in *Selected Letters*, 114. In quoting Oppen's letters and his working papers from the Archive for New Poetry, I follow the editorial principles that DuPlessis delineates in *Selected Letters*, xxv–xxvii.

5. Oppen himself said in his 1968 interview with Dembo: "Pound's ego system, Pound's organization of the world around a character, a kind of masculine energy, is extremely foreign to me" (183). In addition to DuPlessis, "Objectivist Poetics and Political Vision," and Nicholls, see Davidson, *Ghostlier Demarcations*

64–93, and Alan Golding, "George Oppen's Serial Poems," on the political and ethical implications of Oppen's serial form.

6. See Davidson, notes for *New Collected Poems* 380, on the importance of quotation in "Of Being Numerous." Oppen dedicated *Of Being Numerous* and his *Collected Poems* to Mary, stating that her "words . . . are entangled / inextricably among my own."

7. See Subarno Chattarji, *Memories of a Lost War* 40–43, on these major factors that informed antiwar poetry in the United States. In addition to Chattarji, whose book is the most thorough and incisive study of Vietnam War poetry by American writers, see the studies of Vietnam-era protest poetry by Michael Bibby, *Hearts and Minds;* James F. Mersmann, *Out of the Vietnam Vortex;* and Cary Nelson, *Our Last First Poets,* 1–30.

8. For detailed histories of the antiwar movement, see Charles DeBenedetti and Charles Chatfield, *An American Ordeal;* Tom Wells, *The War Within;* and Nancy Zarouli and Gerald Sullivan, *Who Spoke Up?*

9. DuPlessis cites Oppen's involvement in a Washington, D.C., antiwar demonstration in early 1966 (*SL* 126), and Linda Oppen (in an email correspondence with me) has confirmed her father's attendance at demonstrations in Washington and New York. Neither DuPlessis nor Linda Oppen recalls the specific demonstrations that Oppen attended, however. The most specific reference to a demonstration in the *Selected Letters* is from the January (or early February) 1966 letter to June Oppen Degnan. Commenting on the Fulbright hearings, he notes, "A number of people taking care to declare themselves unassuaged by the Johnsonian peace offensive—A veteran's demonstration on Washington, which I'll go to" (*SL* 130). Oppen may be referring to the February 5, 1966, demonstration in which hundreds of veterans marched to the White House to protest the war, with many turning in their war medals and discharge papers. See Andrew E. Hunt, *The Turning,* 6–11, on 1965–66 antiwar activism by U.S. veterans' organizations.

10. As Perloff has written, the poem evokes the modernist topos of the "exile's return." While I disagree with her reading of the poem's trajectory as a withdrawal from human contact, her emphasis on the exiled poet's alienation from the city represents an important corrective to more optimistic claims about the poem's "populist" vision.

11. "The Oxen" exemplifies the theory of memory that informed Hardy's later poetry, the theory of the "exhumed emotion," which he discusses in *Life and Work* 408. His concept of "exhumed emotion" resembles such contemporaneous psychological theories as Proust's theory of involuntary memory or Freud's theory of the uncanny. What makes his World War I poems so resonant, though, is the correspondence of intensely felt personal memory with the apocalyptic public event of war. Like Oppen, Hardy's response to the absurdity of war is informed by a vision of recurrent patterns of destruction that is based on a long lifetime of experience.

Works Cited

Bibby, Michael. *Hearts and Minds: Bodies, Poetry, and Resistance in the Vietnam Era.* New Brunswick, NJ: Rutgers University Press, 1996.

Chattarji, Subarno. *Memories of a Lost War: American Poetic Responses to the Vietnam War.* Oxford: Oxford University Press, 2001.

Davidson, Michael. *Ghostlier Demarcations: Modern Poetry and the Material Word.* Berkeley and Los Angeles: University of California Press, 1997.

———. Introduction. *New Collected Poems.* By George Oppen. New York: New Directions, 2002.

DeBenedetti, Charles, and Charles Chatfield. *An American Ordeal: The Antiwar Movement of the Vietnam Era.* Syracuse, NY: Syracuse University Press, 1990.

DuPlessis, Rachel Blau. "Objectivist Poetics and Political Vision: A Study of Oppen and Pound." Hatlen, *George Oppen* 13–48.

———, and Peter Quartermain, eds. *The Objectivist Nexus: Essays in Cultural Poetics.* Tuscaloosa: The University of Alabama Press, 1999.

Golding, Alan. "George Oppen's Serial Poems." DuPlessis and Quartermain 84–103.

Hardy, Thomas. *Complete Poetical Works.* Ed. Samuel Hynes. New York: Oxford University Press, 1982.

———. *The Life and Work of Thomas Hardy.* Ed. Michael Millgate. Athens: University of Georgia Press, 1985.

Hatlen, Burton. "Opening up the Text: George Oppen's 'Of Being Numerous.'" *Ironwood* 26 (1985): 263–294.

———, ed. *George Oppen: Man and Poet.* Orono, ME: National Poetry Foundation, 1981.

Hooker, Jeremy. "'The Boundaries of Our Distances': On 'Of Being Numerous.'" *Ironwood* 26 (1985): 81–103.

Hunt, Andrew E. *The Turning: A History of Vietnam Veterans against the War.* New York: New York University Press, 1999.

Lowney, John. *History, Memory, and the Literary Left: Modern American Poetry, 1935–1968.* Iowa City: University of Iowa Press, 2006.

McAleavey, David. "Clarity and Process: Oppen's *Of Being Numerous.*" Hatlen, *George Oppen* 381–404.

Mersmann, James F. *Out of the Vietnam Vortex: A Study of Poets and Poetry against the War.* Lawrence: University Press of Kansas, 1974.

Nelson, Cary. *Our Last First Poets: Vision and History in Contemporary American Poetry.* Chicago: University of Illinois Press, 1981.

Nicholls, Peter. "Of Being Ethical: Reflections on George Oppen." DuPlessis and Quartermain 240–253.

Oppen, George. "Discussion of *Another Language of New York.*" George Oppen

Papers. Mandeville Special Collections Library, University of California, San Diego.

———. Interview with L. S. Dembo [1968]. *The Contemporary Writer: Interviews with Sixteen Novelists and Poets.* Ed. L. S. Dembo and Cyrena N. Pondrom. Madison: University of Wisconsin Press, 1972.

———. *New Collected Poems.* Ed. Michael Davidson. New York: New Directions, 2002.

———. *Selected Letters.* Ed. Rachel Blau DuPlessis. Durham, NC: Duke University Press, 1990.

Perloff, Marjorie. "The Shipwreck of the Singular: George Oppen's 'Of Being Numerous.'" *Ironwood* 26 (1985): 193–204.

Wells, Tom. *The War Within: America's Battle over Vietnam.* Berkeley and Los Angeles: University of California Press, 1994.

Whitman, Walt. *The Collected Writings of Walt Whitman: The Correspondence,* Vol. I: 1842–1867. Ed. Edwin Haviland Miller. New York: New York University Press, 1961.

Wittgenstein, Ludwig. *Philosophical Investigations.* Trans. G. E. M. Anscombe. 1953. Oxford: Basil Blackwell, 1967.

Zarouli, Nancy, and Gerald Sullivan. *Who Spoke Up? American Protest against the War in Vietnam 1963–1975.* Garden City, NY: Doubleday, 1984.

v
Receptions

8
Third-Phase Objectivism

Ron Silliman

[*Editor's Note:* Since Silliman's essay is a reception history concerned with the publication dates of particular volumes of Oppen's work, I have retained his page references to the *Collected Poems*, rather than citing the more recent *New Collected Poems*, which is the standard reference point for the present volume.]

Objectivism's third or renaissance period was marked by the resurrection of the works of Zukofsky, Oppen, Basil Bunting, Carl Rakosi, Charles Reznikoff, and Lorine Niedecker to public attention virtually overnight in the early 1960s. This has proven the most problematic of that literary tendency's phases, simultaneously its most influential and least cohesive time, mixing a resurgence of interest in existing texts with the production of new writings. The definition of Objectivism was altered just as that curious rubric was, in turn, being used to rewrite the literary history of the thirties and forties.

Objectivism's absence, the long second phase of neglect, was attributable, at least in part, to the fact that these poets had not created a sufficient network of support—particularly lacking a magazine—before many of them turned their attention elsewhere during the years of the Depression and World War II—and, not coincidentally, because several were Marxists and Jews. Their long "silence" contributed significantly to the extremism of form and content that so many of the New American poets had found necessary to bridge the distance between themselves and those twin sources of a rigorous, open-form, speech-based poetics, Pound and Williams.

Not surprisingly, the return of the Objectivists was to coincide with a tempering and toning down of just this extremism, and the formation of not so much a neo-objectivist movement as a "middle road" halfway between the New Americans and those academics who'd moved on their own toward a poetry founded on speech, both in open form and syllabics. This middle road, which was first to reach the public through the *San Francisco Review*, the third series of *Origin*, *Poetry* during the last seven years of Henry Rago's editorship, and later through a series of tightly edited little magazines, including *Maps, Ironwood, Occurrence, Paper Air*, and *Montemora*, has substantially altered the contours of American verse, although it has received relatively little attention as a phenomenon in its own right.

That the revival period of the Objectivists would prove less cohesive could have been expected. Men and women in their sixties, their aesthetics and work fully formed (and, in some instances, largely behind them), have fewer needs for peer group response than do writers in their twenties. Nor, unlike first-phase Objectivism, did they now have to rely on one another for publication and the other support services that normally characterize any collective literary activity.

The actual products of Objectivism's final period are not many, but they are significant: Bunting's addition of *Briggflats* to an essentially completed oeuvre; Zukofsky's return for only the second time in twenty years (there had been a period of work between 1948 and 1951) to the poem "*A*," composing eleven new sections and adding his wife Celia's *L. Z. Masque* to finish the project; Rakosi's return as a writer of short, witty, lyrical poems; and 95 percent of the works of George Oppen.

It is this last fact, the "return" of Oppen from decades of silence to a place beyond that which he had taken during the earlier periods, that fundamentally defines third-phase Objectivism, transforming it from the aesthetically radical and oppositional poetry of the early thirties to a more conservative (aesthetically, if not politically) phenomenon that then served as the foundation for the ensuing middle road. This transformation is registered most clearly in the *Chicago Review* feature on Objectivism, which is incoherent from the perspective of the first phase, but consistent with this much later version.

There is more to this evolution than the mere addition of new poems gaining one writer greater weight within a collective whole. Oppen's works, from *The Materials* onward, are decisively different than *Discrete Series,* his first-phase volume. This shift is precisely one of stance, and it may well be that a quarter century of struggle, with the constraints of daily life, marriage, parenting, with war and exile, with capitalism and its Frankenstein, fascism, render the later position inevitable. However, it is not difficult to demonstrate that it falls outside the original, loosely held program of phase-one Objectivism. It is only necessary to contrast the later work with a piece such as the review of *Discrete Series* written by Williams for *Poetry* under the title of "The New Poetical Economy," which reads in part:

> The appearance of a book of poems, if it be a book of good poems, is an important event because of relationships the work it contains will have with thought and accomplishment in other contemporary reaches of the intelligence. This leads to a definition of the term "good." If the poems in the book constitute necessary corrections of or emendations to human conduct in their day, both as to thought and manner, then they are good. But if these changes originated in the poems, causing thereby a direct liberation of the intelligence, then the book becomes of importance to the highest degree.
>
> But this importance cannot be in what the poem says, since in that case the fact that it is a poem would be a redundancy. The importance lies in what the poem is. Its existence as a poem is of first importance, a technical matter, as with all facts, compelling the recognition of a mechanical structure. A poem that does not arouse respect for the technical requirements of its own mechanics may have anything you please painted all over it or on it in the way of meaning but it will for all that be as empty as a man made of wax or straw.
>
> It is the acceptable fact of a poem as a mechanism that is the proof of its meaning, and this is as technical a matter as in the case of any other machine. Without the poem being a workable mechanism in its own right, a mechanism that arises from, while at the same time it constitutes the meaning of, the poem as a whole, it will remain ineffective. And what it says regarding the use or worth of that particular piece of "propaganda" that it is detailing will never be convincing.

Beginning with *The Materials,* Oppen, contrary to the admonitions of this highly partisan piece of writing, demonstrated himself to be a master in calling attention to the importance in what the poem says. This he achieved through a variety of devices. The sheer number of the techniques he employed make it evident that this new conceptualization of meaning was, in fact, a difference in position and not (as rigid adherence to the tenets of phase-one Objectivism might lead one to conclude) a decay in skills brought about by decades of disuse:

(1) a formal rhetorical tone, sometimes utilizing inversions of syntax or the parallel construction of examples, each punctuated with an *and,* implying sobriety of context;

(2) the use of adjectives which, value-laden, impart as much of judgment as they do of description;

(3) the use of repetition, which in Oppen's work nearly always carries the tone away from that of speech, positing a supplement of emotion beyond the content of the repeated term itself;

(4) the use of spacing and silence to cast certain terms and phrases into a highly defined frame;

(5) the placement of key terms at critical locales on the line itself (no one in Oppen's generation was so sensitive to the fact that placement itself alters semantics, that the last word in a line carries the greatest weight, but that the first word carries the next most, so that any line beginning *and* & *of* carries a formality beyond that of the words themselves); and

(6) the use of plurals or mass nouns, rather than particulars or individuals, as objects for description and discussion.

Several of these mechanisms can be observed together in the two-stanza fourth section of the sequence "Tourist Eye":

The heart pounds
To be among them, the buildings,
The red buildings of Red Hook! In the currents of the harbor
The barn-red ferries on their curving courses
And the tides of Buttermilk Channel
Flow past the Brooklyn Hardware stores

And the homes
The aging homes

Of the workmen. This is a sense of order
And of threat. The essential city,
The necessary city
Among these harbor streets still visible.[1]
(*Collected Poems [CP]* 43)

They are even more visible in the later poem "Exodus":

Miracle of the children   the brilliant
Children   the word
Liquid as woodlands   Children?

When she was a child I read Exodus
To my daughter   "the children of Israel . . ."

Pillar of fire
Pillar of cloud

We stared at the end
Into each other's eyes   Where
She said hushed

Were the adults   We dreamed to each other
Miracle of the children

The brilliant children   Miracle

Of their brilliance   Miracle
of [2]
(*CP* 229)

Note that final lowercase o.

It is not as if no other Objectivist poet employed such techniques, even to the same ends. Consider *"A"-10*, for example. Yet none went so far as to make them the grounds for an entire poetics, which Oppen did. One can imagine that the response of the partisan Williams of the thirties to this stance would not be positive. "Who," for instance, is the first of the two voices in the 38th section of *Of Being Numerous*, a character created wholly out of the placement of the word *last*, the rhetorical closure of the statements via the repeated terms *You* and *Nurse*, and the increased formality gained by the final use of the word *him* in the third stanza?

You are the last
Who will know him
Nurse.

Not know him,
He is an old man,
A patient,
How could one know him?

You are the last
Who will see him
Or touch him,
Nurse.
(*CP* 178)

But one must remember that Williams was a partisan to a particular cause, that there was the academic tradition in American poetry that was then much more prevalent and substantial, in terms of publications and critical support (and jobs) than anything he, Pound, and these young followers had going for them. There was, in short, a battle being waged which had largely been settled, if not forgotten, by the time *The Materials* appeared, a year before Williams's death. (This should not be confused with the one then being conducted by the New American poets, although this latter confrontation was, in a sense, a direct historic descendant, and the momentary success of their revolt provided the context in which the Objectivists as a whole reemerged.) The problem that confronted George Oppen in the early 1960s was not one of either/or, but rather the possibility of demonstrating to that alternate, conservative tendency in poetry how it might be done better by other principles, specifically Objectivist in origin.

So it is not surprising that Oppen should be the bridge-poet between the tendency known as the New American poetry and those of the middle ground, an accomplishment of third-phase Objectivism that helped to restructure the entire field of American verse.

Notes

1. The poem was originally collected in *The Materials,* published in 1962.
2. The poem was written around 1972.

Works Cited

Black Mountain and Since: Objectivist Writing in America. Chicago Review Special
Issue 30, 3 (Winter 1979).

Oppen, George. *Collected Poems.* New York: New Directions, 1975.

———. *The Materials.* New York: New Directions, 1962.

Williams, William Carlos. "The New Poetical Economy." *Poetry* 44, 4 (July 1934).
220–221.

9
George Oppen and the Anthologies

John Taggart

[*Editor's Note:* This essay first appeared in 1985, in no. 26 of Michael Cuddihy's poetry journal, *Ironwood.* As I discuss in my introduction to the current volume, it is, thankfully, no longer the case that Oppen's poetry is entirely absent from what Taggart labels the "anthologies of influence." Nonetheless, Taggart's meditation on Oppen's "difficulty" remains relevant, and his discussion of Oppen's exclusion from the anthologies marks an important moment in the reception history of Oppen's poetry. For the sake of consistency, page references for the *New Collected Poems* have been provided when Taggart cites Oppen's poetry.]

Having recently returned to George Oppen's *Collected Poems* and having been moved once again by them, I find myself confronted by a question I had not anticipated and for which there may be no ready answer. The question is: why aren't the poems better represented in the anthologies most often used by college classes and carried by most bookstores, the anthologies that for whatever reason have managed to stay in print? A quick check of current editions of *Contemporary American Poetry*, edited by A. Poulin; *the Norton Anthology of Poetry* (both the committee-edited volume and the specifically *Modern Poetry*, edited by Richard Ellmann and Robert O'Clair); *The New Pocket Anthology of American Verse*, edited by Oscar Williams and Hyman Sobiloff; and *The Voice That Is Great Within Us: American Poetry of the Twentieth Century*, edited by Hayden Carruth, turns up no representation at all. There is not a single Oppen poem in any of them. It is as though the poems never existed. While I have talked with Carruth, who simply stated that when he put his together he was familiar only with the early books and that he hadn't derived much pleasure from them, I have no acquaintance with the other editors nor with their selection procedures. What follows, then, is something of a speculation.

I wish to base my speculation on "Ballad" (*New Collected Poems [NCP]* 207–208) a poem from *Of Being Numerous*. The poem's physical dimensions are appropriate for anthology format; it comes from an acclaimed volume (Pulitzer Prize, 1969). Further, its title refers to a recognizable verse form, something that suggests the possibility of ongoing tradition and thus of historical comparison, possibilities an anthology might be thought to encourage. If these external reasons would seem to qualify the poem for inclusion in an anthology, then it follows that we must look at "content" as a rationale for its exclusion.

The poem begins: "Astrolabes and lexicons / Once in the great houses—" (*NCP* 207). These are instruments of measure for the natural world and for language. The nature of each and, together, their relation concerns every poet. Every poem represents a decision made about the two and their relation. The beginning lines might seem nostalgic. They imply that in the unspecified past, unspecified except for not being the present, these instruments may have been common enough property, if limited to the dwellers of the great houses. They also imply that neither that past nor its instruments are available in the present. The question that hinges on this further implication is how one is to live in a time when the great houses are at best relics or uninhabited museums.

The unsurprising and inescapable answer is that people must devise instruments as they can. They must either locate past examples or improvise their own from whatever comes to hand. There is always the risk that past examples will not function in a new present, that the improvisations will somehow not be adequate. The poet is hardly exempt from this risk. Hence the dash at the end of the second line is not incidental. I read it as a lingering punctuation, a lingering over something that might be considered remarkable in history, when once the instruments were available and functional, the equivalent for which must be come upon in what we feel to be the very different conditions of the present. My inclination is to regard the lingering not as nostalgic but as hesitant, a hesitancy in recognition of the difficulty or even impossibility of the task.

These beginning lines are put in a kind of suspension from the rest of the poem by the dash, as well as by their distinct vocabulary and self-contained syntax, so that they become an epigraph or headnote for it. The poem then proceeds as a narrative of the poet and his wife meeting "by chance" a poor lobsterman on Swan's Island, where he was born, and of being driven over the island in an old car by him. There is comment in passing on the lobsterman: "A well-spoken man / Hardly real / As he knew in those rough fields" (*NCP* 207). Attention is given to things of the island, lobster pots and their gear, and then comes something unexpected, breaking up the inventory.

> The rocks outlived the classicists,
> The rocks and the lobstermen's huts
> And the sights of the island
> The ledges in the rough sea seen from the road
> (*NCP* 207–208)

What's unexpected is the word "classicists." Its association with books and study, above all with "culture," remind us of the beginning epigraph lines. Whether they are the owners or not, Jeffersonian aristocrats, the classicists are the likely occupants of the libraries of the great houses. Or if not the occupants, then the contributors to the libraries, the recorders through their books of what has been found admirable and significant in human history.

The great houses at least aspire to contain, if not actively demonstrate, those "records" which can, cumulatively, be considered as an index of what human thought is capable of. This enlargement is justified by the double sense of great houses as admirable, costly structures (as described in "Guest Room" from *This in Which*) and as, say, the house of Atreus, a noble family whose actions are "great" in their effect upon others. The classicists are charged with keeping the memory alive in us of that capability which, per the instruments, is one fundamentally of measure. As these instruments and the great houses, structures and families, are not now readily found, so the items of the natural world, the rocks of the island, have outlived the recorders of admirable human thought. The natural world is triumphant, a dominant ongoing present in comparison with the ever-receding past of the classicists. The lobstermen's huts are not great houses, and the lobsterman himself is hardly real in the present of the rough fields.

One is reminded of the following from no. 26 of the collection's title poem:

> The power of the mind, the
> Power and weight
> Of the mind which
> Is not enough, it is nothing
>
> Against the natural world,
> Behemoth, while whale, beast
> They will say and less than beast,
> The fatal rock
>
> Which is the world—
> (*NCP* 179)

The figure comes from Melville, but the thought differs from his Ishmaelean notion of survival in a treacherous white world, a survival made possible by the deliberate creation of a fictional space through language. The difference is one of degree. In Melville the deliberate fiction of fiction is called to attention—the contradictory placement of "the Town-Ho's Story" in the middle of *Moby Dick,* the contradictory hinting of the narrator in *Pierre,* the contradictory evidence produced at the end in "Benito Cereno" and *Billy Budd*—if indirectly and for more crucial reasons than its recent glib emphasis (metafiction) whereby it becomes merely another technique to be studied by creative writing classes.

In Oppen there is an attempt to use language without subversion of statement and to know the world even as the persistent and perhaps irrevocable difficulties of either are readily acknowledged. Rather than set up structures only to collapse them by internal contradiction or ironic subversion, Oppen builds what might be called tentative structures that remain tentative. His poems betray no confidence in a final outcome, but the voice that emerges from them has a tone that suggests, however intransigent the difficulties, one might still attempt to use language "constructively" and to come to knowledge (measure) of the world.

Yet there is little interest in fiction making per se, if only because the results are unsatisfactory even when "successful." Why concern yourself with fictions when measure obtains only problematically at best? Thus the dissatisfaction, in "Solution" from *The Materials,* with the puzzle, a polychrome "fiction" which completely covers the table without a gap or hold. "The puzzle is complete / Now in its red and green and brown" (*NCP* 45). Even given completion according to its logic of artifice, the puzzle fails to satisfy because it is so patently a reductive covering of the world. There are more than three colors; there are sordid cellars and bare foundations. In Oppen there is still the attempt to use language, to measure the world, even as there is the awareness that the "fatal rock" has been and will continue to be the abiding present and presence of our lives. Far better than Ozymandias, the world mocks every completed puzzle. A shared element in the vision of both Melville and Oppen is this final fatality of the natural world. In view of this final fatality, the term that Oppen supplies in equation with "the human condition" is "precariousness." That the island's rocks have outlived the classicists is but one more instance of the world's fatal power, a power that, in motion, is most often manifested by the sea in Oppen's poetry. The rocks' longevity is the passive equivalent of the sea's terrific and measureless motion. Lived out in the motile presence of this power, our lives can only be precarious.

It is at this point that another hesitation occurs in the poem. For, after moving from the rocks to the sights of the island, Oppen also mentions the island's harbor and post office. These are products of human effort, not belonging to the set of the "outliving" natural world. The harbor may lose its defining contour, the post office face, and eventually fall. The hesitation is registered immediately thereafter: "Difficult to know what one means / —to be serious and know what one means—" (*NCP* 208). The simply exterior is not automatically superior, outliving. One's eye may move easily enough among the sights of the island as among a group of fundamentally like objects, but the mind, finally powerless as it may be, knows that the harbor and post office, while definitely enough there, may well not be there as the rocks and the ledges will continue to be.

The order of the poem suggests that this difficulty, suddenly come upon, is something of a surprise. The mind, not simply the coordinator of the eyes' information, apparently does do something. Perhaps more is involved than a temporary unsuspected contradiction of the poet's assumptions. The problem is how to indicate this something. For the moment I think it can be considered a question of integration and not a fundamental contradiction. That is, the rocks still outlive the classicists. The question is just what sort of life does the mind have? What value, within the larger life of the natural world?

It's put somewhat differently in no. 36 from "Of Being Numerous."

Tho the world
Is the obvious, the seen
And unforeseeable,
That which one cannot
Not see

Which the first eyes
Saw—

For us
Also each
Man or woman
Near is
Knowledge
(*NCP* 185)

There is the possibility of human knowledge; we can learn from each other, but what we learn occurs in a larger context, which, because it is to be seen equally by all and because, relative to our lifetime, it endures beyond us, is superior to the knowledge we would try to gain and to accumulate. We can visit other islands and we can learn from our visits, but what we learn must remain provisional against the outliving constancy of the larger context. What defines the islands is the sea. (Cf. "*The sea that made us / islands*" from "Coastal Strip," *NCP* 73, in *The Materials*.) The world is not to be defined by islandness, but by the surrounding constant sea. The sea is the world revealed in its motive power. The precariousness of our condition results from our having to live with the sea. It is precarious because of the power of the sea and because of its sheer largeness. The world, finally, cannot be seen as held, bracketed by our understanding.

The poem hesitates, but no outright answer to the almost accidentally come-upon dilemma is offered. This is one of the distinguishing features of George Oppen's poetry. It could be called phenomenological. Yet its combination of reportage and active, unrehearsed meditation on that reportage keeps it from being confused with Husserlian projects or for that matter with the flat ironic tone assumed by much postmodernist writing. Perhaps it is this bare combination of reportage and active thought in process, as opposed to the rhetorical finish of most verse, the "commonwealth of parlance," that accounts for Oppen's nonexistence in the anthologies.

In a sense, this is understandable. The typical anthology piece has to stand on its own, self-reflective, not need a reading context beyond what can fit in a footnote or two at the bottom of the page. The poem radiates process at every point, often in a jagged hesitating manner, and frustrates expectations fed on "finished" verse. Such a poem necessarily reminds the reader that the anthology piece, by itself, may not be enough, that much more reading may be required, that there are compositions that will not fit neatly on a page or two, and that, even if their lines will fit, their thoughts won't. Whether an anthology editor would be happy to include work that by its nature throws into question the presumed utility of this form of publication is to be doubted. Whether a flower of process will be included in the garland of finished blossoms is to be doubted. Expressed critically, Oppen's poetry is a continual, if quiet, opposition to the whole conception of rhetorical completion characterized by the closed field of New Criticism, which, despite the ferment of deconstruction, remains the pervasive attitude—expectation and methodology—of our time.

As complication, this opposition is very quiet. It makes no flourish of challenge (an aspect of ceremony and a recognition of the governing attitude, New Critical or not). In fact, it is an opposition that often comes in the guise of the most old-fashioned of nineteenth-century conventions, the capital letter at the beginning of each line, and of our own century, the phonetic spelling of certain words.

The poem hesitates but moves on. What follows appears, atomistically, to have almost nothing to do with what comes before or after: "An island / Has a public quality" (*NCP* 208). My first inclination was to skip over these lines, something their very flatness encourages. On rereading, the key term seems to be "public." By it I think Oppen intends what is exterior and available for inspection by all. This shifts attention away from a time-centered categorization by which, because they are both older and more enduring, the rocks are felt to be superior to the mortal classicists. Those physical things, harbor and post office, that have some connection with the human are somewhat superior to the rocks (the world). This, however, occurs more as a comment in passing, as an aside, rather than as a conclusive answer. It is kept within the meditative movement of the poem, the tentative voice in the poem.

The poem moves on. The wife of the lobsterman, wearing a soft dress "such as poor women wear," rides along with them. She tells the Oppens two things. One is that they (the visitors) must have come "from God"; the other is that more than anything else she likes to visit other islands. Oppen doesn't comment upon her statements, and it is up to us to make what we can of them. In a sense, if only because the poet has chosen to quote them, they can be regarded as parts of his own discourse. I wish to concentrate on the second of the two.

Why should anyone want to visit other islands? The desire, first of all, implies that at some time one has or presently lives on an island of one's own. Islandness, per the "Coastal Strip" poem, is part of the precarious human condition. There is a paradox involved. One visits other islands to relieve the isolation of one's own. Yet visiting them can only promote a heightened feeling, "pluralized," of isolation. To use Oppen's word, perhaps more knowledge of the "public" is gained, but the knowledge is much the same in each case. That is, in the flat, broken phrase of a poem from *Myth of the Blaze*, "knowledge is / loneliness" ("The Lighthouses," *NCP* 256). The rocks outlive the classicists. The world will outlast us, will outlast the instruments we construct in an effort to come to an understanding of the world. The argument isn't with the mind's existence (or, as in philosophy, with the existence of other minds) nor even with the values, supposedly inscribed by the "classics," associated with it. There is no argument. As the flatness of Oppen's diction suggests, this is simply and irremediably how it is.

There is a paradox involved in the visiting of the other islands. The apparent motivation is to alleviate one's feelings of isolation and to add to one's knowledge. What is encountered is just the opposite: the feeling of isolation increases, and the knowledge comes to be a knowledge of its own provisionality. This explains Oppen's frequent reference to "shipwreck." The reference appears as early as "From Disaster" (*NCP* 50, *The Materials*) and as late as "Two Romance Poems" (*NCP* 261, *Myth of the Blaze*). It is particularly concentrated in *Of Being Numerous*, where it occurs as the "bright light of shipwreck." Later, this is often abbreviated to "light," whereby it haunts the poetry with its paradoxical, positive and negative at once, associations. (Cf. "One has not thought / To be afraid / Not of shadow but of light" from "But So As By Fire," *NCP* 232, *Seascape: Needle's Eye*.)

Shipwreck results from collision with the world in its power. The abbreviation of the phrase to "light" indicates more a condition or effect than a literal event. If anything, this has to be a greater cause for fear than any event that, however catastrophic, can only happen once. There is light because of the understanding, inescapable, the collision forces upon the mind of the power of the world. The moment of the mind's understanding is the moment of collision. And once the moment has taken place (not that it is to be reduced to a single occurrence), it colors as a constant and complex condition every other moment of consciousness.

The paradox is that the light of understanding occurs precisely when the "darkness" of the fatal rock is encountered. (Cf. "It is the nature / Of the world: / It is as dark as radar" from "A Narrative," *NCP* 154, *This in Which*.) In terms of isolation and knowledge, the visiting of other islands is an instance of shipwreck. The visiting increases the feeling of isolation.

> The absolute singular
> The unearthly bonds
> Of the singular
> Which is the bright light of shipwreck.
> (no. 9 from "Of Being Numerous," *NCP* 167)

While there can be knowledge gained from other persons as islands, it compels the mind, if not exactly to an increasement, to acknowledge its finite and provisional nature. It is the "virtue of the mind" to cause "to see" ("Guest Room," *NCP* 107), and what is seen is the power of the world against which human life is a precarious balancing that will eventually come to shipwreck. The idea of the numerous as a saving response to shipwreck is an illusion. Multiplication, the people for the singular person, doesn't alter our experience in the world. If anything, the idea, as in the form of cities, disguises and compounds the wreckage. (Cf. "over the city / Is the bright light of shipwreck," from no. 19 "Of Being Numerous," *NCP* 173) Thus there is a brooding apocalyptic harmonic in the "constructive" voice of this poetry.

I had thought the ideal would be to live "responsively" with the world, to recognize its fatal nature and, like Ishmael, to float on the margin of what was disaster for others. Now I doubt if the vision of George Oppen's poetry allows for any such ideal or "right" behavior. However carefully one lives, however skillful in precarious balancing, *there will be shipwreck* if there is any consciousness at all.

The poem ends quietly with the statements of the lobsterman's wife. The second of the two, about liking to visit other islands more than anything else, is not enclosed by quotation marks and ends the poem with an ellipsis. The lack of enclosure is a gentle appropriation so that the words become the poet's own. I take the ellipsis to indicate, not that the woman had more to say than is reported by the poet, but rather that there are implications beyond her speech, perhaps implications she can hardly know. (The opening lines of "A Kind of Garden" in *Of Being Numerous* may apply to her.) The appropriation is not plagiarism but an act of unassuming identification. Knowing full well what the woman is apparently unaware of—the inevitability of shipwreck with its increase of isolation and an increasing sense of knowledge as strictly provisional—the poet still chooses to be identified with those who, "innocent" or not, must undergo this inevitable, inevitably tragic experience, which is not limited to the last scene of the last act. Ishmael floats free on the margin of shipwreck, a spectator. Oppen, knowing the nature of the event and its cause, which is consciousness itself, chooses to join those caught up in the whirlpool. Surely, it is noble to do this.

Historically, Oppen's achievement is to have extended imagist-objectivist poetics to a vision. A poetics that emphasizes the visual and cadential image based on close attention to the particular is transformed into an encompassing vision by an awareness of its own limitations. The more and more scrupulous exercise of attention produces further isolation and knowledge that more and more knows itself to be provisional. It is these quietly encountered and acknowledged paradoxes—paradoxes that should not be confused with those of Donne, bright particular star of New Criticism, which depend for their puzzlelike brilliance on a ground of unquestioned orthodox belief—that, collectively, give Oppen's vision depth, complexity, and nobility. The last comes from his decision not to be superior to his vision of human experience in the world but to be part of it.

I have not chosen to base my speculation on "Ballad" because it is a personal favorite nor because I consider it to be an indispensable key to Oppen's poetry as a whole. The choice of the poem was somewhat arbitrarily based on the publicity surrounding the *Of Being Numerous* book and the fact that, "physically," the poem was not unlike those found in the *Norton* and other anthologies. But Oppen's poems are not to be found in these anthologies. It seems clear at this point that their nonexistence there has little to do with the author's public reputation or with their gross morphology.

What, then, are the other reasons? One could be Oppen's disregard for the conventions of punctuation or his penchant for conjoining lines without warning. Unlike e. e. cummings, the poems do not end up as vehicles for fairly conventional sentiments but with unconventional wrappings. Another could be his disregard for some poetic devices (rhyme, meter) while retaining certain conventions (capitals at the beginning of lines). This brings us back to the poem's title. In its versification appendix, the third-edition *Norton* defines the ballad stanza as consisting of four lines in which lines of iambic tetrameter alternate with those of iambic trimester, rhyming *a b c b* or *a b a b*. "Sir Patrick Spens," "The Rime of the Ancient Mariner," and Emily Dickinson's "I taste a liquor never brewed" are given as examples. Oppen's poem is not written in this stanzaic form, and it does not sound like any of the examples. According to the *Norton*, the poem can't be a ballad; and, by inference, its author is guilty of duplicity.

If the poem can't be a "regular" ballad, what kind can it be? It could be, like a Berrigan sonnet, an un- or antiversion of the form. Yet the poem doesn't deliberately mock the form, nor does it completely ignore at least some poetic conventions. If it is a ballad, then it must be one of "essence," concerned only with what is most essential to the form. And what is most essential to the ballad form is song. If we look to Zukofsky's *Test of Poetry*, where the consideration of song is demonstrated primarily by ballads in all three of its parts, we find song "as musical, poetic form" defined as "a continuous and complete statement of the words." This statement has to do with the meaning and sound of the words. If there is nothing more to be said, if a melody line (cadence) has taken on adequate definition, then there is song that, further, comes *from* the words. (Cf. "the cadence the verse / and the music essential" from "The Lighthouses," *NCP* 256, a poem dedicated by Oppen to Zukofsky, *Myth of the Blaze*.)

To this definition might be added the expectations of rendition. That is, the ballad belongs to folk tradition and is to be sung in an unstudied manner, something that probably wouldn't be performed as such in the great houses. The song of "Ballad" is the statement developed from its beginning two lines and presented as a "story" in the others. In its relative lack of punctuation it is literally continuous, and it is complete in terms of action (the visit to Swan's Island) and vision (the world, people in the world, their fate). As for rendition, the voice that emerges from the poem is conversational, even plain, ready to disturb the flow of its story with an admission of difficulty. To cite Zukofsky again, "simplicity of utterance and song go together."

All of this is consciously apprehended in "Song, the Winds of Downhill" from *Seascape: Needle's Eye*.

"out of poverty
to begin

again"   impoverished

of tone of pose that common
wealth

of parlance   Who
so poor the words

would   *with*   *and*   take on substantial

meaning   handholds   footholds

to dig in one's heels   sliding

hands and heels beyond the residential
lots   the plots   it is a poem

which may be sung
may well be sung
(*NCP* 220)

The poverty is an impoverishment not simply of accumulated literary tradition but also, specifically, of imagist-objectivist poetics. The poem represents, as does Oppen's poetry as a whole, a radical (if quiet) stripping away to reach the essential poem, the essential song.

Perhaps we arrive here at the root cause for the absence of his poetry from the anthologies. (It should be noted that it has appeared in several anthologies, some of which have had reasonably wide distribution, e.g., *The New Naked Poetry*, edited by Berg and Mezey; and *America a Prophecy*, edited by Rothenberg and Quasha. None of these, however, has had the sustained distribution—and the sustained influence—of those anthologies enumerated in my opening paragraph.) In an utterly quiet, utterly unassuming way, George Oppen has taken his imagist-objectivist inheritance and stripped it to the essentials to emerge with a distinguishable voice and with a "complete" vision. As an accomplishment, this bears comparison with that of his contemporary Zukofsky, who is represented in all the enumerated volumes with the exception of the Poulin, and with that of their common master, Pound, who has become a centerpiece of nearly all anthologies.

Zukofsky and Pound, in different but analogous ways, attempt to come to vision by expansion, proliferation of the image. Oppen, alone, consistently accomplishes what he would refer to as clarity by a stripping down that at the same time opens out and takes on depth. It takes time to read such poetry, and it takes time to comprehend an "ars povera" that is deliberate, conscious, and still "art," song. It is a requirement that Oppen himself is not unaware of: "one man could not understand me because I was saying / simple things; it seemed to him that nothing was being / said" (from "Route," *NCP* 197, *Of Being Numerous*). *Nothing is being said* unless there is understanding of the calculated impoverishment that has been undergone and unless the voice that nevertheless emerges from that impoverishment is heard in its quiet nobility. Whatever their selection procedures may be, the anthology editors have neither understood nor heard.

Let me come back to the time required by this poetry. It is a familiar chestnut that work of substance can be returned to without exhaustion. In the case of George Oppen's poetry, I would want to say it applies with a surprising accuracy. I have read it since the late 1960s, I have heard him read it, I have had conversation and correspondence with him about it. I have also done the sort of rereading that reviewing demands. Like the lyrics of Wyatt and Reznikoff running through his mind, Oppen's poetry runs through my own. Yet none of this reduces the requirement of time, the requirement of close attention to the particulars of his poetry, even its admitted difficulties, in order to hear the voice and perceive the vision.

Writing this, which may well repeat some of what I have written about his poetry in the past, has surprised me. For I thought I knew the work and find that I do not. For this reason, it has moved me even as I have to wonder at what further readings will reveal. This is written as an indication that the required time and attention are not to be resolved by research into sources and influences but by thinking itself, the unrelenting effort along the "thought-paths" of Heidegger's description. It is not written, however, to exonerate those who haven't made the effort, who haven't been willing to follow the "handholds" and footholds" to arrive at the substantial meaning and song of this poetry.

Again, I have no knowledge of the selection procedures. Yet, surprised and moved as I find myself, the conviction grows that the anthology editors have neither understood nor heard because they have not thought long or hard enough with the poetry of George Oppen. In his case they haven't been willing or able to stir beyond the customary lots and plots of past poetry. An anthology represents what is supposed to be worth keeping. My claim is that the poetry of George Oppen is eminently worth keeping because of its unique technical accomplishment and because of the vision—deep, complex, noble—made possible by that accomplishment. My hope is that the poetry of George Oppen will appear in the anthologies of influence before it is too late for its own influence to be felt in our time.

Works Cited

Melville, Herman. "Hawthorne and His Mosses." In *Hawthorne: The Critical Heritage*, ed. J. Donald Crowley. New York: Barnes and Noble, 1970.

———. *Moby-Dick; or, The Whale.* Berkeley and Los Angeles: University of California Press, 1981.

———. *Pierre; or, The Ambiguities.* Evanston, IL: Northwestern University Press and the Newberry Library, 1971.

Oppen, George. *The Collected Poems of George Oppen.* New York: New Directions, 1975.

———. *This in Which.* New York: New Directions, 1965.

Zukofsky, Louis. *A Test of Poetry.* Highlands, NC: Jargon/Corinth, 1964. Reprint. New York: C. Z. Publications, 1980.

10
Conviction's Net of Branches

Michael Heller

I

The poetry of George Oppen is one of our most sustained examinations of the characteristic themes of poetry (themes of love and of death, and of a sense of history), an attempt to determine if the very meaning of such words as "love" or "humanity" can be retained in the light of what we have come to know and of what we have become. Indeed, Oppen's work has been to show forth the meanings of these terms by exploring in the deepest sense our need to resort to them.

Oppen sees the poet involved in a task that is as much question and inquiry as it is an order of expression, a task that asks whether the moral, religious, and philosophical notions by which we live, and which have informed our common heritage, are any longer possibilities. His poetry arises from our own ambivalence toward what we know and have come to rely on, a poetry very much aware of the human effort to remain in predictive and utilitarian certainties (aware also of the religious attractiveness they engender). Yet the power of his poems is that they do deliver us by a process of skeptical homage into a world seen afresh, vivified by an emergence from inauthentic and outworn sentiment.

There are certain pressures and attitudes in what we might call the Western mind with which Oppen has been struggling throughout his career. There is that impulse which for better or worse is labeled "metaphysical," that taste

for bedrock
Beneath this spectacle
To gawk at . . .

And there is the contrary of that taste: the hardening of what is intellectually and emotionally grasped into conceptions, into a "Solution," as Oppen ironically entitled an earlier poem about a jigsaw puzzle "assembled at
last" which curiously apes our flawed science and technology:

The jigsaw of cracks
Crazes the landscape but there is no gap,
No actual edged hole
Nowhere the wooden texture of the table top
Glares out of scale in the picture,
Sordid as cellars, as bare foundations:
There is no piece missing. The puzzle is complete
Now in its red and green and brown.
(*New Collected Poems [NCP]* 45)

The irony here is that in addition to its freight of misused benefits and
dangling hopes, this solution too, by virtue of that metaphysical impulse,
begins to look like (to use a recurrent and important expression of Oppen's) "mechanics," and like mechanics ("remote mechanics," Oppen says
in one place), distanced from the human world. Thus, the poet feels that
ever-modern estrangement, where

Perhaps one is himself
Beyond the heart, the center of the thing
And cannot praise it
As he would want to . . .
(*NCP* 112–113)

In this, poet, thinker, contemporary man are co-joined in a time when,
as the critic Erich Heller has noted, "uncertainty along is ineluctably real."
Oppen is among our most profound and eloquent explorers of this
theme, profound because he comes without illusion into the act of writing
poetry, eloquent because the order of his craft cannot be separated from
the order of his perception. In *Seascape: Needle's Eye* he continues an interrogation of reality in language, which has always been at the very center of

his work, continues it, as Wittgenstein warned, against the bewitchment of language itself:

'out of poverty
to begin
again' impoverished
of tone of pose that common
wealth
of parlance
(*NCP* 220)

The word "poverty" provides a peculiarly modern test of articulation, a form of resolve against certain historical and elegiac associations of words or of the convenient knowingness of slang. (Kenner, in *The Pound Era*, speaking of the yet-to-be-written history of the Objectivists, among them Oppen, Williams, and Zukofsky, puts it this way: "In that machine [the poem] made out of words . . . [the word] is a term, not a focus for sentiment; simply a word, the exact and plausible word, not inviting the imagination to linger: an element in the economy of a sentence" [404].) In Oppen, this is a principle raised to a very high degree of thoughtfulness and choice. Indeed, in reading him, it often seems that one is confronting not so much an innovation but a search for the adequation of means and ends, an intuitive feel for what is necessary rather than any sense of experimentation. What is given up (or in Oppen's case, better to say rarely taken up) is the analogical mode in language where image and symbol stand as metaphors for *another* reality. Because of this, Oppen's work seems like a kind of first poetry, not by virtue of any crudeness since it is both a subtle and sophisticated body of verse, but by virtue of the sheer unaccountability of its construction. Its beauty and power derive from the simultaneous apperception of its radical construction and the depth at which it seeks to cohere in sense.

Throughout *Seascape: Needle's Eye,* more so than in his earlier work, there is a heightened sense of the struggle to articulate; the language is starker, more primordial, as is the use of spacing, so that the poems have a feeling of resolution arrived at only *in extremis.* Against the "mechanics" of thought, Oppen poses the world of temporality and fragility, the tragic dimension of which is stasis and death. This encounter is experienced through sight and emotions, that "emotion which causes to see" he terms it in an earlier poem, and it is not the unusual or the novel which one sees, but that one sees attentively, with an intensity of sight[1] that moves

> With all one's force
> Into the commonplace that pierces or erodes
> (*NCP* 212)

Or becomes

> Ob via   the obvious . . .
>   Place
> Place where   desire
> Lust of the eyes the pride of life . . .
> (*NCP* 211)

These last phrases hark back to that epigram of Heidegger's that Oppen has quoted, and which might well be the rubric of Oppen's poetics: "the arduous path of appearance."

II

The world of appearance and the commonality of words (their intersubjective meanings) form the twin aspects of Oppen's poetry. The poems move as dialectical occasions between sight and naming, and the poet's truth—no one else's perhaps—is established in the encounter between what is seen and words, with the poet as mediating agency of the process. To this extent, the encounter is seen by Oppen as one that is extreme in its selflessness. Yet it is not impersonal, not a negation of personality as the word objective might imply; rather, it is a *going through* personality, a testing of the ego:

>   Liquid
> Pride of the living life's liquid
> Pride in the sandspit wind this ether this
> Other this element all
> It is I or I believe
>   . . . no other way
> To come here the outer
> Limit of the ego
> (*NCP* 211)

This is perhaps Oppen's most important working principle in that, as he grasps for adequate language, a sense of existence, of personal and social drama, is defined against the counterfoil of conventional or un-thoughtful language which may offer solace or benumb, yet which in ef-fect distances one from what is actually going on. In the main sequence of *Seascape: Needle's Eye* entitled "Some San Francisco Poems," there is a constant play between these modes of language. The first poem in the se-ries describes the mass migration of young people to a rock concert, even though:

> the songs they go to hear on
> this occasion are no one's own
> (*NCP* 221)

Here "no one's own" implies a sort of mystical and ephemeral feeling of togetherness, a *mystique* that Oppen does not regard as the sole property of the young (though it may be of special importance to him there). Rather, for Oppen, the emotional reality of human longings, feelings of isolation, and so forth, which are easily exploitable (one thinks of nationalistic and cultural versions of such exploitation), must be understood and exposed if history is not to be the series of mistaken movements that it has been.

On the level of language, it is the entire enterprise of symbol mak-ing which Oppen attempts to call into question, taking it from childhood roots where

> Night hums like the telephone dial tone blue gauze
> Of the forge flames the pulse
> Of infant
> Sorrows at the crux
> (*NCP* 212)

The "crux" is an intersection of emotion and the imaginary object it cre-ates to bind it. Thus, in the same poem, "the elves the / Magic people in their world / Among the plant roots," the latent content, as Freud might say, of superstitions and mystiques, are

> hopes
> Which are the hopes
> Of small self interest called

Superstition chitinous
Toys of the children wings
Of the wasp
(*NCP* 212)

That these are, to Oppen, subtly dangerous creations seems implied in that final image of the wasp wings. To live by them leads again to recurrent social failure. Hence, returning to the first poem of the San Francisco series,

as the tremendous volume of the music takes
over obscured by their long hair they seem
to be mourning
(*NCP* 221)

What is manifest here, as in Oppen's earlier work, is a rather important and profound ambivalence toward the creative faculty itself, a faculty which in its power to symbolize and to create empathy toward various conceptions of reality is not within its formal, social, and political dangers. For while it may be true that imagination itself cannot be denied, it can be, in Oppen's opinion, frustrated and misapplied. Oppen would have us believe that there is no morality *per se* in the creative life—this perhaps goes against the notion of the artist as savant or enfant terrible leading us on to spiritual heights—there is only a curious kind of moral possibility within the creative act. He puts this quite bluntly in "Five Poems about Poetry" in *This in Which* (1965):

                    Art
Also is not good

For us
Unless like the fool

Persisting
In his folly

It may rescue us
As only the true

Might rescue us . . .
(*NCP* 104)

For Oppen, this moral possibility lies in the artist's fidelity to that Heideggerian world of appearance and to a language which seeks to make (as he said in his essay "The Mind's Own Place") "clear pictures of the world in verse which means only to be clear, to be honest, to produce the realization of reality and to construct a form out of no desire for the trick of gracefulness, but in order to make it possible to grasp, to hold the insight which is the content of the poem" (MOP ref). We have in Oppen's oeuvre a body of work then whose protagonist is language struggling with the clichéd and unthoughtful language of mass mind and mass fantasy, where the artist's attempt to give voice to the visible world becomes a form of *claritas* by at least offering out the possibility of an intersubjective reality—that is, one in which there will be some occasions in which human beings agree, thus making "truth" provisionally possible. If in Oppen's poetry language is transformed, it would seem to be from individuated literal words into a kind of *supra*literalism consisting of statements which, as Oppen puts it, "cannot not be understood." The mystery of such statements would lie not in their need to be explained, but in the sheet substance of their existence. They would be that "other miracle" that the French philosopher Merleau-Ponty refers to in saying: "it is easy to strip language and action of all meaning and make them seem absurd . . . But that other miracle, the fact that in an absurd world language and behavior do have meaning for those who speak and act, remains to be understood."

III

Intensity of sight, its literal counterpart in language, the clarity in effect which these become are the essential modes in Oppen's work by which reality is grasped. An attitude, an impression, even the deepest expression of an emotion are rendered in terms of the visible. As a modality, sight and transformation via the offices of vision, almost in the manner of Donne and the Metaphysicals, are the agency of a singular and personal love. Thus, in "A Morality Play: Preface," light is played upon, a sort of metaphor of interanimation, like the function of sight in "The Exstasy":

Never to forget her naked eyes

Beautiful and brace
Her naked eyes

Turn inward

Feminine light

The unimagined
Feminine light

Feminine ardor
Pierced and touched
(*NCP* 222)

Here, as with "the commonplace that pierces or erodes," love and the
visible are intertwined, bridging individual lives. The morality play of
the title lies in the distinction between this personal sense of love and
the abstract uses of the word, a juxtaposition that is the development of
a theme previously elaborated in Oppen's important long poem "Of Being Numerous" (1968), where the individual in his isolation both mental
and physical, the "shipwreck of the singular," is transcended not in any abstraction of "humanity," but by attentiveness and curiosity, a form of love
of the visible. Without this attentiveness, "Morality Play" goes on, "Tho
all say / Huddled among each other / Love," there is only the implicit continuous failure of mankind en masse, the apocalyptic image of

This city died young
You too will be shown this
You will see the young couples
Leaving again in rags
(*NCP* 223)

As Dembo's essay suggests, this love *within* clarity or as a form of
clarity is, for Oppen, the central impulse that resolved the dialectic of seeing and naming, an experience very much akin to the philosopher's sense
of wonder:

It is impossible the world should be either
                              good or bad
If its colors are beautiful or if they are not
                              beautiful
If parts of it taste good or if no parts of it
                              taste good
It is as remarkable in one case as the other
(*NCP* 224)

Taken this way, clarity itself is a good that transcends *and thereby tests* our ordinary systems of value. As Oppen tellingly puts it in "Route" (one of the poems in *Of Being Numerous*),

> Imagine a man in the ditch,
> The wheels of the overturned wreck
> Still spinning—
> I don't mean he despairs, I mean if he does not
> He sees in the manner of poetry
> (*NCP* 198)

Recalling that the poet's truth is encountered at the "outer limits of the ego," such clarity becomes a way of bearing witness that is neither academic nor detached; for all of its relation to philosophy, Oppen's poetry has left the ivory tower and gone among men and things both intellectually and emotionally. Thus, in "And Their Winter and Night in Disguise" the world's remarkableness is tempered by the suffering of man, as in war:

>   As against this
> We have suffered fear, we know something of fear
> And of humiliation mounting to horror
> (*NCP* 224)

Yet, it is the uniqueness and power of Oppen's work that he does not leave the matter resting there as yet another image of social horror. Rather, he explores further the ambiguity of bearing witness (another dimension of his ambivalent relation to creativity), suggesting that in seeking out the truth it is also the poet's task to forbear the schizophrenic and vicarious glorifications of both terrors and heroics. Thus the foxholes are "*These little dumps* / The poem is about them," their fascination lying in the fact that "Our hearts are twisted / In dead men's pride" (*NCP* 224). As with other images of mass mind and fantasy, it is not truth but falseness, mystical falseness, which makes an adventure out of these horrors, which makes them both endangering and attractive to the imagination:

> Minds may crack
> But not for what is discovered
> Unless that everyone knew
> And kept silent

Our minds are split
To seek the danger out
From among the miserable soldiers
(*NCP* 225)

If, through recognition of such ambivalence, the truths that Oppen dis-
covers and gives voice to remain partial and speculative, fragile as the shifts
of sight and life itself, it is the depth of Oppen's work, the level at which
he seeks for answers, that make his skepticism never an exercise, never the
hubris of a sophist. Indeed, the poet's search for clarity, the needle's eye of
the title, becomes for the poet finally a way into praise of the world:

conviction's
Net of branches
In the horde of events the sacred swarm avalanche
Masked in the sunset
Needle after needle more numerous than planets
Or the liquid waves
In the tide rips
We believe   we believe
(*NCP* 228–229)

IV

Oppen is unique in American poetry. While he has marked out for himself the burden of the singular, the isolate man, that both more than and
less than Romantic hero of the Western drama of the mind, the one who
in rending the veil finds another and yet another before him, he has never
taken the fashionable position of being "alienated" or messianic. The few
commentators on his work have noted his capacity to remain free of re-
demptive and prescriptive attitudes, to remain at once free and skeptical
even with regard to his own efforts (note the question mark in the first line
below):

'We address the future?'

Unsure of the times
Unsure I can answer

To myself   We have been ignited
Blazing

In wrath we await

The rare poetic
Of veracity . . .
(*NCP* 215)

Yet, there is an aspect of Oppen's work which keeps it continually positive
and human—human in the sense that it aligns itself with a belief in the
value of that exploration of reality by creative effort. There is, for example,
the recognition of that impulse that transcends one's personal death, as in
this passage from the earliest of his mature work ("Image of the Engine,"
in *The Materials*, 1962):

Endlessly, endlessly,
The definition of mortality
The Image of the engine
That stops.
We cannot live on that.
I know that no one would live out
Thirty years, fifty years if the world were ending
With his life.
(*NCP* 40–41)

Oppen here implicitly acknowledges the existence of a community in
which the poet's labor both weighs and joins through language the feeling of shared experience (perhaps in Oppen's case only at that point where
"it cannot not be understood"). In *Seascape: Needle's Eye*, there is an almost elegiac sense of transmittal of the poet's burden, a transmittal to the
young, to the children who will become

                          New skilled fishermen
In the great bays and the narrow bights
(*NCP* 216)

and who will find, he says,

In the continual sound
Are chords
Not yet struck

Which will be struck
Nevertheless yes
(*NCP* 229)

Against the songs that are "no one's own" is the prospective of a life
realized in language, in language bearing the weight of the visible as evidence of its attempt to be clearly understood. Its recurrence possibly in the
young is for Oppen *the* compensatory value:

> We dreamed to each other
>
> Miracle of the children
> The brilliant children   Miracle
> Of their brilliance   Miracle
> of
> (*NCP* 234)

In an age of false gods and false certainties, Oppen's intention to mean,
to seek clarity, transcends our notions of a poetics; it becomes the voice of
our deepest feelings and our deepest doubts, holding, in the face of death
and aging, that the voice itself is valuable, perhaps no more so than at its
most unbearably beautiful and poignant moments:

> How shall we say this happened, these stories, our
>   Stories
> Scope, mere size, a kind of redemption
> Exposed still and jagged on the San Francisco hills
> Time and depth before us, paradise of the real, we
>   Know what it is
> To find now depth, not time, since we cannot, but depth
> To come out safe,   to end well
> We have begun to say good bye
> To each other
> And cannot say it
> (*NCP* 226–227)

I think that Oppen has tried to do nothing more than make this, our
condition, absolutely clear. It is a major achievement. Oppen stands alone
in this regard: that his poetry is not composed of the effects of modern life
upon the self, but that it is rather our most profound investigation of it.

Note

1. For further discussion of the importance of sight and clarity in Oppen's work, see L. S. Dembo's "The Existential World of George Oppen."

Works Cited

Dembo, L. S. "The Existential World of George Oppen." *Iowa Review* 3, 1 (Winter 1972): 64–91.

Kenner, Hugh. *The Pound Era.* Berkeley and Los Angeles: University of California Press, 1971.

Oppen, George. "The Mind's Own Place." *Kulchur* 3, 10 (1963).

———. *New Collected Poems.* Ed. Michael Davidson. New York: New Directions, 2002.

11
Hinge Picture (on George Oppen)

Charles Bernstein

[*Editor's Note:* As with Silliman's essay, I have retained page references to the *Collected Poems*, rather than the *New Collected Poems*—in
this case because Bernstein uses an acrostic procedure keyed to the
former volume.]

George Oppen's *Of Being Numerous* is a poetry of constructive witness: the
witness of a social becoming that "presses on each" (*Collected Poems* 150)
and in which each, all, are impressed.[1]

Oppen's achievement has little to do with speech or sight, but for
speech *as* sight, site of the social. Not perception but *acts of* perception,
not the given but the *encountered*, as Oppen suggests in "The Mind's Own
Place." Sight in Oppen's work is not a passive looking onto the world but a
means of touching that invests the world with particular, site-specific (historical, material) meanings. Without this touching—tooling, tuning—the
world becomes empty, voided.

"Near is / Knowledge" (176). Or, as Hölderlin has it in "Patmos," "Near
is / And difficult to grasp." Oppen's engendering witness stipulates both
the integrity of things seen and their contingency—"the known and unknown." "Because the known and unknown / Touch, // One witnesses—"
(172). The intersection of these vectors of response creates the "here" of a
"real" we confront, a real which we come to know by participating in its
making. ("Here still" [177].) This poetics of participatory, or constructive,

presentness—akin especially to Creeley's—is Oppen's response to "the shipwreck / Of the singular" (151). The "singular" that has been lost is, in one sense, a unitary system of value or knowledge based on reason or theology ("The unearthly bonds / Of the singular" [152].) For Oppen, there is no neo-Nietzschean rejoicing in this loss. Rather, "The absolute singular" is related to what Walter Benjamin has called the Messianic Moment—out-of-time, out-of-history. "To dream of that beach / For the sake of an instant in the eyes" (152). For Oppen, however, there is another singularity, the potential for social collectivity: "one must not come to feel that he has a thousand threads in his hands, / He must somehow see the one thing; / This is the level of art / There are other levels / But there is no other level of art" (168). "Not truth but each other" (173).

Which is to say that, in *Of Being Numerous,* the loss of the "transcendental signified" does not necessitate the abandonment, or absence, of knowledge but its *location* in history, in "people." This view entails both a rejection of the crude materialism of things without history and the crude idealism of history without things. Materials in circumstance, as Oppen puts it (186): the "actual" realized by the manipulation of materials by human hands, tools. It is this process that is played out in Oppen's poetry by the insistence on the constructedness of syntax: the manipulation of words to create rather than describe.

Of Being Numerous forges a syntax of truthfulness without recourse to the grammar of truth—"that truthfulness / Which illumines speech" (173). The poem's necessarily precarious project is the articulation of a form that would address the commonweal, a project most fully realized in the two long poems in *Of Being Numerous.* For Oppen, the demands of the articulation of an ideal communication situation necessitate a winnowing of vocabulary and tone that entails the exclusion of anything that would extend, displace, amplify, distort, burst—indeed, *question*—the vocables of an enunciated truthfulness. At his most resonant, Oppen creates a magnificent, prophetic, imaginary language—less voice than chiseled sounds. His writing evokes not the clamor of the streets nor the windiness of conversation nor the bombast of the "dialogic" but the indwelling possibilities of words to speak starkly and with urgency.

Yet Oppen's often-claimed commitment to clarity, however qualified, annuls a number of possibilities inherent in his technique. He hints at this when he writes, "Words cannot be wholly transparent. And that is the heartlessness of words" (186). ("Clarity," he has just said, "In the sense of *transparence*" [162].) In contrast, it is their very intractability that makes for the unconsumable *heart* (heartiness) of words. Inverting Oppen's criticism that Zukofsky used "obscurity in the writing as a tactic,"[2] I would say that Oppen uses clarity as a tactic. That is, at times he tends to fall back onto "clarity" as a self-justifying means of achieving resolution through scenic motifs, statement, or parable in poems that might, given his compositional techniques, outstrip such controlling impulses.

Oppen's syntax is fashioned on constructive, rather than mimetic, principles. He is quite explicit about this. Carpentry is a recurring image of poem making. His poems, as he tells it, were created by a sort of collage or cut-up technique involving innumerable substitutions and permutations for every word and line choice. The method here is paratactic, even if often used for hypotactic ends. This tension, which can produce the kinetic, stuttering vibrancy of some of Oppen's most intense poems, is at the heart of his use of the line break as hinge. In contrast to both enjambment and disjunction—as well, of course, as more conventional static techniques—Oppen's hinging allows for a measure of intervallic "widths" of connection/disconnection between lines. The typical Oppen hinge is made by starting a line with a preposition, commonly "Of.") At its most riveting, this hinging taps into a horizontally moving synaptic/syntactic energy at the point of line transition.

Discrete Series uses this orchestration of lacunae in the most radical and open-ended way. (Could the twenty-five-year gap between *Discrete Series* and *The Materials* be Oppen's grandest hinged interval?) In some of the later works, he abandons any angularity in his lineation, at the same time allowing an almost symbolic or allegorical vocabulary ("sea," "children") to take hold. Nonetheless, the possibilities of his use of the line as hinge are omnipresent in the work—and influential. Indeed, the hinge suggests an interesting way to sort through aspects of Oppen's influence, since there is some work that may resemble his but which misses the radical (in the sense of root) nature of his lineation.

The following stanzas were generated using an acrostic procedure (G-E-O-R-G-E O-P-P-E-N) to select lines, in page sequence, from *Collected Poems*. I have borrowed this procedure from Jackson Mac Low. That these poems are so characteristically Oppenesque is, I think, less the effect of familiar lines or typical references than the way single Oppen lines can be hinged to "each other" to create the marvelous syntactic music found throughout his work. I hope the structural allegory is apparent: the autonomy of the root, of the individual, allowing for the music of the social, the numerous.

Grasp of me)
Eyes legs arms hands fingers,
On the cobbles;
Reaches the generic, gratuitous
Geared in the loose mechanics of the world with the valves
jumping
Endlessly, endlessly,

Outside, and so beautiful
Populace, sea-borne and violent, finding
Passing, the curl at cutwater,
Ends its metaphysic
Nature! because we find the others

Generations to a Sunday that holds
Exterior. 'Peninsula
Of the subway and painfully
Re-arrange itself, assert
Grand Central's hollow masonry, veined
Eyes. The patent

Of each other's backs and shoulders
Planned, the city trees
Proud to have learned survival
Effortless, the soft lips
Nuzzle and the alien soft teeth

Glassed
Echo like history
One by one proceeding
Rectangular buildings
Growing at its edges! It is a place its women
Early. That was earlier.

Out of scale
Picturing the concrete walls.
Plunge and drip in the seas, carpenter,
Enduring
New in its oil

Good bye Momma,
Each day, the little grain
Of all our fathers

Ring electronically the New Year
Grows, grass
Enterprise.

On the sloping bank—I cannot know
Pours and pours past Albany
Perhaps the world
Even here is its noise seething
Now as always Crusoe

Gave way to the JetStream
Entity
Of substance
Rectangular buildings
Generation
Exposes the new day,

Of living,
Paris is beautiful and ludicrous, the leaves of every
tree in the city
move in the wind
People talk, they talk to each other;
Even Cortes greeted as revelation . . . No I'd not
emigrate,
Now we do most of the killing

Glass of the glass sea shadow of water
Elephant, say, scraping its dry sides
Of veracity that huge art whose geometric
Recalling flimsy Western ranches
Gravel underfoot
Enemies in the sidewalks and when the stars rise

Other
Piled on each other lean
Precision of place the rock's place in the fog we suffer
Early in the year cold and windy on the sea the wind
Night—sky bird's world

Notes

1. All subsequent citations of Oppen's poetry refer to the *Collected Poems*.
2. Burton Hatlen and Tom Mandel, "Poetry and Politics," 45.

Works Cited

Hatlen, Burton, and Tom Mandel. "Poetry and Politics: A Conversation with George and Mary Oppen." In *George Oppen: Man and Poet*, ed. Burton Hatlen. Orono, ME: National Poetry Foundation, 1981.

Oppen, George. *The Collected Poems.* New York: New Directions, 1975.

———. "The Mind's Own Place." *Kulchur* (1963). Reprinted in *Montemora* 1 (1975).

12
"Uncannily in the Open"
In Light of Oppen

Rachel Blau DuPlessis

What is socially decisive in artworks is the content that becomes eloquent through the work's formal structures.

—Theodor Adorno

The word in one's own mouth becomes strange as infinity—even strange as the finite, strange as things. . . . Which means again that the prosody and the 'philosophy' cannot be separated as of course you know.

—George Oppen

I have chosen this topic, yet it is difficult for me to speak about George Oppen, since in a certain light, everything I write is set against his uncompromising sign.[1] When a person writing poems is frightened by George Oppen, she may have started (cf. *Selected Letters [SL]* 123–124). Oppen writes a poetry of negativity and commitment. Like Paul Celan, Walter Benjamin, and Theodor Adorno, Oppen asks in every word how to make art, what art is possible, what must be said given the pressures and demands of our position in history. In their anthology, Jerome Rothenberg and Pierre Joris debate the aestheticized naming of an epoch: "not so much post*modern*—as it would come to be called—as it was post-bomb and post-holocaust" (Rothenberg and Joris 1998, 4). Work, mind, and understanding are inflected with political and social disasters, and with failures of a political and cultural dream of just societies that shadow these events. Charles Bernstein adds a dimension about social mourning to a sense of these popular front hopes variously compromised when he proposes, similarly, that one project of contemporary American radical poetry mourns Auschwitz and Hiroshima; these disasters are encrypted and repressed information at the core of social identities and artistic practices (Bernstein 1992, 193–217).

Theodor Adorno's 1962 essay "Commitment" contains Adorno's elaborate second thoughts, his own midrash, or exfoliating gloss, on his own intransigent, enraged, doomed sententia (dating from 1949) that to write a poem after Auschwitz is barbaric. To argue that such a poem would be an expression of the impulses that created Auschwitz in the first place is a massive accusation about culture, a massive extension of responsibility for Shoah to the whole of German culture, if not to all culture (Adorno 1981, 34). That infamous original statement is motivated in multiple ways; one may see it, in part, as a desire to halt in one's own tracks by stopping a hapless part of cultural production (poetry), and thereby clearing the time to engage in mourning beyond mourning. Adorno is propelled to criticize one genre, poetry, in which mourning is conventionally undertaken (Adorno 1992, 87). The passage from "Commitment" is very intricate, as it would necessarily have to be.[2] At the end of his consideration, Adorno says something quite simple, but rich with the intricacy of his prior argument: that an artist should not produce straightforward political art, engagé art, an art of commitment as this word is conventionally evoked in the postwar context by, say, Jean-Paul Sartre. An artist must understand, rather, that the political has "migrated into" all art, and work with this situation and its implications (Adorno 1992, 93).

Oppen's art is political in this way: commitment has migrated into form. Oppen exposes and explores the riven and fraught nature of subjectivity in a state of political and existential arousal that cannot (yet) be satisfied. His poetry traces the dialectical motion of that arousal. Oppen argues that light is as inadequate as darkness: pure reason as problematic as mysticism. Imagery in his work makes us see that fire or "blaze" exists in a narrow site between hyper-rational, overly bright light and hyper-irrational darkness, obscurity, and obscurantism. Thus tiny "temperate" images of rot, change, smallness, process, human scale ("cozy black iron work"—cozy! *New Collected Poems [NCP]* 230) are so vital.

> We have gone
> As far as is possible
>
> Whose lives reflect light
> Like mirrors
>
> One had not thought
> To be afraid
>
> Not of shadow but of light
>
> Summon one's powers
> (*NCP* 233)

In "The Second War and Postmodern Memory," Charles Bernstein follows the implications of Adorno's critique of the Enlightenment values embodied in claims for European social and intellectual systems: the "war undermined, subliminally, more than consciously, the belief in virtually every basic value of the Enlightenment, insofar as these values are in any way Eurosupremacist or hierarchic" (Bernstein 1992, 198). At the same time he notes the simultaneous problem "of the vatic, the occult, the charismatic, the emotional solidarity of communion" such as one might see in fascism and elsewhere—in any mono-ocular, nonsecular, affirmative belief system (Bernstein 1992, 199). We live in a space (newly inflected by other failures of the West and the East) in which neither positivist enlightenment nor its opposite, positivist antisecularism, is adequate. In his time, Oppen explicitly resisted the mystical irrationalisms prevalent and making revolutionary claims in the 1960s: drug culture, Jungian thinking, and surrealism. If neither the irrational nor the rational is adequate, this effectively ends many binarist oppostions in which we have believed, or at least that we have credited. Where can we stand? What can our writing say or make of this? These were dilemmas that Oppen faced, incited by the sickening political rupture of the 1963–1968 assassinations of U.S. political leaders, including a president, and ignited by the corrosive Vietnam War, with its lies and manipulations in a frayed democratic context.

As close as one gets to "stopping" writing (something Oppen, of course, did, a silence generated and supported variously, a sociocultural act), that temptation and its complex overcoming "expresses negatively" (in Adorno's terms) "the impulse that animates committed literature."[3] But beyond that almost twenty-five years of not talking to the page (1934–1958), Oppen's later poetry seems continuously to be stopping at virtually every line, at every porous white-space caesura, and then picking up the commitment again to go on. His "Adorno-esque" commitment is made precisely against Tendenz literature, but precisely for engagement inside form, in, I will argue, the line itself. Understanding commitment as manifest in form, I want briefly to think through connections between Oppen and certain European thinkers and poets. I am doing so dependent on translations, and despite the fact that I am not versed in philosophy as a tradition, but only in poetry as tradition and practice.[4] Versed, in part, by Oppen. Hence I will begin in memoir, with some of the terms activated by that interchange.

I was a graduate student at Columbia University when I met Oppen in 1965; we were introduced by a fellow student, John Crawford, later the founding editor of the socially committed West End Press. I was fascinated with the work of Pound and Williams, alternative poetries uninteresting to my erstwhile graduate professors. I was beginning an unmentored dissertation (completed 1970) about *The Pisan Cantos* and *Paterson*—under the predictive rubric the "endless poem," investigating how imagist "intensity of seeing" modulated into, demanded, or necessitated such sprawling encyclopedic poems (Pound 1967, 102; *NCP* 167). Later, I wrote a comparison of Oppen and Pound, trying to establish the different historically changing politics of the use of fragment in a poetics of sincerity, and taking, as flashpoint, Oppen's late-career poem about Pound (DuPlessis 1981). Pound's use of fragment and parataxis became a totalitarian and mystical way of carrying out Objectivist poetics ("totalitarian"—meaning totalizing and authoritative is Pound's uncanny term); he used the fragment to headline affirmative ideas he wished to promulgate. Thus he was inadequately investigative, or, rather, held he had already investigated and was declaring (establishing) permanent results. Oppen, in contrast, maintained a use of the fragment negatively, as moving among contradictions and proposed that vectored movement as veridical—constructing situational truth.

My calling card to Oppen was work on *Paterson,* original at that time, regrettably never published. I was awarded a prize for this article, the Bunner Medal, but when I thanked the proper university authorities, I kept on typing "Bummer." Speak of ambivalence. In any event, the paper evoked from George a striking letter about mythoposis and the long poem, a subtle critique of Williams (*SL* 117–118). This was our first exchange. Issues of seriality, long poems, the alternative modernist tradition (mainly male modernists), experimentation, political stances, addressing one's society (or one's "peers," at any rate)—these issues and more were opened (*NCP* 158). I was a sympathetic and willing reader of the rhetorical austerities and the objectivist stances that Oppen exemplified.[5]

Given the ruling counterpoetics in New York City in the mid-1960s—Deep Image, the New York School, both generations, the fascination with French surrealist and absurdist models (in drama and poetry)—what Oppen said rejecting surrealism became annoyingly, provokingly important to me. He took surrealism as a poetic diction or rhetoric, not as a method or an ethos, considering it as yet another one of the "obvious" period styles that he challenged as being inadequate to epistemology: to "asking oneself what one does know and what one doesn't know" (*SL* 121, 120). I was living in a particular 100th Street poetry group within a backwash of surrealist strategies, and George took issue with my fascination in a very didactic way; he truly saw surrealism as a path that should not be pursued, and he mustered a good deal of wit and argument to that end.[6] His own poetic texture of abruptness and unexpected shifts of voice and mode were to become startling, but they were never done for what one might call stylistically avant-garde reasons. Any hint of "manner" was anathema to Oppen.

In his interesting position of old younger poet (his second book published in 1962 at age fifty-four, his third in 1965, at fifty-seven), Oppen made sets of remarks that criticized various contemporary avant-gardes for their poetics—aleatory work in music, such as John Cage's; happenings, the Judson dance scene, and Fluxus-inspired poetry such as Jackson Mac Low's (*SL* 67), "the new dadaisms, the new derangement of the senses"—the Rimbaudian term he hated.[7] Plus Allen Ginsberg, with a too-flip quip, "merely Howling" (*SL* 78), and finally "Deep Image-ists," whom he couldn't quite get a handle on, in part because they were all his friends, but whom he saw as not secular enough, too symbolist and mythic (*SL* 78).[8] Aside from showing the sometimes notorious "Oppen judgment" in the absolutism of these remarks, he is clearly trying to carve a place for himself among the active 1960s counterpoetics when he mostly disagreed with just about everything that was happening in alternative poetry.[9] The resistance to surrealist/dada is based on a principled critique of "irrationalism" as a source for knowledge. In that he was conservative, one might say, or classical (might be better), but he also was engaged in the functional strategic analysis possibly learned in Communist circles: these methods (dadaism, derangement) might be subjectively exciting and tempting, but they were objectively (as it were) counterproductive.

Oppen wrote me forthright corrective statements on surrealism, about how you can't just put an elephant into a poem for reasons of decoration, association, free play, neat juxtaposition, or charming willfulness. That is, "One cannot make a poem by sticking words into it, it is the poem which makes the words and contains their meaning. One cannot reach out for *roses* and *elephants* and *essences* and put them in the poem—the ground under the elephant, the air around him, one would have to know very precisely one's distance from the elephant or step deliberately too close, close enough to frighten oneself. When the man writing is frightened by a word, he may have started" (*SL* 123–124; see also 389–390 n. 21). Thus if the word "elephant" gets there, you have to measure the force and meaning and contexts and solidity of the thing, and what it was actually doing there, not as ornament or shocking pendent of your poem, but as itself, and as whatever brought it into your poem, compelling thought. Compelling a commitment. You had to think about what was true, not just whatever could be sutured or combined together. Oppen's later poem "West" that begins "Elephant, say, scraping its dry sides / In a narrow place as he passes says yes // This is true // So one knows?" I see as Oppen's last word in that debate on the surrealist impulse. In that poem he calls for "The rare poetic / Of veracity"; he probably considered this the opposite of surrealist practice (*NCP* 215).

Oppen once said to me: "why don't you put all of your intelligence in your poems." That is—make poems of thinking. Use poems to think with. They are a commitment to thinking.[10] One must gasp: that was a breathtaking thing to say to a struggling "girl" to whom poetry had been more or less forbidden as a career or vocation by her own formerly wayward, but now rather academic father.[11] Oppen's invitation had a tremendous long-term impact on me. It was certainly a way of honoring the potential of a young woman, a not-otherwise-notable person, and certainly not a person doing much yet (in 1966 to about 1976) with her poetry. In writing to me, or imagining some "me" to write to, he said some pretty remarkable things, "Notes on Prosody?" for example, from which that elephant emerges. I am grateful for whatever it was in the "me" that elicited these remarks. Oppen was about equally attentive to women and men as poets, a very good, a very lucky, and somewhat rare thing to find in an older male person in circa 1965. This didn't mean he had no gender-laden demands, or only positive ones. But he didn't seem to cut women any slack (rejecting, mostly, that buried chivalric condescension), and he was mostly angry when women tried to be "too nice" or "too good." That's what, in his view, ruined Denise Levertov's poetry (which he had at one point somewhat admired)—he was absolutely adamant about this. It was a cutting and admonitory remark. Oppen had no trouble, as I've said, with judgment.

Oppen also read my early struggling work in poetry. This he ruthlessly cut, rejecting large parts of it, teaching me thereby how to hear, read, and listen to a genuine statement that had some grit, some meaning, and how to remove, cut, toss out the rest. After the editing, what was left got linked—one simply linked the genuine material (possibly re-sequencing it). This was his method—making of every poem a "discrete series," and attenuating or cutting the "argument" or the "logic" or the "development" one might so laboriously, so banally, have constructed. Indeed, "discrete series," as we know from a good deal of commentary now, was an epistemological argument Oppen made about reality and knowledge, as well as an implied argument about the ethics of writing. The proposition was that startling and original logic or sequence would emerge from the editing out of the nongenuine, something quite far from the conventional—from the conventional *anything*. You would confront what you really thought in cutting what was inadequate, generic, or "poetic," and try to comprehend the rest in whatever form it emerged, as traces, fragments, phrases, as constellations.[12] It was the opposite—but the reverse image—of a surrealist combinatoire; here it was excision, not association, that created startling juxtapositions. Oppen rejected both language as fill and the decorative, a clarity Poundean in origin, although without its political baggage. This, along with his suspicion of tidy, nice, good-for-you moves at closure, made people's poetry and their conclusions or endings subject to a good deal of correction. He enraged both Jane Cooper (who was polite) and Armand Schwerner (who was not) by his ability to dismiss notable sections of their hard-won words. If you sent him work, if you asked him—he told you. Then you had to live with what he said. Oppen was quite serious about the ethics of writing, and the tactic of such sincerity was uncompromising. He was also, given this austere picture I am limning, one of the wittiest people I have ever met.

About a poem I wrote in 1976, he even said, "can't keep my hands off it" (*SL* 317). This was somewhat chilling and warming at the same time—a displaced Petrarchan freeze and burn. Or was that Pater-rach-an? Was this flattering? Sort of, but it was appropriative and manipulative, too. I wanted to make my mistakes on my own time. It's a wonder I learned anything. Did I know what to do with this remark? Yes, I knew. This comment demanded that I completely reject his interventions into this poem, no matter what, and it marked the last time he intervened thus. The fact that the poem under discussion was a work ("Voyaging") dedicated to Oppen himself, one even might say an elegy before the fact, makes for some intricacy in both the approach and the rejection (DuPlessis 1980). The fact that the exchange elicited from Oppen a remarkable statement about line break and "the vertical dimension" is something, however, from which I still do learn (*SL* 316–317). His ruthless editing was an immeasurable gift, but because it involved judgmental lucidity, it was not an easy gift to receive. Certainly, to say the least, such scrutiny did not encourage fluidity or ease of production. Internalizing such a scrupulous, intransigent standard is a permanent challenge to exclude unmotivated words.

"A good one line poem is not nothing," he once said to me. He meant some poems that were somewhat magical, image-y, and woman oriented, tattered Sappho after the almost complete loss of her oeuvre. This grim "one-line" moment occurred when the combination of my own way-ward, self-quarreling seriousness, my nothing career—a woman in a university was rather endangered then—, my desire for poetry so great that it stopped poetry, and my inchoate quarrel with gender narratives in the lyric. . . . not to speak of the austere Oppen-standard that did nothing for fluency and exposition—all conspired to leave me with the tiniest seed-like works. One-line poems—it was the next worst thing to total erasure. The glass was almost totally empty! (I might mention I was writing my dissertation at that time.) However, from his poetics, Oppen could help-fully, if optimistically, view this attenuation as the proper beginning of a full glass, as material boiled down or taken down to the drop of the essen-tial. *Wells* was published in 1980 by Eliot Weinberger of *Montemora* maga-zine and press. Or, to say this with another inflection, my first book of po-etry was not published *until* 1980. I was then thirty-nine.

Oppen had a horror of the willed, of the forced, of the fake. The main criterion he taught was sincerity. The testing of the words, the emotion, the meanings, the feel of the work by a deep inner ethos and a stubborn inner ear. This was expressed as primary resistance, on the level of vis-ceral stubbornness and intelligent suspicion, to all exaggeration and elo-cutionary rhetorics. His sincerity was, also, simultaneously a political sin-cerity. This involved an ethics about knowledge, accuracy, clarity of mind, a willingness to say what one wanted, for oneself, not speaking for others, but joining others in demands or in speech. What it means to link poetic and political sincerity can be seen in Oppen's critique of Ginsberg: "There need be nothing ephemeral about the lyric poet who responds passionately and in his own way to his own vision, but if the poet begins to ask us to ac-cept a system of opinions and attitudes he must manage the task of rig-orous thought" (Oppen 1962, 329). I remember (1967, 1968 maybe) trying to write a New Year's poem, a poem of vocation called "Calling" in which I was unmaliciously but ignorantly talking about what people in New Jersey thought. ("New Jersey" is a New York topos; I was a New Yorker. I was also awkwardly bumbling after Oppen's commitment to speak of so-cial class in his poetry.) And George called me on it. Calling, indeed! He said I didn't know what those particular people thought; I was faking.

Oppen rejected rhetorical build, free play, automatic writing, epiphe-nomenal linkages (that is, indistinguishably surrealism and dadaism), so-cial flippancy, insouciant faking, too many words, and virtually any mor-alizing whatsoever. This standard simply shrivels 99 percent of what is called poetry, then and now. It was something to face this, because one could never face it down. That's obvious—I'm still talking about what Oppen's work means to me. I also know there might be a counter-way of reading this essay: that Oppen was blocking for me. Let's say he had the faults of his virtues, but his virtues mattered deeply. In 1985–86 I catapulted myself into *Drafts,* incidentally writing the very first words of "Draft 1: It" in 1986 on the Pacific Coast at Solana Beach having just visited the George Oppen Archive at the University of California, San Diego, in La Jolla, and just after the centenary conference on H.D. in Orono, Maine. When this long poem moment arrived and when, a month or so later, I knew it had arrived, I had to get George (who was, of course, already dead) off my back a bit—but he never said *no,* he was just too much there. You might call that "Killing the Uncle in the House."

The problem of writing for me is how to get an ethical literature without any didacticism or political forcing. How to address human issues without being trapped by the ego-, ethno-, phallo-, logo-centrisms of humanism. How to honor choice in a serious way, even an existential way, while somehow allowing for mystery and transcendence (a word I use with some suspicion). And how to write poetry in brackets—meaning barred from whatever merely accomplished poetry we have in our tradition. That is, how to write: not poetry as decoration, not poetry as a recurrent imbedding of problematic gender narratives and iconizations, not poetry as only expressive or simply personal, but some austere, deliberative, materialist, awe-struck art in segmented language. These things—along with how to talk in a "vertical" fashion within a horizontal, extensive, and open worldview—these are things that George often did well. The first Draft I wrote vowed it, using Celan: no more sand poems. "Keine Sandkunst mehr, kein Sandbuch, keine Meister." ("No sand art anymore, no sandbook, no masters"—is how Pierre Joris translated this [1995, 106–107] in *Breathturn/Atemwende.*)

Within the term or cover word "avant-garde"—this is a finding for cultural studies—one might want now to disaggregate particular activities and practices. In the statements in poetics found in the *Selected Letters,* Oppen worked the term "avant-garde" round and round at least three different ways in his own history, and in the process separated it into specific practices. He appreciated aesthetic extremism and intransigence, and yet evinced a suspicion of groups and communities built solely around avant-garde claims.

In a letter to me in 1965, he claims "avanced guard" as a kind of ontological stance within poetry: "the thing that the poetry was for" (*SL* 122). In a letter to John Crawford in 1973, looking over *Discrete Series* (1928), Oppen says that the work was "avant garde alright" because the "old forms" were unusable, but that he doesn't (in 1973, and maybe in 1928) "*live* in an avant-garde." Oppen splits textual issues and questions of poetics away from the choice to live (as the surrealists did, but as the Objectivists really didn't) in and as an ongoing group formation (*SL* 254). Then, in a couple of letters in 1974 to Jerome Rothenberg on the publication of *Revolution of the Word*, one of Rothenberg's crucial anthologies, Oppen implies that he was not really part of those avant-garde formations, and hence didn't feel the book as a "reunion" (*SL* 291). This point is elaborated in a 1974 letter to David McAleavey in which Oppen says, "I cannot remember that I had ever set myself to enter the avant garde on the page - - - - I felt the avant-garde of time, of time itself - - - - if we would rescue love . . . etc but as for avant-gardism of technique - - - - I wrote as I could I found, if I could, and find if I can a way to say it - - - -" (*SL* 291–292). Indeed, an Oppen poem in Pound's 1934 *Active Anthology*, "Brain / All / Nuclei / Blinking / Kinetic / Electric sign" suggests that once upon a time Oppen had attempted a mild avant-gardism of technique but then stopped. Abruptly and decisively (*NCP* 292–293). This complex passage echoes his ontological textual claims—the poems are not avant-garde because this was a fashion, but because they had to be. Here, Oppen adds a dimension—a sense of an extreme historical crisis to which he felt he responded. Three propositions then emerge from Oppen's considerations of the avant-garde. First, textual, formal tactics must answer to necessity, not fashion; second, there are community formations and practices, groups of avant-garde practitioners, but to these he is agnostic. His attempted regathering of some "Objectivists" and his various addresses to the "young" in the 1960s are perhaps paradoxical in this regard, but they were also eclectic and not "groupy." And third, the most essential for his practice of poetry, is his conviction of historical and political crisis—the "avant-garde of time . . . itself" to which work must respond by thought. His sense of time lurching ahead of itself, the sense of being endangered, is located in the cold war's precarious poise of atomic bomb against atomic bomb, the fear of nuclear accident, "the time of the missile" (*NCP* 70).

The impact of Oppen's poetry is not aesthetic only, but a kind of ontological arousal to thinking itself—not to knowledge as such, but to the way thought feels emotionally and morally and processually in time. The way it feels is moving, aching, startling, and barely consoling. Olson's, Pound's, Williams's, even H.D.'s and Eliot's long poems are often knowledge based, written in some measure to give access to new accumulations of insight about researched (suggestive, nonscholarly) materials, they seek to present a general knowledge, one culturally useful, a new information about the way the world works, what brought us to this moment, or some analysis of the elements of culture and history. They often make you feel—even insist upon—the importance of that knowledge, and they often go through a quasi-dialogic process of teaching. Oppen's serial works are based on thinking rather than knowledge (don't misunderstand this): a motivated apparently nontendentious, even random cast into and among materials, which is open-ended and changing: "There are things / We live among 'and to see them / Is to know ourselves'" (*NCP* 163). His work exemplifies Blake's call to make "Mental Fight": a critique, an examination, a readiness to experience the ruptures and possibilities of our place and time.[13] A skeptical wariness combined with a kind of fervent hope—beyond reasonableness, but not beyond reason. This might be summed up by Octavio Paz speaking about Republican Spain and its "desperate hopefulness. . . . The memory will never leave me. Anyone who has looked Hope in the face will never forget it. He will search for it everywhere he goes" (Paz in Howe 1982, 352). I think of Oppen and his choices in the 1930s, and then all his later work as searching for hope wherever he goes, but never imagining it was there when it was not: the work is investigative, not self-deceived. He showed the importance of that "Mental Fight," with a muted critique by citation of Pound and an allusion to the Museum of Modern Art and what it represents of modernist aestheticization, perhaps, or the separation of the art work from its context. "I am a man of the Thirties // 'No other taste shall change this'" (*NCP* 295). But the world being what it is, the condition of "Mental Fight" seems permanent.

It wasn't so much collage that Oppen did (though it sometimes seems to be) as gnomic aphorism pitched past thought by thinking. This is to walk the *via negativa* of poetry. It is "Allegory" in Walter Benjamin's sense— that is, not seeking a totality: "allegory has to do, precisely in its destructive furor, with dispelling the illusion that proceeds from all 'given order,' whether of art or of life: the illusions of totality or of organic wholeness which transfigures that order and makes it seem endurable. And this is the progressive tendency of allegory" (Benjamin 1999, 331 and 329). "Allegory holds fast to the ruins": this, precisely, the negative way: against fusion, totality, rest. If culture means affirmations only, we are doomed to those who want to manipulate us. If it means skeptical hope and secular attentiveness—we can, like Oppen, work against wholeness, positive thinking, delusive ideologies, celebratory visions. "Brush[ing] history against the grain"—a counter poetics, a contestatory resistance, creates a stunned "conception of the present as the 'time of the now' which is shot through with chips of Messianic time" (Benjamin 1969, 257 and 263).

"How this work was written: rung by rung, according as chance would offer a narrow foothold, and always like someone who scales dangerous heights" sounds as if it were written by Oppen, perhaps in reference to the poem "Song, The Winds of Downhill" or perhaps about all of his poems (*NCP* 220). However, it wasn't. The passage, by Walter Benjamin, describes the sensation of constructing *The Arcades Project* (Benjamin 1999, 460). The method of holding on, of casting one set of materials after another, the metaphor of handholds, footholds in the small words, all make one see an overlap in their concerns, the extremity of literary works negotiating the questions: what art is possible after disasters; how we can live in a world in which both Enlightenment consolations and fundamentalist consolations are horrifying, monstrous.

Benjamin brings me, by unapologetic metonymic logic, to the connections I feel between Oppen and another marked European figure. The sensation of reading George Oppen, as of reading Paul Celan, is of being propelled into a space on the edge, of being brought out about as far as one can go by a curious and unique mix of thought and language practices. Both writers offer the sensation of leaving the "poem" as made object with its conventions, leaving the text as contained formula of words, and of leaving the poetic career as a curated artifact, in order to be in the world of statement itself, both beyond language and inside it. The only poem for our time is something that refuses poetry. Both could be called hermetic poets; yet of course both insisted that they were only writing a reality as they understood it. Both used a form of the kenning: more clearly in Celan's fused word nodules, and for Oppen in some of the odd things (I mean words) that end up together, kenning-like, on one line, like "page the magic" (*NCP* 278), or "distances the poem" (*NCP* 281), or "center of the rock image" (*NCP* 271), riddling, mutually illuminating word clusters. Certainly both refuse to console. Both would say, as Celan did, that language in poetry "does not transfigure or render poetical; it names, it posits, it tries to measure the area of the given and the possible" (Rothenberg and Joris 1998, 155).

The January 1958 speech by Paul Celan accepting the prize of the Free Hanseatic City of Bremen offers some terms pertinent to Oppen.[14] For Oppen is, like Celan, a poet of negativity, of ontological intransigence.

The final paragraph of the Celan summarizes his subject place. Even in accepting whatever honor or prize someone has decided to offer, one must be mindful of one's real exposure, an exposure that seems to increase, in modernity, not diminish.[15] Celan will refer, in this passage, to the recently launched Russian satellite *Sputnik*. Its launching was a cold war crisis moment for the West, thereupon compelled to weigh its own technological (and covertly military) prowess and "superiority," the compromises of its educational systems and values. Celan offers an even deeper crisis out of which he writes. "[These lines of thought, the poems, said Celan] are the efforts of someone who, overarced by stars that are human handiwork, and who, shelterless in this till now undreamt-of-sense and thus most uncannily in the open, goes with his very being to language, stricken by and seeking reality" (Felstiner 1995, 116).

Our political, historical time keeps sending us out, in Celan's decisive phrase, "uncannily in the open."[16] Because of this political and existential homelessness and exposure, one must undertake to find in language a strange home, and in reality a subject. Celan's final phrase in German is "*wirklichkeitswund und Wirklichkeit suchend*"—in John Felstiner's close-English gloss, which I prefer for this essay, "Reality-wounded and Reality-seeking" (Felstiner 1995, 117). This phrase, and its close companion, "most uncannily in the open," seem particularly germane to a meditation on George Oppen, and not only because of the accidental onomastic pun. Oppen also spoke of the shelterless subject and the high stakes of the act of writing, the primary act of going to language "Reality-wounded and Reality-seeking."

In the poetics and projects of Oppen there were several intransigent problems—how to achieve a saturated realism, presenting the things that had presented themselves to be comprehended, the "things on the road," the images encountered, but how to do so without what (he felt was) the taint of surrealism, or willful juxtapositions. And second: how to understand the space we are in now, in this particular postwar of modernity: our exposure "uncannily in the open" without the props our civilization and other civilizations have depended upon for hundreds of years: Enlightenment self-justificatory reason or vatic irrational mysticisms of the non-secular, including religion treated as certainty, as religiosity.

Nothing is so simple, but for purposes of this argument I would say that one central instrument of his attention to these issues in and as poetry, is a central formal mechanism: the line, which leads to and engages what I will (following Benjamin, partly) call the "dialectical image" (Benjamin 1999,

462, 464, 466, 473, 474, 475). Sometimes Oppen will use the term "prosody" for this or "music"—together these terms denominate a formal cluster that is also an intellectual, ontological, and epistemological cluster. To begin to analyze this, we have to acknowledge "line" as a crucial communicative means of poetry itself.

Something fairly straightforward, but highly distinctive, separates and distinguishes poetry from nearby modes like fiction and drama that also unroll in time and use sequencing tactics of various kinds. The word *narrativity* evokes the central aspect of storytelling—making sequenced events with some point unroll in represented time. *Performativity* means making elements of coded and decodable gestures in special space and time. What, on this model, is the fundamental activity of poetry?

Both of these now-familiar neologisms (narrativity and performativity) indicate the practice of sequencing event, gesture, and image. Poetry also sequences; it is the creation of meaningful sequence by the negotiation of gap (line break, stanza break, page space). Although the other practices may have periodicities or gaps, these are more constitutive and systematic in poetry. Poetry can then be defined as the kind of writing that is articulated in sequenced, gapped lines and whose meanings are created by occurring in bounded units, units operating in relation to chosen pause or silence. The line segment creates meanings. The acts of making lines and making their particular chains of rupture, seriality, and sequencing are fundamental to the nature of poetry as a genre. Fundamental to what can be said in poetry, as poetry. To write poetry is, as George Oppen said, to control the "sequence of disclosure" by segments that have a strong relation both to melos and to meaning: "separating the connections of the progression of thought" (Oppen 1984, 26, and Dembo interview 167).[17] *Segmentivity*—the ability to articulate and make meaning by selecting, deploying, and combining segments—is the underlying characteristic of poetry as a genre. Narrativity and performativity summarize the particularities of fiction and drama, but segmentivity distinguishes poetry.

How does Oppen deploy the precise textual resources of poetry to sustain being "Reality-wounded and Reality-seeking"? In Oppen, matter, the substantive, the "thing" (in its sense of an object) is deeply engaged in time (with "things" in the sense of events), and the effect of all these things is to be both solid in time, and streaming, broken up, interrupted with other connections in time to other objects and events. Oppen is eloquent about the line. His attention to things happening is created through the line—"a sense of the whole line, not just its ending" including "the relation between lines, the relation in their length . . . the relation of the speed, of the alterations and momentum of the poem . . . the shape of the lines and the pulse of the thought which is given by those lines" (Dembo interview 167). Oppen remasters and changes the lyric, proposes a subjectivity ("Reality-wounded and Reality-seeking") by historicizing (and temporalizing) not only the speaking subject of poetry but the line itself, the material practice of poetry.

To see in "The manner of poetry" is to penetrate what is primary (thus such Oppen-inflected words as *primitive, the materials, the obvious*), what presents itself as such, obdurately and irrevocably (*NCP* 198). The statement "All that was to be thought / Yes / Comes down the road" (*NCP* 213) is the "same" as the anti-surrealist statement "the image is encountered, not found" (Oppen 2003, 175). That is—it is what you cannot not see; it is not a trouvaille or wrought wit: it is the "narrative" (that is, the pedagogy) of "things."

> In the starlight things the things continue
> Narrative   their long instruction and the tide running
> Strong as a tug's wake   shorelights'
>
> Fractured dances across rough water a music
> Who would believe it
> Not quite one's own
> With one always the   black verse   the turn and the turn
> (*NCP* 213)

There are a number of allusions to, and metaphors for poetry and the poetic line in this passage: "narrative" (amusingly), "long instruction," "a music," "dances,"—not the least of which is "the black verse the turn and the turn." This can allude to blank verse (that is, to epochal poetic form in the humanist period), to the dark ink of writing on the page, to the darkness of water at night, and the dark side of modernity's unfounded optimisms. It also alludes to the mechanism inside verse that makes it "turn," to make the next furrow of work—precisely the etymological meaning of verse. By layering the encrypted words *blank verse* underneath *black verse,* the old humanist line is alluded to and surpassed, and a new ethical and formal space for a post-humanist "black verse" line "uncannily in the open" is suggested. "Black verse" could, without too much overstatement, allude to poetic tactics chosen when one is faced with the dark events of recent history, wounded by that darkness, and yet "Reality-seeking." It is at once the prosody of and the ethical calling into the *via negativa*. "The black verse" is always in motion, because it derives from the play of waves, the play of historical time, the play of the poetic segment. "Black verse" is Oppen's metaphor for his poetry of negativity: an unconsoled poetry of turning and searching, an unconsoling poetry of hope. That is, to go back to Adorno's terms, "black verse" is form for a poetry of commitment. To turn, as I will, to Benjamin, "black verse" constructs a dialectical image. To repeat Celan, "black verse" leaves one "uncannily in the open."

Especially in his later poetry, Oppen achieves a nonsurrealist, but continuous combinatoire—a realist but destabilizing combinatory movement, by junctures along the line, openings inside the line, and by hinges created by line break. The strained, open, gnomic, and aphoristic line of his later poetry gives to him, but with a different ethics, a different epistemology, what surrealism gives to others: an investigatory tool to explore how the world may be put together differently by setting certain materials in combination. This is not a magical irrationalism in Oppen, but it does create a sense of unresolvable oddness at the core of the real.

Once upon a time I happened to use the word dizzy, meaning vertiginous, to George in describing the effect of his later poems on me, something I think that he misunderstood. When, in a letter to Robert Duncan, Oppen defended himself, a little proudly and happily, from the burden of my dizziness, he said something germane to this discussion: "But I thought I was simply pointing to things—and clearly enough or accurately enough" (*SL* 300). Still half-talking to the dead, let me say that I belatedly comprehend what this vertigo entailed: what Adorno called (in Robert Kaufman's words) "a quasi-cognitive, quasi-experiential otherness in art" sensed through a "shaking of the subject in aesthetic experience" (Kaufman 2002, 49).

Adorno proposed this as "a breaking through of reified consciousness" in "aesthetic experience" that allows one to "exercise . . . those faculties whose development contributes to sociopolitical critique and praxis" (Adorno 1997, 196; Kaufman 2002, 48, 49). Or even, "a liberated society . . . is enciphered in art and is the source of art's social explosiveness" (Adorno 1997, 227). The vertigo of these unrolling line turns of "black verse" propels one magnetically down the road of negativity, skepticism, and resistant hope. This is the goal of Oppen's saturated-realism (the opposite of surrealism), and he achieves this not by combining image-based words, but by the startling combinatoire of his line breaks. These line breaks offer a sense of another space, the space of awe and the inexpressible. For an attenuated sense of transformation enters in the turn of many of Oppen's lines. It is, as he says in "Myth of the Blaze," the "blaze // of changes" (*NCP* 248).

One aspect of the "uncanny open" is, then, Oppen's vertiginous sense of statement, syntax, and space. The spaces of the poem are like the universe of stars, and of human losses. A poem swings from the smallest to the largest terms at once, a netting of the void. The open is also the historical and dialectical swing of statement, where the lines are like thesis and antithesis, and where any "synthesis" is like the beginning of a new dialectical formulation. Oppen's work is confluent with Benjamin's *The Arcades Project*, which is itself a suggestive, collaged, intense, raggedy, frustrating, startling text, porous by virtue of its refusal to construct argument.

"Method of this project: literary montage. I needn't say anything. Merely show. I shall purloin no valuables, appropriate no ingenious formulations. But the rags, the refuse—these I will not inventory but allow, in the only way possible, to come into their own: by making use of them" (Benjamin 1999, 460). I cite this for the untoward suggestiveness of its confrontative praxis; it is more suggestive than I can say, even understanding that in its apparent refusal of anything but pointing, it has made a strange, strange claim. *The Arcades Project* was in large measure conducted exactly as these words propose. To collect and set forth scraps of insight and fact, to rupture the academic and journalistic arguments from which these facts had been gleaned, would, Benjamin claimed, allow a myriad of flashes to be generated over the whole texture of the project. This juxtaposition of deictic plenitudes made an anti-systemic and anti-triumphalist texture, fractally opened to a space beyond argument, to sheer suggestiveness. One of Benjamin's great ironies is how he uses positivist collection of fact against itself, for anti-positivist ends. With cinematic, though not narrative design, Benjamin proposed that a montage of images on certain topoi offered instantaneous meaning in a modernist flash, but he also modified this desire for instant epiphany by a focus on "intervals of reflection" or "distances lying between" his cited and sometimes, though rarely, glossed materials (Benjamin 1999, 458 and 456).[18] Those words ("intervals" and "distances") insist on the creation of structure by interactive space between the blocks of fact, very much the poetics of seriality, as in Oppen.

Benjamin spent some time in section "N" working through the "dialectical image" (Benjamin 1999, 462–475). "Where thinking comes to a standstill in a constellation saturated with tensions—there the dialectical image appears. It is the caesura in the movement of thought. Its position is naturally not an arbitrary one. It is to be found . . . where the tensions between dialectical opposites is greatest. Hence, the object constructed in the materialist presentation of history is itself the dialectical image" (Benjamin 1999, 475). But this is quite odd when applied to poetry, as one might immediately desire to, led by the words "caesura," not to speak of "image," "constellation," or even "thinking." Benjamin seems to propose a poetics of modernist presentation (maybe applied to history)—the still moment, the held object, the formed thought emerging from a field of conflictual materials. The "dialectical image" "is dialectics at a standstill" (Benjamin 1999, 475, 462). But isn't the point of dialectics its ongoingness, its movement in time, its rejection of stasis, its situated repositioning of primary materials? It's as if Benjamin named something using a terminology that honored the play of temporality and movement, but in his descriptive definition of the constellation, he produced a modernist freeze-frame "hold." Further, for Anglo-American readers, Benjamin's definition "thinking [at] a standstill in a constellation saturated with tensions" recalls Pound's famous capital *I* and quotation marked "'Image'" from 1913: "an 'Image' is that which presents an intellectual and emotional complex in an instant of time," and also recalls the methods of field and/or ideogram construction used in Poundean poetries (Pound 1954, 4).[19]

It is hard to parse this and honor its complexity. In Oppen, one might say, "thinking" never comes "to a standstill." Oppen's poetry thus offers a critique of Benjamin's modernist, freeze-frame poetics, yet it can perfectly illustrate another definition of the "dialectical image." Adorno seems to double back on Benjamin's insight when he says, "the artwork is both the result of the process and the process itself at a standstill," showing how an artwork is dynamic and objectified at once, perpetually "in a process of becoming" (Adorno 1997, 179, 178). Putting words like dialectical and historical near the word "image" illuminates the poetry of Oppen and poetry in general.[20] Thus, using the same key words differently, I want to say: "where thinking in poetry is both poised and ongoing, in a streaming of lines that one could read as a constellation, but which also embodies the experience of temporality and ceaseless questioning, there the dialectical image appears. It is the caesura in the movement of thought, a caesura paradoxically both in the full poem as a unit, and inside a line of poetry, as an actual caesura, white space or pause, in the pressure of the line break or turn of the line."

In the section of *Aesthetic Theory* called "Toward a Theory of the Artwork," Adorno comments on the dialectic of constellation as both stasis and motion. "Artworks' paradoxical nature, stasis, negates itself. The movement of artworks must be at a standstill and thereby become visible" for "it is only as finished, molded objects that they become force fields of their antagonisms"; thus stasis is necessary to the sense of transformative movement (Adorno 1997, 176). Line break in poetry—visceral and visual—expresses this lively tension between eloquent stasis and driven becoming.

One may thereby theorize Oppen's distinctive practice of hovering and enjambment, a practice achieving ethical and emotional effects from poetic segmentivity, as this dialectic constellation. These bidirectional, even multidirectional line segments in later Oppen compel a practice of reading that makes fluid and ambiguous what part of the line segment to read with what other part. Or how to read and reckon with enjambment and *apo koinou* (Quartermain 1992, 113, 215). Through the various answers to the open-ended question what line segments go with what, hovering, hinges, and bridges are created that make double or triple readings plausible. Thus from any one later Oppen poem, one has several shadowy poems (more "black verse"), and the intellectual, emotional, and structural mobility of the lines in the reading process, their modular quality, create a sense of temporality (even historical time, large time, time in motion) inside the poem as object. These aspects make reality multidimensional and offer a sense of "occurrence" or the things we are among, and our sense of exposure "in the open" to those things. The thinking poetry achieves is created within the texture of poetry.

Oppen's poems are precisely dialectical images in this sense—in a temporal sense, not at a standstill (except insofar as they are in finished poems).[21] They are dialectical images both in individual lines and particulars and in the total poem. To say "I believe // in the world // because it is / impossible" is formally a constellation saturated with tensions that changes temporally as you read the lines (*NCP* 248). The lines seem to have one meaning if you stop with line break, another meaning if you continue. The statements (I believe in the world because it is; I believe in the world because it is impossible) propose dialectical, ongoing thought by using the deepest formal mechanisms of poetry. These kinds of moments are not the only ones in Oppen, but these tactics set the tonality and pitch for readers.

In their use of fragmented phrases, Oppen's lines are not static, but the phrases, taken as objects, seem to stream toward each other in a desire for connectedness in the "between" created by the poem. This desire is never quite fulfilled. Oppen's later poems are something between full statement and attenuated absences, plenitude in opacity, bridging between the two states in a literal demonstration of the between. One reads the potential condensation of any one thought into finality, but as more possibilities are created, the sense of a "black verse" overwritten with itself, also increases. The phrases move along on the same "speaking plane," but they turn both toward and away from each other as the stream of language moves along. There is very little settled (there is, indeed, very little final punctuation or commas), and nothing seems to end, even at the conclusion of any given poem. Yet many of the statements have the force of enormous pronouncements. This is black verse; this is the dialectical image, completeness in motion.

The statements "and the music essential" then "clarity plain glass ray" (*NCP* 257) are final, but the statement created by line break "and the music essential // clarity plain glass ray" changes things ("essential clarity"? "essential clarity plain"?). Not to speak of the addition of the final line "of darkness ray of light" (*NCP* 257). In many (though, of course, not all) of the relationships of line to line in Oppen, there are alternative determinate meanings palimpsested as the poem releases itself into its temporality dialectically, as the lines change in relation to each other, repositioned as synthesis or as new thesis, and then antithesis. One changes or extends the statement by imagining "periods" or puncted marks after various words. One changes or extends the statement by imagining alternative relationships of apposition among the elements. But finally (something that makes later Oppen hard to read aloud, as it makes him hard to excerpt), the poem is a chain with modular links built to surround or net something ungraspable, unnettable, unassimilable. There is a relative, though not absolute attenuation of syntax creating horizontal equality among the elements, as if they were being scanned along a changing horizon.

One is often straining for meaning as it shifts, via line break, right under your eyes. Indeed, any given line may have two centers—a completed thought and an incompleted thought (in the swing to the next line). This is a plausible condition of poetry in general, one might say, but Oppen pushed this potential of the poetic line very far. Finally often in the later work, the poem never ends but simply stops, leaving us where we are: and by this we know we are "uncannily in the open." (I have of course, echoed both Celan's phrase and Oppen's own line, "by this we know it is the real // That we confront"; *NCP* 202.) The uncanny open of Oppen exists in the tensions between surface and depth, between conclusion and endlessness; between sententia/aphorism and the breaking of those vessels not by force, but by the direct continuance of thinking itself. This is Oppen's saturated realism, a mode of practicing "combination" that makes a critical answer, in form, to surrealist practices of the image, allowing for alternative combinations, pointing to real things. Oppen wants to show that claims of our materiality are the same as claims of our mystery: "I suppose it's nearly a sense of awe, simply to feel that the thing is there and that it's quite something to see" (Dembo interview 164). Where materiality and mystery join dialectically along the line, there is the uncanny light of his poetry.

Notes

1. Written originally as a lecture for my receipt of the Roy Harvey Pearce / Archive for New Poetry Prize (2002).

2. He agrees, for example, with the critique of his absolute position offered by Hans Magnus Enzensberger "that literature must resist precisely this verdict, that is, be such that it does not surrender to cynicism merely by existing after Auschwitz"; Theodor Adorno, *Aesthetic Theory* 88. He further argues that it is unthinkable to engineer "transfiguration": "By this alone an injustice is done the victims, yet no art that avoided the victims could stand up to the demands of justice" (ibid. 88). However, turning the victims into "works of art, [they are] tossed out to be gobbled up by the world that did them in," an ethical nightmare of the aesthetic. Furthermore, he rejects the "dreary metaphysics" of a humanism (and presumably journalism) that "shows us humanity blossoming in so-called extreme situations"—a "cozy existential atmosphere" whose implications are happier for "the executioners" than the victims. The impulse to make such literature would then be—intransigent self-questioning and lacerating judgment unto blockage.

3. On the silence, see Rachel Blau DuPlessis, "'The familiar / becomes extreme'"; on its impact on others, see Weinberger, Preface to *New Collected Poems,* vii–viii. Charles Bernstein has also commented on Riding's and Oppen's stopping writing: how political grief and thinking about human social disasters, a grief so strong it is almost blocking, affected them obliquely (Bernstein 1999, 257–59).

4. I will bracket the issue of the translation of these works as interpretive practices and any reader's dependence on translations.

5. With a number of literary historical models possible (from George Oppen to Langston Hughes), serial poems are sectional or modular works whose argument is built by the order of the parts, by the nature and montage cut of the parts (image, phrase, line, word), by the shape of blankness or space in relation to

the parts, and by the varied intellectual and emotional relations of suture and leap among these parts. Seriality proceeds by vectors, adjusting to pressures on all sides and coming out with a situational path.

6. Eliot Weinberger notes Oppen's "obstinate blindness to all forms of surrealism, which he saw as an escape from, and not a way into, current realities" (*NCP* x). In an important set of comments in an email of May 6, 2003, the poet and critic Andrew Joron notes the degree to which surrealism "haunts" my essay, first by virtue of the fact that surrealism serves as a "constitutive moment" for both Benjamin and Celan, as Margaret Cohen argued in *Profane Illumination* (1993), and second by virtue of the terms I come to use: "vertiginous" and the "uncanny," all of which have serious uses in surrealist thought. Third—and here I will cite Joron, whose defense of surrealism deconstructs Oppen's resistance: "At the same time I remain convinced of the French movement's relevance and vitality, especially with regard to a negative poetics (aren't Oppen's valorizations, for example, of austerity and clarity conditioned by their relations to opposites, their repressed others, namely jouissance and obscurity? Poetic meaning, at some level, must conjure and agonistically embrace its repressed Other, a contradiction that cannot be resolved or thought through, perhaps, so much as lived through, 'uncannily in the open')." I thank Joron for these penetrating remarks and for permission to cite them.

7. For a corrective view of the career of John Cage, see Joan Retallack's essays in *The Poethical Wager.*

8. In the year of his second book, Oppen wrote on Olson, McClure, and Ginsberg, praising Ginsberg's *Kaddish* in strong terms for its lack of "preciousness" and its breadth. But he takes issue with the overdone quality of "declamatory form" in the shorter poems, with the temptation of "riding 'no hands'" in that poetics, and finally with Ginsberg's putting opinions into poetry without subjecting them to "rigorous thought" (Oppen 1962, 329–330). The review, which always tempers criticism with allusions to the better work of those poets, frankly criticizes his serious and well-received peers.

9. The stakes were very high and his sense of isolation from "Bohemia" is patent in his 1963 essay "The Mind's Own Place."

10. This is the point—poems tracking the graph of thought—at which a "projective" poetics as in Olson, Creeley, and, differently Duncan and Blaser meet the "objectivist" tendency.

11. For his part, Oppen told me repeatedly I should leave the university, something I also ignored.

12. In a remarkable letter (1976), Oppen enunciates the "principle" of working "to connect each word at BOTH ENDS" (which in his view demands a major cutting of superficial syntactic connections)—and indicates thereby how, out of a purely horizontal and paratactic poetics, he achieves the "vertical dimension" (*SL* 316).

13. Blake's poem "from Milton" beginning "And did those feet in ancient times." That Oppen is a kind of meditative poet about class might explain why he (mis)cites George Herbert's anti-Platonic pastoral "Jordan (I)," ("Shepherds are good people let them sing," *NCP* 250, for "Shepherds are honest people; let them sing"); that he is a kind of revolutionary poet suggests why he miscites Shelley (?) (Oppen's "of the world's deed this is the young age," *NCP* 240, derives possibly from *Hellas*: "The world's great age begins anew"); that he is a poet of essences of insight explains his Western Wind citation; that he has a scrupulous, brilliant aphoristic quality and a social vision might explain why Blake was so important to him. These were talismans.

14. There is even a curious coincidence of dates, for 1958 was a turning point: Oppen returned to poetry after interior and exterior exile, after choices of other work.

15. This is akin to Oppen's refusal to commodify himself immediately after winning the Pulitzer Prize for Poetry in 1969, although that prize offered the potential for some fame.

16. The twentieth-plus century keeps on exposing us. The satellite, a stunning and moderately positive event, is just one more of the events of the twentieth century that Celan explicitly says have made him shelterless—exposed. Those "called" to look upward in earlier times could look at the stars without ambient light, without airplanes, without the (evocative) satellites of human science and militarism. Oppen was quite stunned by the moon landing, by the threats of military prowess he saw immediately in it.

17. All of Oppen on prosody is about this. See "note by note the prosody carries the relation of things and the sequence" (Oppen 1984, 26). Important remarks on prosody and the line occur in the Dembo interview. "I do believe in a form in which there is a sense of the whole line, not just its ending. Then there's the sense of the relation between lines, the relation in their length; there is a sense of the relation of the speed, of the alterations and momentum of the poem, the feeling when it's done that this has been rounded. . . . The meaning of a poem is in the cadences and the shape of the lines and the pulse of the thought which is given by those lines. The meaning of many lines will be changed—one's understanding of the lines will be altered—if one changes the line-ending. It's not just the line-ending as punctuation but as separating the connections of the progression of thought in such a way that the understanding of the line would be changed if one altered the line division. And I don't mean [line break as] just a substitute for the comma; I mean with which phrase the word is most intimately connected—that kind of thing" (Dembo interview 167).

18. Benjamin 1999, 462. The material is rather similar to the sense of the Image that Pound offered in 1913, but adds a temporal aspect that does rather transform it. "It's not that what is past casts its light on what is present, or what is present its

light on what is past; rather, image is that wherein what has been comes together in a flash with the now to form a constellation." Image is the crystallization of historical forces or temporal forces otherwise in movement.

19. In the same way the Benjaminian word "constellation" offers the interplay between elements in a field poetics or a multiple array of a thicket of materials.

20. "Only dialectical images are genuine images (that is, not archaic); and the place where one encounters them is language" (Benjamin 1999, 462). Not archaic means "genuinely historical" (Benjamin 1999, 463).

21. Here one could comment how in later Oppen the modular movement of lines and materials from site to site (keeping the poems experimentally unfinished or open) is a kind of indication of the force of thinking temporally with the words for Oppen. Thus, at the end of his career, poems float into each other, something discussed by Michael Davidson at several junctures (*NCP* xl; Davidson 1997).

Works Cited

Adorno, Theodor. *Aesthetic Theory.* Trans. Robert Hullot-Kentor. Minneapolis: University of Minnesota Press, 1997.

———. *Prisms.* Trans. Samuel and Shierry Weber. Cambridge, MA: MIT Press, 1981.

———. *Notes to Literature,* vol. 2. Trans. Shierry Weber Nicholsen. New York: Columbia University Press, 1992.

Benjamin, Walter. *The Arcades Project.* Cambridge, MA: Harvard University Press, 1999.

———. *Illuminations.* Trans. Harry Zohn. New York: Schocken Books, 1969.

———. "N [Re The Theory of Knowledge, Theory of Progress]." In *Benjamin: Philosophy, Aesthetics, History,* ed. Gary Smith, trans. Leigh Hafrey and Richard Sieburth. Chicago: University of Chicago Press, 1989.

Bernstein, Charles. "The Second War and Postmodern Memory." *Apoetics.* Cambridge, MA: Harvard University Press, 1992. 193–217.

———. *My Way: Speeches and Poems.* Chicago: University of Chicago Press, 1999.

Celan, Paul. *Breathturn [Atemwende].* Trans. Pierre Joris. Los Angeles: Sun and Moon Press, 1995.

Cohen, Margaret. *Profane Illumination: Walter Benjamin and the Paris of Surrealist Revolution.* Berkeley and Los Angeles: University of California Press, 1993.

Cope, Stephen, ed. *Selected Prose, Daybooks, and Papers.* See Oppen.

Davidson, Michael. *Ghostlier Demarcations: Modern Poetry and the Material Word.* Berkeley and Los Angeles: University of California Press, 1997.

DuPlessis, Rachel Blau. *Wells.* New York: Montemora, 1980. Duration Press Online Out of Print Book Archives, 1999. http://www.durationpress.com.

———. "Objectivist Poetics and Political Vision: A Study of Oppen and Pound." *George Oppen: Man and Poet,* ed. Burton Hatlen, 123–148. Orono, ME: National Poetry Foundation, 1981.

———. *Drafts 1–38, Toll.* Middletown, CT: Wesleyan University Press, 2001.

——— "'The familiar/ becomes extreme': George Oppen and Silence," *North Dakota Quarterly*, special issue ed. Sherman Paul; 55, 4 (Fall 1987): 18–26.

———. *Blue Studios: Poetry and Its Cultural Work.* Tuscaloosa: The University of Alabama Press, 2006.

———, ed. *The Selected Letters of George Oppen*; see Oppen.

Felstiner, John. *Paul Celan: Poet, Survivor, Jew.* New Haven, CT: Yale University Press, 1995.

Howe, Irving. *A Margin of Hope: An Intellectual Autobiography.* San Diego: Harcourt Brace Jovanovich, 1982.

Kaufman, Robert. "Aura, Still." *October* 99 (Winter 2002): 45–80.

Oppen, George. Review of Ginsberg, Olson, and McClure. *Poetry* 110, 5 (August 1962): 329–330.

———. "The Mind's Own Place (1962)." *The Selected Poems of George Oppen.* Ed. Robert Creeley. New York: New Directions, 2003. 173–182.

———. *Selected Prose, Daybooks, and Papers.* Ed. Stephen Cope. Berkeley and Los Angeles: University of California Press, 2007.

———. "Interview with George Oppen," conducted by L. S. Dembo on April 25, 1968. *Contemporary Literature* 10, 2 (Spring 1969): 159–177.

———. "Statement on Poetics." *Sagetrieb* 3, 3 (Winter 1984): 25–27.

———. *The Selected Letters of George Oppen.* Ed. Rachel Blau DuPlessis. Durham, NC: Duke University Press, 1990.

——— *New Collected Poems.* Ed. Michael Davidson, preface by Eliot Weinberger. New York: New Directions, 2002.

Pound, Ezra. *Literary Essays of Ezra Pound.* London: Faber and Faber, 1954.

———. *Pound/Joyce: The Letters of Ezra Pound to James Joyce.* Ed. Forrest Read. New York: New Directions, 1967.

Quartermain, Peter. *Disjunctive Poetics: From Gertrude Stein and Louis Zukofsky to Susan Howe.* New York: Cambridge University Press, 1992.

Retallack, Joan. *The Poethical Wager.* Berkeley and Los Angeles: University of California Press, 2003.

Rothenberg, Jerome, and Pierre Joris, eds. "Introduction." *Poems for the Millennium: The University of California Book of Modern and Postmodern Poetry, Volume 2: From Postwar to Millennium.* Berkeley and Los Angeles: University of California Press, 1998: 1–18.

13
George Oppen
A Radical Practice (excerpt)

Susan Thackrey

Introduction

George Oppen exercised a very specific form of poetic practice that was meant to permit and show forth true, and truthful, lived experience. It is easy, given his reading in Heidegger and Merleau-Ponty, to label this "existentialist" and be done with it. In the philosophical shifts of the last thirty years the premises of existentialism have been often stereotyped and considered passé. The political disillusionments of the late 1960s have given rise to a philosophical turning toward the insights of Structuralism, post-Structuralism, and postmodernism, which have analyzed the structures of power and other forms of intent. This shattering of form itself has become a new definition of truth; Lacan said that the existentialist observation revealed negativity but continued to rely on a subject who was falsely unified. I think this can probably be argued with, but in any case, at the heart of Oppen's own poetic practice there is an extraordinary identification of several understandings of what authentic experience is, an identification which seems to be unique to him, and is certainly instructive for us.

Probably every person has experienced moments when habitual ways of being and experiencing have just suddenly disappeared, and something is "just there," as is the person in that moment. Probably every poet has experienced those times when a poem or some piece of a poem is just there, or just arising, as is the poet. And certainly everyone knows and inhabits various moments of past experience, seemingly consequential or inconsequential, that arise as terms of the present, as does each person at that moment. Oppen's practice recognized all these forms of experience and recognized how feeling at the same time moves within them, selecting and shaping. As if in answer to Lacan's objection about the unified subject, over time it was the very literalness of his lived experiences that allowed Oppen's poetics to become more and more capable of including the very gaps and discontinuities of human perception and experience.

An art critic has recently written that "The essential revelation of modern art was that literalism could have an emotional impact" (Perl). Applied to Oppen's practice, this statement puts back in place what Oppen was trying to undo. For him the literal actuality of the moment of perception and experience does not operate on a perceiver—that division disappears. This literalness, for Oppen, can actually overcome the curse of reflection. So for him the desire for the reader, in his words, to "find me" in the poem, as well as the practice of exploiting experience to produce the personally symbolic poem, are both pernicious. His practice circumvents both narcissistic and gnostic reflecting.

In his practice Oppen simply refused a poetics that was based anywhere other than in this present experience. If in fact this practice can be found to be in any way limiting, it has nevertheless given us the great gift of a poetry and a poetics that can be radically trusted.

Oppen's Practice

George Oppen was afraid that he would be read as a simple realist—someone not only kicking stones to prove that they exist, but then talking *about* the experience of kicking stones. At the watershed moment of his later career, he wrote to Michael Heller, in a draft: "I begin to understand that the earlier books have been taken to be a simple realism - - I was in those books speaking of Being: I had thought I could arrive at the concept of Being from an account of experience as it presents itself in its own terms - - Needle's eye . . . will be taken as less than I meant it to be if it is not taken in the light of the previous books. . . . I was sure I had said, managed to say - - - - - - *Being* - 'the most obvious thing in the word' [*sic*]" (*SL* 410).

In at least one very sophisticated instance Oppen's fears have been justified. When Ron Silliman wrote about Oppen in *The New Sentence*, he saw a loss of the original Objectivist "identification of method with content," and any linkage between this and a broader social vision. "What is missing is precisely its challenge to the perceptual limits of the reader," which had been based on a presumption "that perception itself is not possible within the confines of social norms" (Silliman 136 and 132). Instead, Silliman says, "Beginning with *The Materials*, Oppen . . . demonstrated himself to be a master in calling attention to *the importance in what the poem says*." This, he goes on, is directly contrary to what W. C. Williams had said in the preface to Oppen's very first book (*Discrete Series*). Here is Williams: "[The] . . . importance cannot be in what the poem says, since in that case the poem would be a redundancy. The importance lies in what the poem *is*. Its existence as a poem is of first importance. . . . It is the acceptable fact of a poem as a mechanism that is proof of its meaning and this is as technical a matter as in the case of any other machine" (Silliman 138). This emphasis on a subject matter is, Silliman goes on to say, a conscious change of stance for Oppen, revealed by his use of multiple techniques to achieve it.[1] This was to have, in Silliman's view, far-reaching and not particularly salubrious effects on American poetry.

There is no doubt that the poems in *The Materials* were different from those of *Discrete Series*, or that Oppen's technique had changed in some respects. But, in Oppen's poetry it is a *given* that cultural norms render perception impossible—this is one of the things that makes his series "Of Being Numerous" so intensely tenuous; how is it possible to find relation to existence as it is embodied in other human beings, when so many are embroiled and entangled in a network of rigidly defined perceptions—if an attempt to perceive without prior definition is one's basis for truth? Here is the last verse of an early poem from *The Materials*.

> . . . And yet at night
> Their weight is part of mine
> For we are all housed now, all in our apartments,
> The world untended to, unwatched.
> And there is nothing left out there
> As night falls, but the rocks
> ("Myself I Sing," from *The Materials*, NCP 57)

As for Williams's point—which Silliman says Oppen's later poetry contradicts—that the poem is empty if its importance lies in what it says, since in that case the poem is a redundancy, let us turn to Oppen in early

1959, in a letter to his sister as he begins to write poetry again. "Maybe I admire myself . . . for simply not attempting to write communist verse. That is, to [write] any statement already determined before the verse. Poetry has to be protean; the meaning must begin there. With the perception. Eliot . . . thinks of himself as deliberately finding the 'objective correlative' to substantiate a body of thought" (*SL* 22).

What is the difference here, if Oppen is so much in agreement about the absolute necessity that the poem not participate in any sort of predetermined meaning? The key is in the words "Poetry . . . must begin . . . With the perception." That is to say—a freed perception is possible for one—for a human being—for a poet. It is there that truth arises. I think what is confusing (and occasionally, in his less successful poems, confused) in Oppen, is that only in the very earliest poems of *Discrete Series* does perception refer to purely sensory perception of an outside, objectifiable world. Thoughts, in the sense of whatever might arise in one—sensations, cognitions, feelings, percepts, memories, and not least, words—are part of what is perceivable, part of world, in which mind is. It is a shift of perceptual focus.

Oppen was fully aware of the shift. In 1966, in a letter to John Crawford, he speaks vehemently against "the machine of words" to which Williams had pointed in his preface. Oppen goes on to say that since "Words cannot be wholly transparent . . . In despair, so many turn to 'the machine of words' and arrive, if anywhere, at the Hermetic . . . the 'machine of words' which resolves everything - - - until one steps out the door" (*SL* 144–145). "We awaken at the same moment to ourselves and to things," he quoted at the beginning about *The Materials*, and to try to remove words, or the poem itself, from this moment of awakening leads to a situation, "where it becomes like all machines a kind of poisonous frenzy, the mind locked in its cage" (*SL* 145). Hermetically sealed. Always, always, in experience mind and world arise together.

Oppen wrote to his sister: "Whereas the point is something else, the point is the mind operating in a marvel which contains the mind . . . *It* can really not be thought about because *it* contains the thought, but *it* can be felt. *It* is what all art is about" (*SL* 90; emphasis added). The poem is mind in the world, coming into being—not mind or world, not one being a content or about the other.

I have emphasized the word "it" in this quotation because of its great importance to Oppen, always indicating a perception arising in awareness, but which cannot be captured and caged. In this understanding signifier and signified are already free of each other; this aspect of the post-structuralist project is already accomplished.

A use of language which blocks referentiality and contextuality, so that cultural norms can become visible as constructions, which makes the attempt to undo hierarchy and a spurious unification of the writing, speaking subject, is without question an enormously ethical project. It is just not Oppen's project. He had come to a point where he did not wish to operate *upon* the political construct, and since his political credentials in the earlier years of his life are impeccable, his entire life going into the fight against fascist authoritarianism, his political integrity must not only *not* be at issue, but his own project must have another significance.

A wonderful quotation from Oppen describes the always originary act of perceiving: "suppose, instead of an 'instant archaeology' that imagines a personification of things already known, one imagines the first objects to become *object* to living consciousness - - their force is that among sensations they emerged as *objects*——— can we suppose, in the history of the Sacred, a greater moment? this is the ground the poems meant to stand on" (*SL* 248). Again, if one is able to write from this point, then that person has moved, by definition, beyond the socially and culturally imposed order of words—it implies, in art, another kind of capability of freedom.

Oppen's procedure for accomplishing this can be more or less worked out from his letters and poems, although it cannot be reduced to linear steps. It amounts to a literal *practice* of perception, which in his poetry, over time, became capable of including more and more into its ground, its world of *objects* as they are in the act of perception. In 1960 he said, in a letter to Cid Corman, "I think that poetry . . . must be made of the clarity of the perceptions, of emotion as the ability to perceive" (*SL* 40). Later, in 1965, writing to Rachel Blau DuPlessis, he said—"There are certain things, appearances, around which the understanding gathers. . . . they are one's sense of reality and the possibility of meaning. They are there, in the mind, always. One can sit down anytime and sink into them - - can work at them, they come into the mind" (*SL* 123).

It is possible to drop into the mind, and find there things, appearances that are most central, most important; they can also leap on us, choose us, and we can choose to occupy them. In other places Oppen said that the poem makes the words, and that if a man feels himself afraid of a word, he may have started, and that he didn't know where the line or the word itself came from (*SL* 123). Sometimes he would find himself trying to fit words to the felt perception, but "one can't really find the words. It simply springs into the mind." And, he went on, "There is, in some places, at some times, for some people - - the simple intuition of existence. Of one's own existence, and in the same instant the intuition, the pure intuition of the existence of things, absolutely independent of oneself. . . . It is *that* intuition first of all which is assuredly 'a thought' and which does not occur in words" (*SL* xx).

In this sense image remained primary for Oppen. In his essay "The Mind's Own Place" he said, "Modern American poetry begins with the determination to find the image, the thing encountered, the thing seen each day" (*Montemora* 132). In fact, that is how so many of his poems actually compose—always remembering *his* sense of image—as a shining moment of unfolding appearance of both consciousness and world, in which words arise. Later he said in a letter to Robert Duncan, quoting Heidegger: "'the Word comes to existence, and for the last time, as language'" (*SL* 273).

This most fundamental moment is at the basis of Oppen's truth of perception. It is remarkable that it should constitute a practice of such clarity. It had its predecessors, in Husserl's phenomenology, with its examination of consciousness, but Husserl wanted to find the universal structure of intention, beyond the empirical, and Oppen was adamant in his attention to the empirical—the actualness of lived experience. We also know that Oppen read Merleau-Ponty (*SL* 311), who insisted that lived experience is bodily, and always taking place in an embodied world. But Oppen's practice is fruitful and completely specific—it includes the always arising poem, issuing from true experience. This, he said, is its own kind of thinking, and will be recognized as such in the future (*SL* 99). If, as both Laura Riding and more recently Leslie Scalapino have said, poetry has become philosophy, it is in this sense of nonreflection—a thinking that arises rather than reflects, true to its own experience of itself; and that has nothing to do with the two primary moves of what the philosopher John Searle in a recent lecture sees as inherent in the intentionality of both language and consciousness—an accommodation of subject to world, or of world to subject. In an essay of Heidegger's that was, as we shall see, the location of an extraordinary experience for Oppen, Heidegger calls for a thinking that is not a "nachdenken"—a thinking back, a reflection—but a "vordenken," a thinking forward, which is *not* the same as a planning or a calculating. Oppen copied those sentences into his notes (*SL* 136; see Heidegger, trans. Leidecker 32, and trans. Stambaugh 41).

I would call Oppen's practice an ethics of perception if Oppen did not consistently use the word "ethics" for an already constituted set of principles, which can be articulated, and which one knows are there because one acts on them. But admitting and permitting, acknowledging what is actually appearing as most central, also constitute the ground of truthful action.

In an interview in 1968 with L. S. Dembo, Oppen aroused some consternation in his interviewer by saying "that there is no life for humanity except the life of the mind" (Dembo 172 ff.). Pressed he said: "I mean the awareness . . . simply to feel that the thing is there. . . . I was anticipating as its opposite . . . all the struggles for happiness, all the search for a morality of altruism, all the dependence on the poor to confer value." (And we must be reminded here of Blake's words: "Pity would be no more / If we did not make somebody Poor" [Blake 217]). Oppen went on: "I don't mean that there isn't anything to do right now, but I was thinking about a justification of human life, eventually, in what I call the life of the mind." Pressed again, he said that "the ethic isn't permanent and it isn't going to answer the problem"—that is, the problem of what human beings actually are about. And yet again, he said that he himself had a commitment to an ethic, and "therefore I do something about it." As indeed his biography proves that he did.

> Wars that are just? A simpler question: In the event,
> will you or will you not want to kill a German. Because,
> in the event, if you do not want to, you won't.
> ("Route (part 6)," from *Of Being Numerous, NCP* 196)

I want to notice that the possibility that ethical commitment might be a viable human creation in history was actually there in Oppen's poetry. Oppen said that he had included the words "amor fati," love of fate, in section 8 of his sequence "Of Being Numerous," and that this *is* "the center of the poem, its meaning" (*SL* 111). It is human history of which he is speaking here. "Amor fati" is a term Nietzsche used to refer to the absolute necessity for a human being to love her own fate, all that has come before the present moment, if that person is to achieve freedom. For Oppen here it refers to "the concept of humanity," and a love of our fate, to where we have come—not excluding from awareness the cruel, the manipulations of power, the automatisms of what he called the stone universe, and the glassed-in modes of perception and consciousness which dominate.

I, says the buzzard,
I—

Mind

Has evolved
Too long

If 'life is a search
For advantage.'

'At whose behest

Does the mind think?' Art
Also is not good

For us
Unless like the fool

Persisting
In his folly

It may rescue us
As only the true

Might rescue us, gathered
In the smallest corners

Of man's triumph. *Parve puer.* . . 'Begin,

O small boy,
To be born;

On whom his parents have not smiled

No god thinks worthy of his table,
No goddess of her bed'
("From Virgil," from *This in Which, NCP* 104–105)

At the end of this poem from *This in Which*, indeed, the final lines, translated from Virgil's Fourth Eclogue, generate for Oppen a profound and personal sense of how a human being becomes ethical—in his history of being within the circle of human relation. It is part of Oppen's extraordinary poetics that here it is both a personal questioning of himself, and also an arrival at an understanding that this is not just something "in the genes," but in human history. Oppen faced history, he recognized that particular actions have had particular effects, and that we live in the history of our physical being. A wolf removed as a cub from her family cannot hunt, a monkey removed from her mother cannot later have fruitful sex, a child removed cannot later learn to speak. This is wolf history, primate history, human history. We include all three. The small ones of perception, the small boy, can be born, but the term of purely physical survival is, for many years, a counterweight to the term of true perception for Oppen.

In any case, he saw it as a contradiction that Socrates died for an *abstraction,* even of ethical principle, and not in direct ethical action impelled by feeling (Dembo 178). Oppen was clear that his looking toward the kind of truth he was talking about did not mean setting up a dichotomy between art and human life. Truth in perception, informed by feeling, permits ethics and art to *not* split from one another.

This is, in fact, related to another aspect of true action for Oppen. He said, both in his essay "The Mind's Own Place" and in a letter to John Taggart (*SL* 287): "there are things we believe or think we believe or want to believe which will not substantiate themselves in the concrete material of the poem." That is, the moment of absolute particularity, the appearance of the "thing" in the concrete materials of the poem, as it arises as an "instance of being in the world," will not support generalities of any sort. Notice that this is neither technique nor stricture: it is practice—what the actual moment of perception that manifests a poem brings forth.

Related to this is Oppen's often repeated and powerfully held understanding that Symbolism was an attempt to convert actual "things," actual "objects," into "symbols of interior sensations" (*SL* 249). This technique would, of course, obviate the very foundations of Oppen's practice—world would disappear, as would the possibility of any originary experience. Surrealism, too, which was based for Oppen in a "derangement of the senses" (this is Rimbaud's term), removes one from the encounter, from "the arduous path of appearance." In another letter he says, "We HAVE only our sight" (*SL* 56). That is, we have only our practice of perception. We have only truth in that sense.

In a culture in which the capture of individual attention has become the principal means of coercion and power—computer screens, television screens, windshield screens—as earlier the imposed focal points of the machine age were production lines, cinema, windows of rapidly moving trains—tiny territories in which our attention is grabbed—we learn to, literally, *pay* attention. It is the price of political survival, survival within a political entity.

As Jonathan Crary has found, the project of many visual artists, beginning with the Impressionists to whom Oppen felt so strongly related, was to respond by acts of actual perception. Near the beginning of Oppen's only essay are the words "the passion of the Impressionists to see and to see past the subject matter and the attitudes of the Art Academy" (*Montemora* 132). In Crary's analysis, it was Cézanne who was able to include both the actuality of multiple forms of perception and of the gaps and lapses of perception into his work—by actually looking (Crary 281ff.). My own talismanic quotation from Cézanne for a number of years has been: "Painting from nature is not copying the object. It is materializing one's sensations." Among other things this is a politically and ethically charged statement, and it is directly parallel to Oppen's own practice.

Oppen and Heidegger

Oppen's practice of perception found an affinity in the thought of Martin Heidegger, and his reading in Heidegger was generative for him throughout the time of his writing. It does seem that the slippage in Heidegger, from passionate existential apprehension of beingness and beings, to Idealist reification of Being and even of a myth of Being, was not a particular temptation to Oppen. He refused, as we have seen, to consider experience that was not rooted in conscious perception, in particulars. But Oppen had honed in on what is most crucial in Heidegger's thought: that *truth is no longer defined as the congruence of a concept and a thing but as the ongoing disclosure of "beings"* (or "things" or "entities," depending upon the translation). There are three primary and explicitly named points where Oppen felt that his work was touched by Heidegger's, and there are a number of others where the contact seems clear.

The first of the three is one that occurred after the fact, but seemed mysteriously synchronous to Oppen, and he often referred to it. His first published poem, the start of *Discrete Series,* written in 1929, began, he felt, at precisely the same moment of time, and with the same kind of realization as did Heidegger's 1929 address, which was entitled "What is Metaphysics." This moment entailed the recognition of boredom as an absolutely crucial mood or feeling—because out of it comes the *indifference* (that is, literally, lacking differentiation) in which habitual and conventional networks of perception and thought disintegrate, permitting the possibility of new perception. That poem was the site of a new awareness—the road for Oppen, at that point, out of the stifling mores of family and class, and out of conventional space. Some thirty years later, Oppen in the first poem of his next book, *The Materials,* was again moving out of a no longer formal living room, invoking the particulars.

The men talking
Near the room's center. They have said
More than they had intended.

Pinpointing in the uproar
Of the living room

An assault
On the quiet continent.

Beyond the window
Flesh and rock and hunger

Loose in the night sky
Hardened into soil

Tilting of itself to the sun once more, small
Vegetative leaves
And stems taking place

Outside—O small ones,
To be born!
("Eclogue," from *The Materials, NCP* 39)

The second point of contact is in the quotation from Heidegger that prefaces Oppen's next book, *This in Which* (1965). The phrase he chooses to use is "the arduous path of appearance." I found that these words come from Heidegger's book, *An Introduction to Metaphysics,* published in paperback in English in 1961. It is the culmination of a passage in which Heidegger is talking about the question of appearance and how it relates to beings; put most simply, how is it possible to connect to beings, when what we perceive are appearances? Plato's answer was through the Ideas, an answer that Heidegger rejects. The full quote from Heidegger is "superior knowledge . . . is given only to the man who has known the buoyant storm on the path of being, who has known the dread of the second path to the abyss of nothing, but who has taken on himself the third way, the arduous path of appearance" (Heidegger 96). This is an explication of a passage from Parmenides, and hinges, as always, on a sense of living and struggling with "things" as they *appear* to us, in both senses of the word "appear"—both as how something merely *seems,* and as how it is *suddenly there* for us in our perception. It means that in perception the "thing" is simultaneously complete as a being, incomplete, and arriving. Not really too mysterious when we permit ourselves to be aware of our own actual perceiving. Appearing, as well as being, is powerful, and in order to avoid the pitfalls of Plato's split, confrontation with it is absolutely necessary. But truly arduous, taken as a real path, because it is without the certainty, the anchor, of completed presence.

Two short quotations from Heidegger's book illuminate the affinity of his thinking for Oppen. Heidegger says, "The realm of being . . . is *physis* . . . defined as that which emerges and endures. It is experienced primarily through what . . . imposes itself most immediately on our attention" (Heidegger 14). And, "We oppose the psychic, the animated, the living, to the 'physical.' But for the Greeks all this belonged to *physis* . . . they contrasted it with . . . rule in the sense of *ethos* . . . not mere norms but mores" (Heidegger 13).

In the face of the ever-arising multiplicity of appearances, "the arduous path," Oppen sometimes found himself slipping into the chase to capture truth. These are the opening lines from "Leviathan," the last poem of *The Materials.*

Truth also is the pursuit of it:
Like happiness, and it will not stand.

Even the verse begins to eat away
In the acid. Pursuit, pursuit;

A wind moves a little,
Moving in a circle, very cold.

How shall we say?
In ordinary discourse —

We must talk now. I am no longer sure of the words,
The clockwork of the world. What is inexplicable

Is the 'preponderance of objects.' . . .
("Leviathan," from *The Materials, NCP* 89)

After this comes the book *This in Which,* with the phrase from Heidegger on the flyleaf, and then the first poem of that book, where Oppen talks of

The 'inch-sized
Heart,' the little core of oneself,
So inartistic,

The inelegant heart
Which cannot grasp
The world
And makes art

Is small

Like a small hawk
Lighting disheveled on a window sill. . . .
(lines from "Technologies," *NCP* 93)

Here it is the heart that chooses and that does not grasp. In Oppen's practice the problem is not that we have to make it new, but that in appearing "it" is always new, sometimes overwhelmingly so. The image here is clear and simple, both in the Imagist sense of what is called up in the mind, and in the Objectivist sense as the shape it moves and rests in, in the mind. The image is not the appearance, but where consciousness and appearance move together. Not a reflection, an action.

In 1966, a few months after this book appeared, Oppen wrote in a letter: "I think that poetry which is of any value is *always* revelatory. Not that it reveals or could reveal Everything, but it must reveal something . . . and for the first time. . . . it is a knowledge which is hard to hold, it is held in the poem, a meaning grasped again on re-reading" (*SL* 133).

This letter was written the day before Oppen's most clearly recorded connection with Heidegger, a crux of emergence. At this point Oppen had finished the primary series "Of Being Numerous" for his next book, which would bear that title, and was working on the astonishing series called "Route," which ends that book. On June first, by his own carefully written report, Oppen had, the previous day and that afternoon, been reading an essay of Heidegger's entitled "Identity and Difference." In the afternoon he fell asleep and dreamed that he was taking notes on sheets of paper typical of his actual poetry notes. He was taking these notes of two conversations simultaneously, one that he was listening to on a telephone held between head and shoulder, in which the speaker seemed to be "a gambler of some kind," and one which was taking place at a table nearby—"a sort of conference" where "decisions" were being made. On awakening he felt he "had dreamed several phrases which seemed . . . very important . . . and found they had dissolved" (*SL* 134). He did make a note from memory of a phrase from Heidegger's essay, part of which seemed to him to be his own, part Heidegger's.

That night he read and reread the essay. "It was very difficult for me to grasp the extreme Idealist assumption on which it was based. When I had grasped it, I turned it over and over in my mind for a long time, unable to accept the assumption, but convinced that a part of the statement was of crucial importance to me, of such importance as to alter the subjective conditions of my life, the conditions of my thinking, from that point in time. I got out a poem I had been working on and had been unable to finish adequately, and wrote into it . . . the statement . . . the phrases which I took to be my own, and the phrases which were from Heidegger . . . which reference, in Heidegger, and now, in the poem, was simply the acceptance of the inevitable final death of mankind - - an actual acceptance, a dealing with it - - The poem with these lines, seemed to me the most important I had written, at least the most important to me" (*SL* 135–136).

Oppen awoke next morning depressed because he felt suddenly that he had plagiarized the lines—but then could not, and could never, find them in the essay. "As I started hunting through the essay the third or fourth time, I didn't know if I was in the real world or not" (*SL* 137).

The unfindable lines as they appear in the poem are these: "'Substance itself which is the subject of all our planning.' // And by this we are carried into the incalculable." This is the entire poem that Oppen finished with such excitement.

Department of Plants and Structures—obsolete, the old name
In this city, of the public works

Tho we meant to entangle ourselves in the roots of the world

An unexpected and forgotten spoor, all but indestructible
    shards

To owe nothing to fortune, to chance, nor by the power of
    his heart
Or her heart to have made these things sing
But the benevolence of the real

Tho there is no longer shelter in the earth, round helpless belly
Or hope among the pipes and broken works

'Substance itself which is the subject of all our planning'

And by this we are carried into the incalculable
("Route (part 13)," from *Of Being Numerous, NCP* 200–201)

Simply put, the recognition on which Heidegger's essay depends is that human beings are creating a technological world, which in Heidegger's sense means that every "thing," everything, is to be planned and calculated (Stambaugh trans. 35). In the modern world, he says, a human being is "the rational animal who is the subject for his objects"—rather than being open to the "things," the beings, of this world (Stambaugh trans. 32). The lived moment has disappeared. It is this situation that is most basic and crucial and not answered by an ethics dealing with the uses of technology, however necessary that may be. Without moving into Heidegger's philosophical arguments, it is possible to see how Oppen would have found arising in himself an overwhelming recognition of the possibility of the end of humankind: either because the world of "beings," of "things" belonging to themselves and not only to human beings, is in the process of vanishing in a technologically determined world, where everything is within the human mind: or because the human mind itself disappears along with human beings in a nuclear "chain-reaction" (the words often used by Oppen). World disappears into Mind or Mind disappears into World. The crucial relationship of mind in world is no longer possible.

If man (*sic*) is the unfinished animal, as Nietzsche said, then the rational animal who is the subject of his technological objects is finally finished. Literally done with. The next poems in the series "Route" were among the most pessimistic Oppen ever wrote, in which he spoke of a "radical depopulation of the earth" (*NCP* 201). The balance of radical survival and radical perception had, for the moment, tilted.

In 1958, as Oppen had first begun to write again, he had said in a letter to his sister: "we have to recognize that people have been confronted with the idea of chain-reaction, the destruction of the world. . . . No one can help thinking *something* - - once the subject is raised. And experience so far has not indicated that it will help him much to be a professional philosopher - - tho it may be fatal not to be. I don't mean naturally that I'm trying to elaborate a philosophy in a poem: I mean that these thoughts are part of one's feeling about everything - - it can't just be kept out, except by the purest of artiness" (*SL* 18–19). And in *The Materials,* as he published those new poems, the first, "Eclogue," was an invocation to the start of a world, the second, "Image of the Engine," of an ending beyond the death of our own automatic engine selves. There he wrote: "I know that no one would live out / Thirty years, fifty years if the world were ending / With his life" (*NCP* 40–41).

I would like to go back now to those particular lines that arose for Oppen in reading Heidegger and that appeared so crucial to him. "'Substance itself which is the subject of all our planning' // And by this we are carried into the incalculable." "Incalculable" is Oppen's word. In checking the translation he used, the word as it appears is "immeasurable," and in the German is actually "unabsehbare," "unforeseeable." But "incalculable" is poetry, both in the lift and drift of the sound, as well as in its eliding meaning of overwhelm. "Incalculable"—what we can't figure out. But also "incalculable"—something that our planning and calculating isn't able to touch. Undefined, unknown to hope or despair.

These last poems in *Of Being Numerous* stand, it seems, at a watershed point for Oppen. He had written three books since 1958, and there were three books to come, although these new poems constitute just about a third of his work in terms of length. He couldn't be clearer about what he was doing. In 1959 he wrote in a letter: "all of the poems are about this same thing. . . . 'The eye sees' Poems about the human vision which creates the human universe. . . . but it is - - - O, I do blush . . . talking about 'being'" (*SL* 30–31). In 1972, shortly after his book *Seascape: Needle's Eye* appeared, he wrote (as quoted earlier): "I had thought I could arrive at the concept of Being from an account of experience as it presents itself on its own terms" (*SL* 410). A "concept of Being" for Oppen means of course what can be found *in* the poem—as it is read, reread, experienced not just again, but anew—the moment of perception. Being as noun, Being as verb. When George Oppen was trapped in a foxhole with his dead companions he recited, over and over again, the poem of Charles Reznikoff containing the line "the girder, still itself among the rubble" and the poem of Wyatt's starting with the line "They flee from me that sometime did me seek." He was arriving at a concept of Being, over and over. These are the stakes, and this is his practice.

Ditch

It is impossible to read through Oppen's work without finding, arising in the mind, the word "ditch," which occurs a number of times throughout the poetry. First in the last poem of *This in Which* (*NCP* 159), then in poems 8, 9, and 12 of the series "Route" (*NCP* 198–200), in the book *Of Being Numerous*, then in the third poem of "Some San Francisco Poems" in *Seascape: Needle's Eye* (*NCP* 224), to reappear for the last time in "The Speech at Soli" in *Myth of the Blaze* (*NCP* 238–239). Read in sequence these passages appear as ever-closer approaches to a moment of despair, of a turning over, a being upside-down, that leads to another mode of perception, another mode of language.

> Failure, worse failure, nothing seen
> From prominence,
> Too much seen in the ditch.
>
> Those who will not look
> Tho they feel on their skins
> Are not pierced;
>
> One cannot count them
> Tho they are present . . .
> ("World, World—" from *This in Which, NCP* 159)

> 8.
> Cars on the highway filled with speech,
> People talk, they talk to each other;
>
> Imagine a man in the ditch,
> The wheels of the overturned wreck
> Still spinning—
>
> I don't mean he despairs, I mean if he does not
> He sees in the manner of poetry
>
> 9.
> The cars run in a void of utensils
> —the powerful tires—beyond
> Happiness
>
> Tough rubbery gear of invaders, of the descendents
> Of invaders, I begin to be aware of a countryside
> And the exposed weeds of a ditch . . .

12.

. . . .

wheeled traffic, indifference,
the hard edge of concrete continually crumbling

into gravel in the gravel of the shoulders,
Ditches of our own country

Whom shall I speak to
("Route," parts 8, 9, and 12, from *Of Being Numerous, NCP* 198–200)

'And Their Winter and Night in Disguise'

The sea and a crescent strip of beach
Show between the service station and a deserted shack

A creek drains thru the beach
Forming a ditch
There is a discarded super-market cart in the ditch
That beach is the edge of a nation . . .
(first verses from "Some San Francisco Poems (part 3)," in *Seascape:
Needle's Eye, NCP* 224)

"The Speech at Soli"

. . . .

the return of the sun there are actors'

faces of the highways the theatre
greets itself and reverberates the spirit
goes down goes under
stationary
valves of ditches the chartered
rivers threats in stones
enemies in sidewalks and when the stars rise
reverse ourselves regions of the mind

alter
mad kings

gone raving . . .
(from *The Myth of the Blaze, NCP* 238–239)

I think these must in all likelihood be poems that stem from the mortal accident that Oppen precipitated at the age of nineteen. The "ditch" functions in some related way to the "fox-hole," which also recurs many times in Oppen's later poetry. "These little dumps" is a line from #3 of "Some San Francisco Poems," a poem that includes both experiences. "Dumps"— middens, junky places, piles of shit. Why is the ditch here in the poems? Because it arises—it occurs—not because it *was* a thing, an occurrence, but because it *is* a thing, appearing in consciousness, chosen by feeling. Which makes it not a trauma, not an element of a psychology, not a symbol of an inner state, and not a piece of narrative biography. Together these "ditches" make up an embedded "discrete series" of disclosures of perception, each arrived at empirically.

George Oppen titled his very first book carefully, calling it *Discrete Series,* a mathematical term meaning, as he said in a letter, "a series in which each term is empirically justified rather than derived from the preceding term" (*SL* 122). That is, every poem starts from its own image—it is itself. At this point in time, about 1931, the image is still within the Imagist and Objectivist definitions; Imagism for Oppen being the direct treatment of the "object," defined by him as that "moment, an actual time, when you believe something to be true," an "intensity of vision" that is "a position of honesty" (Dembo 173–174). And Objectivism, for him, being the actualized form of the poem, the image materialized as itself. In *An "Objectivist's" Anthology,* published in 1932, Zukofsky in his introduction went to Pound's definition of the "image as that which presents an intellectual and emotional complex in an instant of time" (Zukofsky 18). What Zukofsky added to this was *his* sense of the image "as the existence of the shape and movement of the poetic object" (Zukofsky 18). But Oppen's own addition, even at this early point, is the importance of the fact that the image is empirically true—it is really experienced, and not merely reflected.

What seems to happen in the almost thirty years until Oppen's next book is an extraordinary refining of this empirical image in Oppen's mind and understanding. Here is Oppen in 1974: "Whatever may be doubted, the actuality of consciousness cannot be doubted. 'Therefore consciousness in itself, of itself carries the principle of actualness.' . . . It can happen in the poem. Perhaps this should have been the meaning of 'objectivism'" (*SL* 290). The adherence to actualness, to discrete and empirical acts of "perception" in which mind and world always, always arise together, began to produce a poetry in which that principle became more and more thoroughgoing. Phrases and words also began to stand more and more on their own, discretely. (All the meanings of the word "discrete" stem from the Latin word "discernere"—"cernere" meaning literally "to sift," figuratively "to perceive," with both senses being present in Oppen's usage.) In 1968, Oppen noted that from the beginning he had not wanted to use syntax to make a "comment" on the image, the "substantive," and elsewhere he said that he did not "predicate" (*SL* 178–180); again, he was not interested in statements *about* truth or syllogistic forms that *defined* truth. Later he described to a translator how a particular word in a poem moved with many subjects: "all that goes before - - - the words, the rain's small pellets small fountains that live, the face of the water, dilations, the heart of the republic - - are the subject of the verb *skips*" (*SL* 329).

As the words themselves began to stand more and more on their own, they also began to work more polyvalently with one another, backward and forward, creating an intricate web of disclosure that was not linear, causing a constant refocusing in the reader, while the image continued to shine. This is the "arduous path of appearance," where something both suddenly is and seems to be, at the same time. And starting with *Seascape: Needle's Eye* the late work includes white spaces, gaps that begin to open on the page—the caesura embodied. The poetry becomes at times one of a most radical caesura, meaning stopping at each phrase, sometimes each word, flashing multitudinously so that enjambment is often created throughout a poem. As with the word "ditch," many words work throughout the discrete series of Oppen's entire body of work. Some of these are "leaves," "sun," "words," "wind," "bare ground," "stones," "pavement," and of course "sea." Starting and stopping, involved with one another.

The effect is one of an ever-ongoing *dis*-closure ("perception," says David Abram, "thwarts closure" [Abram 49]), and of an ever-increasing clarity—not a clarity of abstract concept, but one that includes the profusions of perception in touch with the world, as more and more is included. This is a poetry that is *always* stopping and starting, as perception does. Two phrases can illustrate how this works. One is from the first poem of *The Materials,* called "Eclogue," referred to earlier, the other from one of the last poems in *Primitive,* called "If It All Went Up In Smoke." (The latter is a reference to a line of Heraclitus, for whom all things changed.)

The last lines of "Eclogue"—"Outside—O small ones, / To be born!"—already contain a multiplicity of meanings, not as allusion, but as shifts that manifest the multiplicity of awareness. "O small ones" can be the "vegetative leaves and stems," it can be indeterminate, it can be the moments of awareness themselves, from later poems we can look back and see "small ones" as words, and it is besides, very playfully, a direct translation of a line from Virgil's Fourth Eclogue, believed for many centuries to be a prophecy of the Nativity. And as I noticed earlier, it was used again in the poem "To Virgil," where it concerns the very possibility of ongoing life.

The words "To be born" likewise can refer to the small ones, or to the presumed speaker, or to something or someone indeterminate. It can be felt as exclamation, as a fact about the "small ones," as a play on the words "born" and "borne." And this is not an exhaustive list of possibilities.

In the poem "If It All Went Up In Smoke," this tendency becomes even more fluid, more multitudinous:

> . . . the poem begins
>
> neither in word
> nor meaning but the small
> selves haunting
>
> us in the stones and is less
>
> always than that help me I am
> of that people the grass
>
> blades touch
>
> and touch in their small
>
> distances the poem
> begins
> ("If It All Went Up In Smoke," from *Primitive, NCP* 274)

Here, to take one small group of phrases—"help me I am / of that people the grass // blades touch"—where any phrase can be joined or not joined to what went before. "Help me I am" on its own is a purely lonely cry of existence, or a cry to being itself, that modulates into "of that people," where "that people" can refer to "small selves" or to those who are the location where the poem begins, or just "the people" of earlier poems, or to the Israelites in their relation to God—all these and again others are possible syntactically in this poem, and in relation to the poems directly previous in this book.

There is then no break between "of that people" and the words "the grass," which also bring us to the words of the prophet Isaiah: "Surely the people is grass" (Isaiah 40:7). And back again to the small leaves of "Eclogue." I won't go on—it is exhausting to analyze where the reverberations of meaning and syntax are supposed to stay active and alive.

But the intense density of these transformations continues throughout *Primitive*—a sometimes deeply painful experience of being born and being borne—suffered in the generating power of a poem arising from perception itself. These words refuse to constitute a singular identity or reform a subject. They cannot be calculated, they cannot become counters in a defined game, and they cannot be counted upon. They are finally, as Oppen wanted them to be, incalculable.

As Oppen's poetry moved, it moved to include more and more—true perception became more possible—more could be seen. As in composition by field, where anything could come into the field, anything could arise in the true perception of appearance, and enter into the discrete series. Finally, in the poems of *Primitive*, the disclosure includes the apprehended reality of the working of the poem itself—not as an invented text but as a power.

The last time the word "ditch" appears is in "The Speech at Soli" (*The Myth of the Blaze*, NCP 238–239). (Soli, by the way, is the ancient city where the inhabitants spoke a grammatically incorrect Greek; it's the origin of the word "solecism," and so this is where the language changes, the syntax breaks.) Immediately after it occurs come the words "and when the stars rise // reverse ourselves regions of the mind // alter." "Hidden starry life it is not yet," Oppen had said earlier in *Seascape: Needle's Eye* (*NCP* 233), but now "the stars rise," beginning a new discrete series. In the title poem from Oppen's "Myth of the Blaze" the series continues to arise.

      . . . . . . what names
      (but my name)

      and my love's name to speak

      into the eyes
      of the Tyger   blaze

      of changes . . . 'named

      the animals'   name

      and name the vigorous dusty strong

      animals gather
      under the joists   the boards   older

than they   giving
them darkness the gifted

dark tho names   the names   the 'little'

adventurous
words   a   mountain   the   cliff

a wave are taxonomy I believe

in the world

because it is
impossible   the shack

on the coast

under the eaves
the rain barrel flooding

in the weather and no lights

across rough water illumined
as tho the narrow

end of the funnel what are the names
of the Tyger   to speak
to the eyes

of the Tiger   blaze
of the tiger   who moves in the forest leaving

no scent

but the pine needles' his eyes blink

quick
in   the shack
in the knife-cut
and the opaque

white

bread each side of the knife
(from *Myth of the Blaze, NCP* 247–249)

These eyes of the Tyger *are* the stars, as we know from a letter of Oppen's contemporaneous to this poem: "The Blaze being 'all the Galaxies,'

the night-sky, Blake's Tyger" (*SL* 275), and as we know from Blake himself: "In what distant deeps or skies / Burnt the fire of thine eyes?" (Blake 217). This is the power of the poem entering, the distance itself as a power entering. If we weren't sure this was Blake's Tyger we know from the first spelling—Big "T" and little "y" *Tyger*, which then shifts to big "T," little "i" *Tiger*, and then to little "t," little "i" *tiger*. These are the names of the tiger as it enters the physical and particular world, moving in the forest leaving no scent, his eyes the small leaves of the ordinary world. Those eyes of the Tyger are horizontal like the needle's eye of the horizon from Oppen's previous book, *Seascape: Needle's Eye*. It is that needle's eye that Oppen saw as the gap, the space between sea and sky through which he must pass— old gent, old camel, he said in a letter (*SL* 249)—sea and sky being those two most important and visible elements of the sea-going Oppen's world, the experience of the open, before definition ("my childhood was the sea," he wrote twice to Duncan) (*SL* 238 and 251). So the needle's eye *is* the distance, as Oppen wrote some years earlier in 1966, describing how his practice worked. He spoke of "the need to be able to shift focus, depth of focus, with precision, to control distance, real distance, . . . and get at the crucial moments right on top of the thing" (*SL* 144). But then in 1973 he wrote to Duncan of how consciousness itself is absolute in his vision, and "by itself carries the conviction of actuality," *except* for "the wealth of distance" (*SL* 251). So the Tyger's eye enters from the distance, from Blake's "deeps," and blinks vertically too. The pupil of the tiger's eye is vertical, as the needle's eye is actually vertical, and Oppen wrote to Rachel Blau DuPlessis in 1976 that in the poems "speaking to divinity" *is* the vertical dimension: "'vertical dimension': one of the things the line-break is *for*. . . . when one is talking only to the reader, the lines *lengthen*" (*SL* 316). (This is an insight parallel to, but seemingly uninfluenced by, that of Roman Jakobson on how poetry works.) The eyes of the Tyger blink vertically *and* horizontally, and the power of the poem enters as a power *here*. It is the opposite of indifference, since it differentiates truly as it arises in the last words of the poem: "but the pine needles' his eyes blink // quick // in the shack / in the knife-cut / and the opaque // white // bread each side of the knife."

The power of the poem enters right here—a discrimination.

Oppen's last book was called *Primitive*—meaning originary, native. The entire book is about this new power in perception, the perceived power of the poem. Each poem in it is about poem—it is about itself. The essay of Heidegger's which Oppen felt changed his own conditions of thought, begins with an analysis of the principle of identity, $A = A$, which in Heidegger's thinking is the foundation of Western thought. It is a principle stating that some thing could, for the sake of coherence, be the same as some thing else. Indifference. This is not possible, said Heidegger—it is simply a redundancy (Stambaugh trans. 23–24). Instead, he says, the original meaning in Greek is *A is A,* and he goes back to Plato to find that this means that A is related to itself, there is a relationship within it, it is being itself—*being* itself. When Freud traced the patterning of the unconscious he came up with the concept of metaphor—something like, my love is a rose even when he's not, because we are always looking for the thing that once satisfied our desire and are always finding it; that man must be the man of my dreams. And what else is that but another, hallucinated form of $A = A$? But what Oppen is doing with these last poems is permitting them to be utterly themselves, not identified with, or equal to, something else. John Thorpe said as much in an essay on the prosody of these poems some years ago (Thorpe 50–58). He wrote that the understanding of poetic metre as a fixed unit—based on the artificial bar of musical notation, which implies that some unit of time can actually be equal to some other unit of time—had been utterly overcome by Oppen in these poems. This prosody was due, Thorpe said, not to age, but to purpose. Any thing can come into these poems, and become the poems—even Oppen's disability, an inability to recognize an old neighbor. Which would mean that these poems are working in language not as conscious language, $A = A$, in the law of identity, or unconscious language, $A = A$, in the law of metaphor, but in a language of being itself, the action of being itself—being, as it always is in Oppen, the arising of perception, awakening in the same moment to ourselves and to things—language in the caesura, occurring in discrete series.

In his recent book, *Remnants of Auschwitz,* the philosopher Giorgio Agamben takes up the possibility of testimony and of poetry, in the face of the reduction of human beings to the purely, the utterly, organic, in the camps, and in contemporary medical practice. In that state, he says, fact and the comprehension of fact, experience and language, seem to become irrevocably split, so that witness becomes impossible. But testimony, he believes, can be constituted. One can "establish oneself in a living language as if it were dead, or in a dead language as if it were living" (Agamben 161). One can exist outside the language as what has already been said, because the truth is we are capable of *not* having language—of starting over from that place, and testifying to it.

George Oppen's work, from *Discrete Series* through *Primitive,* was a radical practice of this capability. In one of his last poems in *Primitive* the figure of Job arises in the series. Job, who was chosen and not chosen, heard God speak out of the whirlwind (and let us remember that cold wind "moving in a circle" from his earlier poem "Leviathan") after his friends tried to use platitudinous, used-up language to impose a false understanding of his experience. In an essay that must use reflective language to talk of Oppen's poetry, it seems best to end with this poem.

The Tongues

of appearance
speak in the unchosen
journey immense
journey there is loss in denying
that force the moments the years
even of death lost
in denying
that force   the words
out of that whirlwind his
and not his strange
words surround him
(from *Primitive, NCP* 275)

Thank you.

Note

1. Silliman analyzed a series of four techniques of rhetoric which he sees Oppen as utilizing (*The New Sentence* 139). My own sense is that Oppen does not use the observed stylistic means in order to embody intention, to bring his readers into consonance with a preestablished order, which is something *directly* contrary to his understanding of truth. Instead, they work as placements of perception, articulations of shifting awareness, as described in this essay. Word placement at the beginning and end of lines investigates disclosure, word repetition invites shifts in perception of the "same" sound and image meaning, white spaces are gaps in any presumed continuous flow of perception and feeling, while the use of the word "and," although very occasionally sentimental, more often bodies forth reverberations of shifts in perception: in perception juxtaposition is almost never clean—the previous continues to echo, unless we are traumatized into shock and cannot hold what went before.

Works Cited

Abram, David. *The Spell of the Sensuous*. New York: Random House, 1997.
Agamben, Giorgio. *Remnants of Auschwitz: The Witness and the Archive*. New York: Zone Books, 1999.

Blake, William. *The Complete Writings of William Blake.* Ed. Geoffrey Keynes. New York: Oxford University Press, 1966.

Crary, Jonathan. *Suspensions of Perception: Attention, Spectacle, and Modern Culture.* Cambridge, MA: MIT Press, 1999.

Dembo, L. S., and Cyrena N. Pondrom. *The Contemporary Writer.* Madison: University of Wisconsin Press, 1972.

DuPlessis, Rachel Blau, and Peter Quartermain. *The Objectivist Nexus: Essays in Cultural Poetics.* Tuscaloosa: The University of Alabama Press, 1999.

Hatlen, Burton, and Tom Mandel. "Poetry and Politics: A Conversation with George and Mary Oppen." In *George Oppen: Man and Poet,* ed. Burton Hatlen. Orono, ME: National Poetry Foundation, 1981.

Heidegger, Martin. *An Introduction to Metaphysics.* Trans. Ralph Manheim. New York: Doubleday, 1961.

———. *Essays in Metaphysics: Identity and Difference.* Trans. Kurt F. Leidecker. New York: Philosophical Library, 1960.

———. *Identity and Difference.* Trans. Joan Stambaugh. New York: Harper & Row, 1969.

———. "What Is Metaphysics?" In *Existence and Being,* trans. R. F. C. Hull. Chicago: Henry Regnerie, 1949.

Jakobson, R. "The Metaphoric and Metonymic Poles." In *Fundamentals of Language,* ed. R. Jakobson and M. Halle. The Hague: Mouton, 1956.

Oppen, George. *New Collected Poems.* New York: New Directions, 2002.

———. "The Mind's Own Place" (1963). *Montemora* 1 (Fall 1975): 132–137.

———. *The Selected Letters of George Oppen.* Ed. Rachel Blau DuPlessis. Durham, NC: Duke University Press, 1990.

Oppen, Mary. *Meaning a Life: An Autobiography.* Santa Barbara, CA: Black Sparrow Press, 1978.

Perl, Jed. *The New Republic,* December 4, 2000, 34.

Scalapino, Leslie. *The Public World / Syntactically Impermanence.* Hanover, CT: Wesleyan University Press, 1999.

Silliman, Ron. *The New Sentence.* New York: Roof Books, 1987.

Thorpe, John. "Prosody and George Oppen's *Primitive.*" *Convivio: A Journal of Poetics* 1 (1983): 50–58.

Young, Dennis. "Conversation with Mary Oppen." *Iowa Review* 18, 3 (1988): 18–47.

Zukofsky, Louis, ed. *An "Objectivists" Anthology.* Le Beausset, France, and New York: To Publishers, 1932.

14
if it fails—

Theodore Enslin

I am thinking of George Oppen, and I am thinking of George Oppen's poetry. I think of them both, I can say without exaggeration, every day—at least that often. And to think of one *is* to think of the other. They cannot be divided, and it would be rank stupidity to try to separate them. In great measure, Oppen is a conscience of our time, no less a poetic conscience than a moral one. There is sadness, and there is an inexorable admonition in that voice—perhaps anger, though the anger is never shrill, is always touched with kindness. Wisdom? But what constitutes wisdom? If you will say that wisdom stems from a life fully handled, and fully lived, in which, as I once said of him, he is at home, I will agree with you. It is never necessary for him to reach far to find life. He has it all around him and he knows it. In the poetry, the choice of words says as much. If a precise word were an uncommon one, he would not hesitate to use it but where a simple word will do, will hold the weight, he will use that one, no matter how many times it has been debased before by an improper or an imprecise use. It is not beneath him to breathe new life into a word such as "beautiful"—to use so simple a vocabulary that it hardly seems that we are listening to words at all. It is like one of those rare days when a man steps outside and finds that the sun and air and he himself are in such agreement that it is impossible to say where the tips of the fingers end and the air around them begins. To have sustained such a climate throughout a lifetime is Oppen's genius. In all those years when he did no writing, having, as he says, "other things to do" he was, in sober fact, writing—was contributing that unique part of himself that is the whole of him. Anyone who has had the privilege of sailing with him in that tiny boat in which he explores Penobscot Bay could get more than a hint of his quality. He sits listening and feeling for the merest capful of wind on a hot July morning, goes on from what had seemed becalmed until that puff fails and he must begin again. Deceptively simple and easy. Another time, when we were both listening to an open reading of student poetry—not as gruesome an experience as that can be, and often is, there was a vague feeling of uneasiness, which I think many of us shared. George put his finger on it: "They don't like themselves enough." Oppen lives the life in his poems, and he lives it well. That is where the poems come from. It takes no virtuosity. There is no need for that. He has all of the dexterity, but he allows what he has to say to carry him with it. Five books in a period of forty years. What he has had to say, he has said, and he is still saying it, where and as it needs to be. Reading these poems, even if a sympathetic reader has never heard his voice before, he *would* hear it. There is no other way to find what he is saying, except through that quiet, compassionate voice that will never be raised for effect—so quiet at times that we strain to hear everything. It is well worth the strain. There is never a doubt as to what is meant. From the first ones in *Discrete Series:*

> Drawing
> Not by growth
>   But the
> Paper, turned, contains
> The entire volume
> (*New Collected Poems [NCP]* 33)

to this, from *Seascape: Needle's Eye:*

> Exodus
> Miracle of the children   the brilliant
> Children   the word
> Liquid as woodlands   Children?
>
> When she was a child I read Exodus
> To my daughter   'The children of Israel—'
>
> Pillar of fire
> Pillar of cloud

We stared at the end
Into each other's eyes   Where
She said hushed

Were the adults   We dreamed to each other
Miracle of the children
The brilliant children   Miracle

Of their brilliance   Miracle
of
(*NCP* 234)

The last stanza of that marvelous poem, "The Forms of Love," from *This in Which*:

Beginning to wonder
Whether it could be lake
Or fog
We saw, our heads
Ringing under the stars. We walked
To where it would have wet our feet
Had it been water
(*NCP* 106)

Those terrifying lines of admonition:

Love in the genes, if it fails
We will produce no sane man again
(*NCP* 192)

Lines that I can never hear or remember without a chill, far more than something more immediately horrifying in an ecological report. Or, from that same poem, "Route":

Clarity, clarity, surely clarity is the most beautiful
 thing in the world,
A limited, limiting clarity
I have not, and never did have any motive for poetry
But to achieve clarity
(*NCP* 193)

And this is the summation that does not sum up. There is more to be said, and Oppen will go on saying it—only those things that a man might take if he were going on a long and dangerous journey and must travel light.

15
Excerpts from "'Because the Known and the Unknown Touch'
A Reading of Oppen's 'Of Being Numerous'"

Henry Weinfield

1
There are things
We live among 'and to see them
Is to know ourselves'.

Occurrence, a part
Of an infinite series,

The sad marvels;

Of this was told
A tale of our wickedness.
It is not our wickedness.

'You remember that old town we went to, and we sat in the
ruined window, and we tried to imagine that we belonged to
those times —— It is dead and it is not dead, and you cannot
imagine either its life or its death; the earth speaks and the salamander speaks, the Spring comes and only obscures it ——'
(*New Collected Poems [NCP]* 163)[1]

One of the two epigraphs to *The Materials* (1962)—the poems Oppen
collected following his return to poetry after the long hiatus in which, as
he was fond of saying, he was involved with other things—is taken from
Jacques Maritain's *Creative Intuition in Art and Poetry:* "We awake in the
same moment to ourselves and to things."[2] In the lines that open "Of Being Numerous," self-knowledge is predicated on the act of seeing or witnessing the things among which we live. Whether or not we exist outside
of the world of objects, as Descartes thought, is not in question; but certainly we cannot know ourselves apart from an interaction with the things

of the world. Oppen's presentation of this fundamental starting point is much more radical than my gloss on it, however. "There are things / We live among": the fluidity of the statement is undercut by the line break, which, in arresting the eye, obliges us to read in at least two ways. "There are things": what is, is plural; and the only approach to being is through becoming; the only approach to the One through the Many.

Oppen's concern with knowledge at the beginning of the poem indicates an initial suspension of the epistemological quandaries that will hover over the poem. "There are things / We live among": so much is clear; and we are simply told that "'to see them / Is to know ourselves.'" Beyond the immediacy of the statement, however, the predication of knowing on seeing suggests that we are inevitably submerged in time, in the temporal occurrences that make up an infinite series. Each of these occurrences is "a part," and we are partial, because we do not come to know ourselves apart from them. Insofar as they can be isolated from the continuum—insofar as the "actual" can be isolated, as Oppen will say in section 27 (180)—they present themselves as "sad marvels"—miracles, really, of our knowing.

The beauty of Oppen's prosody, here and throughout the poem (indeed, throughout the great poetry of the middle period), results from a conscious process of *deceleration,* so that phrases we would ordinarily pass by because of their familiarity are replenished, as if with their original meaning. "There are things we live among and to see them is to know ourselves." Oppen's great gift is to allow utterances of this kind—the simplest utterances, but for that very reason pregnant with meaning—to be heard, as if for the first time. It is in this way that he puts his signature on language, and not through any conscious striving after originality. There are deep constraints on his language, however, and when words finally break through to the surface they resonate against a great well of meaning. What gives the simple phrasing of the opening passage such resonance, especially when we have worked our way through the poem a number of times, is the depth of the meditation in which it is embedded and out of which it emerges.

The beautifully subtle allusion in section 1 to the story of Adam and Eve initiates the poem's intertextual dimension. The allusion is interesting both for what it says about Oppen's poetic technique and for what it says about the poem's philosophical content. There is something marvelous, first of all, in the nonspecificity of the reference ("Of this was told / A tale of our wickedness"), and then in the definitiveness of the conclusion that follows ("It is not our wickedness"). The disjunctive leaps that the poem employs, both in its own narrative and in the cultural narratives to which it alludes, contribute to its strangeness and its resonance as poetry. With regard to the poem's philosophical content, moreover, the story of Adam and Eve has a specific resonance for Oppen for a number of reasons. One aspect of Oppen's project, as the opening lines indicate, is to see the world anew and, as far as possible, in its simplicity, without the social, historical, and philosophical projections with which it is habitually encumbered. Thus, in section 36 of the poem, alluding once again to the Genesis story, Oppen will assert that the world is that which "the first eyes / Saw" (185). For Oppen, however, to see the world anew entails going back to origins and rethinking the foundational myth of Western civilization, with its emphasis on Original Sin. And for Oppen, as for Lucretius, it is not our wickedness, it is the way things are; or, as he writes in "A Narrative," "It is the nature / Of the world" (154).

Typescript drafts of section 1 of "Of Being Numerous," when it was still entitled "Another Language of New York,"[3] indicate that Oppen had originally written the following in the second and third stanzas:

> An event, a part
> Of an infinite series.
>
> Of this indeterminancy
> Was told a tale of our wickedness.
> It is not our wickedness.[4]

The revision is fascinating and masterful. The substitution of "Occurrence" for "An event" conveys the suggestion of indeterminacy and thereby eliminates the need for the word itself. But the original emphasis, considered in relation to the Adam and Eve story, suggests the following thought process: (1) Our reality is constituted by indeterminacy; (2) this is precisely what "human kind cannot bear" (to borrow T. S. Eliot's phrase in *Four Quartets* [118]); and (3) because it cannot tolerate a reality which is indeterminate, it constructs a foundational myth of Original Sin as a way of circumventing this reality.

The use of juxtaposition (i.e., the placement of heterogeneous elements side-by-side and without logical transition) is crucial to Oppen's poetic technique in "Of Being Numerous"; and here, a prose passage in quotation marks that seems to be of a personal nature ("You remember that old town we went to") is juxtaposed against lines of verse that evoke

the foundational myth of the West. The obscurity of the passage resonates against a struggle to imagine or penetrate to the heart of experience
without falsifying it ("It is dead and it is not dead, and you cannot imagine
either its life or its death"); but what is clarified in and through the passage
is precisely the obscurity of things ("the earth speaks and the salamander
speaks, the Spring comes and only obscures it"). The passage thus brings
to light—both through its content and in juxtaposition with what has
come before—the impenetrability of the world, which is a crucial aspect
of what Oppen uncovers in the poem. In Oppen's *via negative*, "the known
and the unknown / Touch" (182); for indeed, a part of what is known (poetically) is the unknown.

16
'. . . he who will not work shall not eat,
and only he who was troubled shall find rest,
and only he who descends into the nether world shall
    rescue his beloved,
and only he who unsheathes his knife shall be given
    Isaac again. He who will not work shall not eat . . .
but he who will work shall give birth to his father.'
(*NCP* 172)

Section 16, consisting in its entirety of a quotation from Kierkegaard's
Fear and Trembling, is nevertheless central to the poem as a whole.[5] Oppen said of this passage that "the context of the entire poem alters [Kier-
kegaard's] meaning" (*Selected Letters* [*SL*] 129), and we shall see that this
is indeed the case. Although the quotation clearly underlines the necessity of work and struggle in the process of forging an identity, we must
understand it against the larger background of *Fear and Trembling* in order
to grasp its significance to Oppen's poem. First of all, it occurs in a context in which Kierkegaard establishes a dichotomy between the "external
world," subject to "the law of indifference," and the "world of the spirit,"
in which "an eternal order prevails" (27). At the beginning of the "Preliminary Expectoration" to the "Problemata" (in other words, at the beginning of the body of the work), Kierkegaard makes the following crucial
distinction: "From the external and visible world there comes an old adage: 'Only one who works gets bread.' Oddly enough, the adage does not
fit the world in which it is most at home, for imperfection is the fundamental law of the external world, and here it happens again and again that

he who does not work does get bread, and he who sleeps gets it even more abundantly than he who works. In the external world, everything belongs to the possessor. . . . It is different in the world of the spirit. Here a divine order prevails. Here it does not rain on both the just and the unjust" (27). In Oppen's appropriation, the polarities of Kierkegaard's radical idealism are muted because Oppen does not distinguish between "the external and visible world" and "the world of the spirit"; but what is especially ironic is that Oppen's ellipses also have the effect of muting what we might call the "materialist" counterpart of the argument, which Kierkegaard openly expresses when he admits that in the external world "he who does not work *does* get bread."

In this undoing of the Kierkegaardian polarities, Oppen was apparently attempting to reconcile tensions and ambivalences that are played out in both his poetry and his life. It is only in this fashion that Kierkegaard can be accommodated; otherwise he would pose too serious a danger of "escapism." For actually, a great deal more is at stake in Oppen's appropriation of the Kierkegaard text than is immediately apparent from the quotation. What is at stake is the dialectical engagement between Kant and Hegel, on the one hand, and Kierkegaard, on the other, an engagement that the latter himself inscribes in *Fear and Trembling*. For Kant and Hegel, the universal status of the ethical allows for no exceptions, but for Kierkegaard, as a result of what he calls the "paradox of faith" (70), there can be a suspension of the ethical for the sake of a higher end. Abraham, the "knight of faith" in Kierkegaard's conception, stands for a "teleological suspension of the ethical," according to which "the single individual is higher than the universal" (70). Thus, if we may translate Kierkegaard's conception to the language of "Of Being Numerous," Abraham (ironically, the "father of his people") represents the "absolute singular / The unearthly bonds / Of the singular" (167), which cannot merely be swept up into and subsumed by the universal.

"Abraham cannot be mediated," asserts Kierkegaard; "in other words, he cannot speak. As soon as I speak, I express the universal, and if I do not do so, no one can understand me" (60). One can hear this echoed in several of the passages in "Of Being Numerous" that precede the Kierkegaard quotation. In section 11, in lines that echo Horatio's address to the Ghost, Oppen writes: "Speak // If you can // Speak" (168). If "speech" expresses the universal and pertains not only to ordinary communication but to the realm of philosophical generalization, it follows that there is something irreducibly specific and particular in both art and history. In the concluding lines of section 14, Oppen refers to "The People" (a philosophical abstraction) "Who are that force / Within the walls / Of cities // Wherein their cars // Echo like history / Down walled avenues / In which one cannot speak" (171). As Wittgenstein writes at the end of the *Tractatus*, "What we cannot speak about we must pass over in silence" (151).

Abraham does not represent the aesthetic in Kierkegaard's conception,[6] but rather a mystical faith that establishes its singularity and that Oppen translates to the aesthetic. To Kierkegaard, given the terms of his radical idealism, this conception of singularity does not pose the same problem of elitism and escapism that it does to Oppen; for if one splits apart the world of spirit and the external world, and if to the spiritual world, "No one who was great . . . will be forgotten,"[7] then it scarcely matters what happens in the external world. To Oppen, however, committed as he is to "the arduous path of appearance," it matters a great deal; so there can be no question of leaving the polarities intact: one must strive to reconcile them. And yet, as we see, the Kierkegaardian polarities are by no means foreign to what Oppen struggles with in "Of Being Numerous."

27
It is difficult now to speak of poetry ——

about those who have recognized the range of choice or those who have lived within the life they were born to ——. It is not precisely a question of profundity but a different order of experience. One would have to tell what happens in a life, what choices present themselves, what the world is for us, what happens in time, what thought is in the course of a life and therefore what art is, and the isolation of the actual

I would want to talk of rooms and of what they look out on and of basements, the rough walls bearing the marks of the forms, the old marks of wood in the concrete, such solitude as we know ——

and the swept floors. Someone, a workman bearing about him, feeling about him that peculiar word like a dishonored fatherhood has swept this solitary floor, this profoundly hidden floor —— such solitude as we know.

One must not come to feel that he has a thousand threads
   in his hands,
He must somehow see the one thing;

This is the level of art
There are other levels
But there is no other level of art (180)

In section 27—which, significantly, except for its final stanza, is written in prose—Oppen arrives at his fullest and clearest understanding of the nature of poetry. He develops a philosophical conception of poetry in this section, but one that is given, paradoxically, in the context of a poem and that therefore cannot be divorced from poetry. The conception that Oppen develops does not shirk from difficulty ("It is difficult now to speak of poetry," he begins), but at the same time it recognizes that in order for poetry to be poetry it must attain the "determinate simplicity" that Hegel calls for in his *Aesthetics*.

The difficulty of speaking of poetry for Oppen—and of speaking of it *now*, in (and for) the present—is both historical and epistemological. It apparently has to do, in some not fully explained way, with "those who have recognized the range of choice" and "those who have lived within the life they were born to." Though this might seem reductive, I would argue that Oppen is here developing a Marxist conception of poetry akin to the one Theodor Adorno articulates in his essay "Lyric Poetry and Society." For Adorno, the voice of humanity can be heard "in the poem's solitude" (1.38); and for Oppen, in section 27, the poet is linked to the figure of the "workman." In the previous section, Oppen had written that we "stand on / That denial / Of death that paved the cities" (178), and in this section the poet (the one who has "recognized the range of choice") recognizes that he "stands"—in an equally metaphorical way—on the "solitary floor" that the workman (the one who lives "the life [he was] born to") has swept. The relationship between the poet and the workman is thus an aspect of the relationship between the one and the many. "It is difficult now to speak of poetry," however, because the poet is as isolated from the workman as the workman is from the poet; neither is able to "find / [his] generation," and thus both are in danger of "[withering] in the infirmaries // And the supply depots, supplying / Irrelevant objects" (178). Note the repetition of the phrase "such solitude as we know," which here applies equally to the workman and the poet. The entire section should be read in apposition to section 10, where Oppen had lamented the failure of the solitary poet ("And he fails! He fails, that meditative man!" [168]).

That Oppen is here developing a Marxist conception of poetry—that is, one in which poetry depends on a relationship (veiled and attenuated, to be sure) between the poet and the "productive forces"—does not mean that he is asserting anything like a univocal conception of truth or that "the one thing" of the concluding stanza of section 27 stands for a philosophical truth that could be universalized and articulated. This would be to turn Oppen into an epistemological Stalinist, which he clearly was not.[8] On the contrary, for Oppen "the one thing" cannot be grasped cognitively or rationally, but only as an *intuition* of completeness and formal precision. What allows the poet to weave unity out of the "thousand threads in his hands" (the image is astonishingly precise) or to "see the one thing" is a capacity that is neither rational nor a product of sense perception, in a simple sense. The emphasis should be on the word "somehow" ("He must *somehow* see the one thing")—as if to say that we don't know how it happens or how it can be explained, only that it *does* happen and that the existence of art is the proof that it does. Oppen had earlier described this moment or quality of seeing (but seeing is partly metaphorical here) experientially as "an instant in the eyes, // The absolute singular // The unearthly bonds / Of the singular" (167); but he now has the confidence to give it an expression that risks being philosophical because it is rooted in a poetic context. "This is the level of art / There are other levels / But there is no other level of art," he writes. "It is difficult now to speak of poetry," among other reasons because we are skeptical of philosophy—because no discourse on poetry is able to attain to the *singularity* that poetry attains; and yet, in the conclusion to section 27, Oppen rises to a formulation of poetry that is itself poetry, and, in its determinate simplicity, represents genuine knowledge, knowledge appropriate to its time.

36
Tho the world
Is the obvious, the seen
And unforeseeable,
That which one cannot
Not see

Which the first eyes
Saw ——

For us
Also each
Man or woman
Near is
Knowledge

Tho it may be of the noon's
Own vacuity

—— and the mad, too, speak only of conspiracy
and people talking ——

And if those paths
Of the mind
Cannot break

It is not the wild glare
Of the world even that one dies in. (185–186)

There is a fascinating intertextual connection embedded in the first half of section 36 that not only helps us grasp Oppen's meaning but also furnishes us with crucial insight into the movement of his thought and his relation to poetic technique. Consider the syntax of the third stanza (which itself is enjambed to the fourth):

For us
Also each
Man or woman

Near is
Knowledge.

As they so often do, Oppen's line breaks indicate syntactical doubling, so that in this case "each man or woman near is knowledge" but also "near is knowledge." The latter possibility echoes the opening lines from Friedrich Hölderlin's great poem "Patmos," and this, I believe, provides us with one of the most important keys we have to Oppen's work. I give the passage from Hölderlin both in the original and in the Michael Hamburger translation, which I strongly suspect is the one that Oppen, who had very little German, knew (it is the only translation of Hölderlin I am aware of that renders the first line of "Patmos" "Near is"):

Nah ist
Und schwer zu fassen der Gott.

Near is
And difficult to grasp, the God. (463)[9]

That Oppen is involved in a crucial dialogue with the Hölderlin of "Patmos," one that also carries the overtones of his engagement with Heidegger and Wittgenstein, seems clear. Patmos is the Greek island on which Saint John the Divine is said to have received the vision that resulted in Revelations, and in Hölderlin's "Patmos" what is celebrated and lamented is the simultaneous nearness and distance, approach and withdrawal, of the gods (or, in this case, God), which is this poet's great and perennial theme.

In Hölderlin's conception, the potential for vision—both religious and poetic (for they essentially amount to the same thing)—is underwritten by the simple fact that "Christ lives yet" and that "known / To him are all his works from the beginning" (475). To Oppen, on the contrary, "the world / Is the obvious, the seen / And unforeseeable, / That which one cannot / Not see." It cannot be foreseen or revealed because it contains no hidden mysteries, nothing beneath the surface to foresee or reveal. Whereas Hölderlin attempts to hold onto the departed gods, for Oppen even this is no longer possible: the gods have departed forever, and therefore the systems of salvation we have entertained in the West, throughout our history, must finally be set aside. Oppen's powerfully syncopated rhythms underline the point: the world is "that which one cannot / Not see // Which the first eyes / Saw." The allusion to Adam and Eve, recalling the earlier allusion to the Genesis story in section 1, strengthens the point about human beings as a species.

The conception that Oppen is here developing would seem to borrow from or at least run parallel to the later Wittgenstein, for whom the idea that there are hidden truths or mysteries that philosophy is capable of revealing or unearthing is fallacious. "Philosophy, as we use the word," Wittgenstein writes, "is a fight against the fascination which forms of expression exert upon us" (*The Blue and Brown Books* 27). If the world is the obvious, then, as Wittgenstein will argue, the task of philosophy is to rid us of the need to do philosophy in the old way.

The first half of section 36 is framed by two *although* clauses ("Tho the world / Is the obvious"; "Tho it may be of the noon's / Own vacuity"), which have the effect of tempering what is said about knowledge. Eliminating some of the subordinate clauses (all of which, of course, are important to the poetry), we can reduce the passage to two statements formulated in bare prose: (1) "Though the world is the obvious, for us also each man or woman near is knowledge, though it may be of the noon's own vacuity"; and (2) "Though the world is the obvious, near is knowledge, though it may be of the noon's own vacuity." In the first case, each man or woman near (us) confers knowledge—but the knowledge pertains to what is *obvious* and, it may be, to the *vacuity* of existence. In the second case, more simply, the knowledge we grasp is of the obvious—hence of the vacuity of existence. In both cases, "the known and the unknown / Touch" (182).

For Hölderlin, again, "Near is / And difficult to grasp, the God," whereas for Oppen, "Near is / Knowledge"—the knowledge that the God *cannot* be grasped. Therefore, for Oppen, the knowledge that can be grasped, the knowledge that is near, is "the obvious" and (it may be) the knowledge "of the noon's / Own vacuity"—in other words, of the darkness and emptiness of Nature. (The *v*'s in *obvious* and *vacuity* emphasize the way in which knowledge is being framed.) Now, in hearing the lines, "Near is / Knowledge," the reader of Oppen immediately wants to add, as a substitute for "Tho it may be of the noon's / Own vacuity," "The knowledge not of sorrow, you were / saying, but of boredom"—the first lines of the Maude Blessingbourne poem, which Oppen will himself quote at the beginning of the next section of "Of Being Numerous" (187) and with which his first book, *Discrete Series,* begins (5).

Heidegger is clearly implicated in this section of the poem, perhaps even more so than Wittgenstein. For Heidegger, in "What is Metaphysics?," the inaugural lecture he gave after being appointed to the chair of philosophy at Freiburg, boredom "draws all things, all men and oneself along with them, together in a queer kind of indifference. Thus, boredom reveals what-is in totality" (364). But Oppen's relationship to Heidegger is mediated, in this case, by his relationship to Hölderlin and by Heidegger's relationship to Hölderlin—and we should remember that in Heidegger's famous turn to poetry in his later writings, Hölderlin is the most important presence. In his great essay "What Are Poets For?" of 1946 (an essay in which the central focus falls on Hölderlin), Heidegger writes that knowledge of the abyss is the precondition to a renewed contact with Being. Human nature, he asserts, "lies in this, that mortals reach into the abyss sooner than the heavenly powers. Mortals, when we think of their nature, remain closer to that absence because they are touched by presence, the ancient name of Being" (*Poetry, Language, Thought* 93).

For Heidegger, "To be a poet in a destitute time means: to attend, singing, to the trace of the fugitive gods" (*Poetry, Language, Thought* 94). For Oppen, however, the attempt to hold onto a spiritual or numinous realm can only be through poetry itself—in this case, through an echo of

Hölderlin that has the simultaneous effect of upholding and negating (or at least, revising) what the German Romantic poet says about the gods. Oppen attends, singing, not so much to the trace of the fugitive gods as to the trace of a trace he finds in an earlier poet.

Hölderlin went mad, and the second half of section 37 raises the specter of madness. The ancient Greeks saw a connection between madness and prophecy, *manike* and *mantike,* and thus for them (as in Plato's *Phaedrus*) madness can have the positive connotation of lifting us to the divine. But the madness Oppen addresses in this context seems wholly negative. The poet moves from "the noon's / Own vacuity" to "and the mad, too, speak only of conspiracy / and people talking." In that associative leap, Oppen is raising the possibility that the theological *emptying out* (or vacuity) that one associates with the crisis of modernity is dangerously connected to madness. "There is madness in the number / Of the living," he writes in section 17 of the poem: "'A state of matter' // There is nobody here but us chickens // Anti-ontology" (172). If the gods have departed and there is "nobody here but us chickens," but we still have the need for the gods, madness may be the inevitable result. "And if those paths / Of the mind / Cannot break," the poet concludes, "It is not the wild glare / Of the world even that one dies in" (186). In other words, if at this late stage of history we are unable to break out of the mental grooves we have inherited—if we are unable to face the "wild glare" of reality (one of Oppen's finest epithets) without resorting to myth, we will bring death on ourselves as a species (through nuclear holocaust, for instance); moreover, the death we bring on ourselves will not have been necessary: it will not come from the world as it necessarily is, but rather from our own insane projections.

Notes

1. These excerpts are drawn from chapter 2 of my forthcoming study, *The Music of Thought in the Poetry of George Oppen and William Bronk* (Iowa City: University of Iowa Press). All citations from Oppen's poetry are to *New Collected Poems* and will hereafter be given by page number only.

2. The epigraph is apparently not an actual quotation from *Creative Intuition,* but very close to the conception that Maritain develops in chapter 1 of the work, "Poetry, Man, and Things" (3–30), where he argues—against Cartesian dualism—that the self emerges only in the context of its prior immersion in the things of the world. In a letter to Michael Heller of 1975, in which Heller had referred to Merleau-Ponty, Oppen writes: "More moved by Maritain—Maritain of the *Creative Intuition in Art and Poetry*— only that book of his, in fact" (*SL* 311).

3. The title "Another Language of New York" follows an earlier sequence-poem, "A Language of New York," which was included in *This in Which* and which contains material Oppen simply inserted into "Of Being Numerous" (see 114–119).

4. See Reel 19, "The George Oppen Papers," Mandeville Special Collections of the University of California at San Diego. The line, "The sad marvels," does not appear on the typescript page containing this passage.

5. Oppen made use of the now out-of-print and difficult-to-find Robert Payne translation of *Fear and Trembling,* changing the wording slightly. The passage that Oppen borrowed reads as follows in the Payne translation: "for here it is true that only he who works has bread, only he who is troubled finds rest, only he who descends into the nether-world rescues the beloved, only he who draws the knife obtains Isaac. He who will not work has no bread . . . But he who will work gives birth to his own father" (29–30). In my discussion, I shall cite the edition and translation of *Fear and Trembling* made by Howard V. Hong and Edna H. Hong.

6. "Esthetics allowed, indeed demanded, silence of the single individual if he knew that by remaining silent he could save another. This alone adequately shows that Abraham is not within the scope of esthetics" (112).

7. "No one who was great in the world will be forgotten, but everyone was great in his own way, and everyone in proportion to the greatness of that which *he loved.* He who loved himself became great by virtue of himself, and he who loved other men became great by his devotedness, but he who loved God became the greatest of all. . . . Everyone shall be remembered, but everyone was great wholly in proportion to the magnitude of that with which he *struggled*" (16).

8. On this issue, see my debate with Ross Feld in *Sagetrieb.* Feld writes: "In his own thin-man way, Oppen may have been our most ideological poet. Not just because he seemed to have been an unreconstructed Stalinist but because he operated within that changeable mode of loftiness that in his best-known poem, 'Of Being Numerous,' . . . allows him with a straight face to call truth knowledge and vice-versa. 'Truthfulness / which illumines speech,' he writes—a formula that like a machine extrudes a braid: 'One must not come to feel that he has a thousand threads / in his hands. He must somehow see the one thing'" ("Some Thoughts about Objectivism" 67). In my response, I argued that "the one thing" to which Oppen refers is an intuition, not an ideological position ("'A Thousand Threads' and 'The One Thing': Oppen's Vision [A Reply to Ross Feld]" 79–87).

9. In his preface to the 1967 edition of the *Poems and Fragments,* Hamburger notes that his initial selection, *Poems of Hölderlin,* had appeared in 1943; and thus it is entirely possible that Oppen would have known the poem in this edition. Hölderlin is not mentioned in Oppen's *Selected Letters,* but Oppen would certainly have taken a strong interest in his poetry—among other reasons because Hölderlin is so central to Heidegger. I suspect that Oppen was strongly attracted to Hölderlin for a number of reasons—not only for the substance of what he has to say but for for his style and prosody. As a philosophical poet, Oppen could very

well have viewed Hölderlin's prosody as a road to free verse that bypassed the American one of Whitman, Pound, and Williams. Hölderlin's attempt to imitate Greek quantitative measures led him to forego rhyme and to develop a prosody that, in the context of the German accentual-syllabic system, was tantamount to free verse. Heidegger's attraction to Hölderlin was partly predicated on the sense that Hölderlin represented a return to the pre-Socratics, for whom philosophy and poetry were one and the same thing and had not yet become detached as separate disciplines.

Works Cited

Adorno, Theodor W. *Notes to Literature.* 2 vols. Trans. Shierry Weber Nicholsen. New York: Columbia University Press, 1991.

Eliot, T. S. *The Complete Poems and Plays.* New York: Harcourt, Brace, and World, 1971.

Feld, Ross. "Some Thoughts about Objectivism." *Sagetrieb* 12, 3 (Winter 1993): 65–77.

Heidegger, Martin. *Existence and Being.* Trans. R. F. C. Hull and Alan Crick. Chicago: Regnery, 1949.

———. *Poetry, Language, Thought.* Trans. Albert Hofstadter. New York: Harper & Row, 1975.

Hölderlin, Friedrich. *Poems and Fragments.* Trans. Michael Hamburger. Ann Arbor: University of Michigan Press, 1967.

Kierkegaard, Sören. *Fear and Trembling.* Trans. Howard V. Hong and Edna H. Hong. Princeton, NJ: Princeton University Press, 1983.

———. *Fear and Trembling.* Trans. Robert Payne. London: Oxford University Press, 1939.

Maritain, Jacques. *Creative Intuition in Art and Poetry.* Cleveland, OH: Meridian Books, 1954.

Oppen, George. "The George Oppen Papers." Mandeville Special Collections of The University of California at San Diego.

———. *New Collected Poems.* Ed. Michael Davidson. New York: New Directions, 2002.

———. *The Selected Letters of George Oppen.* Ed. Rachel Blau DuPlessis. Durham, NC: Duke University Press, 1990.

Weinfield, Henry. "'A Thousand Threads and 'The One Thing': Oppen's Vision (A Reply to Ross Feld)." *Sagetrieb* 12, 3 (Winter 1993): 79–87.

———. *The Music of Thought in the Poetry of George Oppen and William Bronk.* Iowa City: University of Iowa Press (forthcoming).

Wittgenstein, Ludwig. *The Blue and Brown Books: Preliminary Studies for the "Philosophical Investigations."* New York: Harper & Row, 1958.

———. *Tractatus Logico-Philosophicus.* Trans. D. F. Pears and B. F. McGuinness. New York: Humanities Press, 1969.

Acknowledgments

I would like to thank my parents David Shoemaker and Patricia Thacker, my wife Suzanne, and my son Nicholas, for their untiring support during the rather lengthy process of preparing this book for publication. Authors dream of having "ideal readers;" I have been lucky enough to be married to one. And I have also been fortunate enough to benefit crucially from the generosity and insights of many other readers as well. In particular, I would like to thank at the University of Virginia Jerome McGann, who got me started on Oppen, and Christopher Bush, who, along with the other members of the Harvard Expository Writing Program's "Writers' Group," helped me revive my work on *Discrete Series* in the spring of 2002. I'd also like to thank the staff at The University of Alabama Press for their diligence, and the Press's anonymous readers for their trenchant reports. For her much appreciated typing and proofreading at certain key moments along the way I thank the invaluable Joyce McDaniel. And finally, I am grateful to the contributors, who taught me a great deal about "Oppen"— the man, the poet, and the poetry.

—Steve Shoemaker

Michael Davidson's essay originally appeared in *Postmodern Genres,* University of Oklahoma Press, 1988.

Part 1 of Peter Nicholls's "Oppen's Heidegger" is reprinted from his *George Oppen and the Fate of Modernism* (Oxford: Oxford University Press,

2007). We are grateful to the publisher for giving permission to include it here.

Forrest Gander's essay originally appeared in *No: A Journal of the Arts*, edited by Deb Klowden and Ben Lerner. http://www.nojournal.com/.

John Lowney's essay contains material reprinted from his book *History, Memory, and the Literary Left*, with the permission of the University of Iowa Press.

Ron Silliman's essay originally appeared in *The New Sentence* (1987), published by Roof Books.

John Taggart's essay originally appeared in *Ironwood* 11 (1978), edited by Michael Cuddihy. It also appeared in *Songs of Degrees: Essays on Contemporary Poetry and Poetics* (1994), published by The University of Alabama Press.

Michael Heller's essay is reprinted from *George Oppen: Man and Poet*, edited by Burton Hatlen and published by the National Poetry Foundation.

Charles Bernstein's essay is reprinted from *My Way: Speeches and Poems* (1999), published by the University of Chicago Press.

Rachel Blau DuPlessis's essay is reprinted from *Blue Studios: Poetry and Its Cultural Work* (2006), published by The University of Alabama Press.

A slightly longer version of Susan Thackrey's essay "George Oppen: A Radical Practice" was previously published by O Books (2001), and was originally presented in San Francisco on December 7, 2000, as the 16th annual George Oppen Memorial Lecture, sponsored by the Poetry Center, San Francisco State University.

Theodore Enslin's essay originally appeared in *Ironwood* 5 (1975), edited by Michael Cuddihy.

Henry Weinfield's essay consists of excerpts drawn from chapter 2 of his book, *The Music of Thought in the Poetry of George Oppen and William Bronk*, forthcoming from the University of Iowa Press.

Contributors

Charles Bernstein's essays are collected in *Content's Dream; Essays 1975–1984, A Poetics,* and *My Way: Speeches and Poems.* His poetry collections include *Girly Man* and *Republics of Reality: 1975–1995.* He is Regan Professor at the University of Pennsylvania. More info: epc.buffalo.edu.

Michael Davidson is a Distinguished Professor of Literature at the University of California, San Diego. He is the author of four books of criticism and the editor of *New Collected Poems of George Oppen.* His most recent book is *Concerto for the Left Hand: Disability and the Defamiliar Body.*

Rachel Blau DuPlessis is involved in an ongoing long poem project called *Drafts* and is also the author of several books of literary criticism and essays on modern and contemporary poetry. She edited *The Selected Letters of George Oppen.*

Theodore Enslin writes: "Since I have become an octogenarian, I don't write that much, and nothing specifically for publication. That means that whatever comes is for friends. I have made a series of twenty cds, an overview of sixty-odd years of whatever I did. There are three connected short stories, which I think of as a quasi-autobiography. What else? Old pitchers tend to break."

Forrest Gander is a professor of English and Comparative Literature at Brown University. His most recent books include the novel *As a Friend,* the poetry collection *Eye Against Eye,* and a translation of the selected poems of Mexican poet Coral Bracho, *Firefly Under the Tongue.*

Lyn Hejinian is a poet, essayist, and translator; she was born in the San Francisco Bay Area and lives in Berkeley. Published collections of her writing include *Writing Is an Aid to Memory, My Life, Oxota: A Short Russian Novel, The Cell, The Cold of Poetry,* and *A Border Comedy;* and a collection of her essays entitled *The Language of Inquiry.* Her most recent book of poetry is *Saga/Circus. The Language of Inquiry,* a collection of essays addressed to poetics and epistemology, was published in 2000. She is one of the authors of the projected ten-volume project titled *The Grand Piano: An Experiment in Collective Autobiography, San Francisco, 1975–1980.* She teaches in the English department at the University of California, Berkeley.

Michael Heller is a poet, essayist, and critic. He has published eight volumes of poetry, the most recent being *Eschaton.* His most recent critical work is *Speaking the Estranged: Essays on the Work of George Oppen.*

John Lowney is a professor of English at St. John's University. He is the author of two books on twentieth-century American poetry: *History, Memory, and the Literary Left: Modern American Poetry, 1935–1968* and *The American Avant-Garde Tradition: William Carlos Williams, Postmodern Poetry, and the Politics of Cultural Memory.* He is currently pursuing research on jazz, internationalism, and African American modernism.

Peter Nicholls is a professor of English and American Literature at the University of Sussex. His publications include *Ezra Pound: Politics, Economics and Writing, Modernisms: A Literary Guide, George Oppen and the Fate of Modernism,* and many articles and essays on literature and theory. He recently co-edited with Laura Marcus *The Cambridge History of Twentieth-Century English Literature,* and he is editor of the journal *Textual Practice.*

Kristin Prevallet is a poet and the author, most recently, of *Shadow, Evidence, Intelligence* and *I, Afterlife: Essay in Mourning Time.* She edited and introduced *A Helen Adam Reader,* and she is the recipient of a 2007 New York Foundation for the Arts fellowship in poetry. She lives in Brooklyn.

Steve Shoemaker is the director of the Roth Writing Center and assistant professor of English at Connecticut College. He has taught literature and writing at Harvard University and Yale University and is currently working on a book entitled *The Poetics of Embodied Mind.* His poems have been published in various magazines, including *First Intensity* and *Fulcrum.*

Ron Silliman is the author of more than thirty books, including most recently *The Alphabet*. *Silliman's Blog*, his weblog, recently saw its two thousandth post and has had over 1.7 million visitors since it began in 2002. He is a market analyst in the computer industry and lives in Chester County, Pennsylvania.

John Taggart has published thirteen volumes of poetry, the most recent of which is *There Are Birds*. He has also published a collection of essays on contemporary poetry and poetics, *Songs of Degrees*.

Susan Thackrey is a poet who lives and works in San Francisco. Her poetry has been widely published, among other magazines in *Apex of the M, Talisman,* and *Hambone,* and her first book is *Empty Gate.* She was a keynote speaker and reader for the George Oppen Centennial Conference at SUNY Buffalo in April 2008.

Henry Weinfield is professor of Liberal Studies at the University of Notre Dame. His most recent books are *The Music of Thought in the Poetry of George Oppen and William Bronk* and *Without Mythologies: New and Selected Poems and Translations*. His translations include versions of Mallarmé and Hesiod.

Index